"Offering a compelling feminist engagement with the Lacanian left, this book allows reconfiguring the notion of the sexual position in ways that question and decenter the Master's Discourse. In so doing, it grapples with stimulating questions of subjectivation, oppression, symbolic identification, and the act, while remaining committed to the possibility of developing a critical analysis of how political subjects emerge within unequal power relations. Attending closely to feminist theories of performativity and precariousness, Alicia Valdés provides an engaging meditation on the complicated questions and conditions that might articulate a feminist Lacanian left as an alternative framework for contemporary political theory and praxis."

Athena Athanasiou, *Professor of Social Anthropology, Panteion University of Social and Political Sciences, Greece*

"Tracing a feminist and intersectional reading of the political Left, Valdes deploys fundamental Lacanian concepts (structure, sexuation, jouissance, fantasy, object a, the four discourses) to offer a critical analysis of contemporary Left politics and the discourses that support them. Aiming at a meaningful intersectional ontology, the book foregrounds the tendency of discourses, including Leftist ones, to non-inclusivity. The feminine "not-all" is posed as both revealing the androcentric 'all' and as an alienator and disrupter of a seamless masculinity, and is what proffers a social bond that is more collectivist and inclusive. Read this book to bolster a psychoanalytically-informed feminist political consciousness fit for the twenty-first century!"

Eve Watson, *Senior Lecturer at Institute of Integrative Counselling and Psychotherapy (IICP), Ireland*

Toward a Feminist Lacanian Left

While traditional feminist readings on antagonism have pivoted around the sole axis of sex and/or gender, a broader and intersectional approach to antagonism is much needed; this book offers an innovative, feminist, and discursive reading on the Lacanian concept of Sexual Position as a way to problematize the concepts of political antagonism and political subjects.

Can Lacanian psychoanalysis offer new grounds for feminist politics? This discursive mediation of Lacan's work presents a new theoretical framework upon which to articulate proposals for intersectional political theory. The first part of this book develops the theoretical framework, and the second part applies it to the construction of woman's identity in European politics and economy. It concludes with notes for a feminist political and economic praxis through community currencies and municipalism.

The interdisciplinary approach of this book will appeal to scholars interested in the fields of psychoanalysis, feminisms, and political philosophy as well as multidisciplinary scholars interested in discourse theory, sexuality and gender studies, cultural studies, queer theory, and continental philosophy. Students at Master's and PhD level will also find this a useful feminist introduction to Lacanian psychoanalysis, discourse, and gender.

Alicia Valdés works as an associate lecturer at the University of Barcelona and research technician at Rovira I Virgili University in Spain.

The Lines of the Symbolic in Psychoanalysis Series

Series Editor:
Ian Parker, Manchester Psychoanalytic Matrix

Psychoanalytic clinical and theoretical work is always embedded in specific linguistic and cultural contexts and carries their traces, traces which this series attends to in its focus on multiple contradictory and antagonistic 'lines of the Symbolic'. This series takes its cue from Lacan's psychoanalytic work on three registers of human experience, the Symbolic, the Imaginary and the Real, and employs this distinctive understanding of cultural, communication and embodiment to link with other traditions of cultural, clinical and theoretical practice beyond the Lacanian symbolic universe. The Lines of the Symbolic in Psychoanalysis Series provides a reflexive reworking of theoretical and practical issues, translating psychoanalytic writing from different contexts, grounding that work in the specific histories and politics that provide the conditions of possibility for its descriptions and interventions to function. The series makes connections between different cultural and disciplinary sites in which psychoanalysis operates, questioning the idea that there could be one single correct reading and application of Lacan. Its authors trace their own path, their own line through the Symbolic, situating psychoanalysis in relation to debates which intersect with Lacanian work, explicating it, extending it and challenging it.

Psychoanalysis Under Nazi Occupation
The Origins, Impact and Influence of the Berlin Institute
Laura Sokolowsky

Toward a Feminist Lacanian Left
Psychoanalytic Theory and Intersectional Theory
Alicia Valdés

The Marx Through Lacan Vocabulary
A Compass for Libidinal and Political Economies
Christina Soto van der Plas, Edgar Miguel Juárez-Salazar, Carlos Gómez Camarena and David Pavón-Cuéllar

Toward a Feminist Lacanian Left

Psychoanalytic Theory and Intersectional Politics

Alicia Valdés

Routledge
Taylor & Francis Group

LONDON AND NEW YORK

First published in 2022
by Routledge
2 Park Square, Milton Park, Abingdon, Oxon OX14 4RN

and by Routledge
605 Third Avenue, New York, NY 10158

Routledge is an imprint of the Taylor & Francis Group, an informa business

British Library Cataloguing-in-Publication Data
A catalogue record for this book is available from the British Library

Library of Congress Cataloging-in-Publication Data
A catalog record has been requested for this book

ISBN: 978-0-367-76571-2 (hbk)
ISBN: 978-0-367-76572-9 (pbk)
ISBN: 978-1-003-16758-7 (ebk)

DOI: 10.4324/9781003167587

Typeset in Times New Roman
by Deanta Global Publishing Services, Chennai, India

A Guillermina y Atalí, mi abuela y mi madre.

Contents

Figures

Series Preface

Ian Parker, Manchester Psychoanalytic Matrix

We must face the uncomfortable fact that, as some cruel left Lacanians like to remind us, that Lacan was not a man of the left. He himself delighted in reminding us of this, and it is all the more curious that the phrase 'Lacanian Left' should resonate in social theory and even in clinical debates over psychoanalysis. We often try in vain to summon up the names of Lacanians who really are on the left, though it is indeed true that many of those 'Lacanians' and 'Leftists' are often men. This book shows us the task that confronts us, and the steps that we must take to move beyond wish fulfillment to a genuine political engagement with the reality of power and its real stakes. We need to be able to situate ourselves in the competing symbolic frames that give to men and women different locations in the world, grasp how those symbolic parameters are refracted through the imaginary domains of dominant macho and subaltern feminist 'experience', and orient ourselves in relation to the real bedrock of oppression and resistance.

A single monolithic theoretical assault on what appears to be a single monolithic entity – the institution of patriarchy relayed through the nuclear family and demeaning images of women as if indeed they barely existed – is not enough to tackle this task. Alicia Valdés Lucas shows us, in this innovative, passionate and reasoned account of where we are and where we need to go, that a constellation of dimensions of oppression and resistance holds women in their place and that this constellation can only be addressed by systematic engagement with intersectional politics.

Intersectionality, this book reminds us, is not a cumulative story of the consequences of compound oppression, as if gender, sexuality and 'race' can simply be added together to give a full reckoning. That way would lie the lures of a positivist numeration of harms and an equally positive fantasy of a 'metalanguage' that would explain everything. Intersectionality is as much about life at the intersection of different forms of oppression as it is about the multiple identities that are mobilized in political resistance and that are attended to in the singularity of psychoanalytic clinical experience.

This book traces its way carefully through a tradition of theory that seemed to listen to women – in Freud's work with hysterics, who were not actually all women at all – a tradition that has so much of the time reproduced rather than challenged patriarchal rule. It mines the resources we need from within Lacan's return to Freud, and polishes them up, fashioning them into something that really speaks for women in their singularity and within their competing overlapping collective identities rather than against them. If psychoanalysis is really to connect with feminist theory and practice, it must do so by reinvigorating critique inside psychoanalysis and in politics. Then it will be possible to speak of the 'Lacanian Left' because it will be fully intersectional, and then also be a 'feminist Lacanian Left' worth the name.

Psychoanalytic clinical and theoretical work circulates through multiple intersecting antagonistic symbolic universes. This series opens connections between different cultural sites in which Lacanian work has developed in distinctive ways, in forms of work that question the idea that there could be single correct reading and application. The Lines of the Symbolic in Psychoanalysis series provides a reflexive reworking of psychoanalysis that transmits Lacanian writing from around the world, steering a course between the temptations of a metalanguage and imaginary reduction, between the claim to provide a god's eye view of psychoanalysis and the idea that psychoanalysis must everywhere be the same. And the elaboration of psychoanalysis in the symbolic here grounds its theory and practice in the history and politics of the work in a variety of interventions that touch the real.

Acknowledgments

This book has a long trajectory of thinking and learning. While this book is a revision of my Ph.D. dissertation, my intricate relationship with the Lacanian corpus traces back to my Master's degree. I have to thank Jordi Ibáñez and Sonia Arribas for being the professors that created the conditions for my first contact with Lacan's work. I owe them much of the theoretical background I now possess. I want to thank you for how you taught me to develop my ideas. I also want to thank Yannis Stavrakakis, Sonia Arribas, and Fabio Vighi for the time and energy they spent reading my articles, listening to my ideas, and allowing me to grow while discussing the heterodox nature of my work.

This book and its prior version in the form of a Ph.D. dissertation have taken all of me in economic and emotional terms. I could not have survived all these precarious years without the help of my mother, who has always encouraged me to pursue my goals, whether they fit with her vision of the good life or not.

I will also be eternally grateful to Paula for her constant emotional support over the Ph.D. Inhabiting the university as a feminist researcher with a heterodox approach is not easy, but I have found a safe space in the middle of this rigid structure. I want to thank Sara Cagliero for her unconditional friendship, constant support, and kind words. Moreover, I want to thank Barbara Biglia for trusting my potential in every single way.

I also want to thank Sara Torres for her comments and delicate review, for creating temples for friendship in every space she enters. Sara's constant inspiration creates the space for personal feminist growth. I also want to thank Luna Miguel and Sara Torres for creating a place for friendship and coalitions, the one that I inhabit with you.

Lastly, I especially need to thank Ian Parker for offering me the opportunity to be part of this series and challenge me to revise my work in such a radical manner. The flattering and scary moment in which such an author offers you the opportunity to publish in such a relevant editorial will inhabit my memories forever. Thank you for taking the risk of publishing such a heterodox work without any doubt.

They don't realize we're the plague.

Introduction

The Freudian approach to sexuality and women imprinted a stigma upon psychoanalysis that has difficulted the feminist approximation to psychoanalysis. His biologicist reading on bodies and sexuality created a wide gap between gender studies and psychoanalysis. Nevertheless, this book aims to illustrate how a feminist and discursive mediation of Lacanian psychoanalysis provides feminist politics of a new variable for feminist political analysis.

However, there have been several previous attempts to apply Lacanian and Freudian theory to feminism and politics. A special mention is owed to women such as Luce Irigaray, Jessica Benjamin, Elisabeth Grosz, Julliet Mitchell, and Jacqueline Rose for their diverse feminist readings and appropriations of psychoanalysis and Lacanian psychoanalysis. On the other hand, Judith Butler, Jason Glynos, Chantal Mouffe, Ernesto Laclau, Yannis Stavrakakis, Fabio Vighi, Slavoj Žižek, among others, have been able to introduce Lacanian psychoanalysis to the field of politics. This second set of authors are part of what Yannis Stavrakakis defined as the Lacanian Left (2007), which refers to a set of authors situated in the left-wing (with heterogeneous points of views on political praxis) and widely influenced by Lacan's work in their research on contemporary political theory and critical analysis (Stavrakakis, 2007).

There are thus two different approaches to Lacan that collide at the same time that they overlap: a feminist reading on Lacan from the perspective of psychoanalysis and a political reading of Lacan from political philosophy. Being the author of this book, a feminist political scientist specialized in political philosophy, the approach to Lacanian psychoanalysis comes from the study of the Lacanian Left as the political translation of Lacanian psychoanalysis, specifically from the discursive mediation articulated by the Essex school. In this sense, the reason for this book to focus on Lacan's theoretical corpus is that there can be a feminist appropriation of the discursive mediation that the Lacanian Left introduces.[1]

However, although this book springs from a feminist reading of the Lacanian Left and not on a psychoanalytical reading of feminist politics, it is relevant to highlight some aspects from various feminist, psychoanalytical readings on Lacan that allow finding the crack within Lacanian psychoanalysis. This crack allows its subversion and the development of a feminist unorthodox political reading.

DOI: 10.4324/9781003167587-1

In her book *Jacques Lacan: A Feminist Introduction*, Elizabeth Grosz affirms that "[t]he *fin de siècle* upheaval could be summarized by three names – Nietzsche, Marx, and Freud – [...] each decentred the individual's pretension to sovereignty, self-knowledge and self-mastery" (1990, p. 1). However, this decentering of the subject did not imply man's decentering as the ideal and standard for the category of the human being. The lack of questioning of the androcentric subject is also present in Lacan. Grosz points out the phallocentric dimension of Lacanian psychoanalysis "in its perspectives, methods and assumptions" (1990, p. 3). However, as Grosz affirms, "[t]he framework of sexual difference provides a conceptual and political position, not quite outside of psychoanalysis nor simply within its terms, from which Lacanian psychoanalysis can be critically assessed" (1990, p. 4). Furthermore, when analyzing Kristeva's and Irigaray's approach to Lacanian psychoanalysis, Grosz points out three reasons why Lacan's work "can be defended (at least up to a point) by feminists" (1990, p. 147). These reasons can be summarized as follows: (a) "Lacan's critique of the Cartesian *cogito*" (Grosz, 1990, p. 147); (b) his introduction of "questions about sexuality to legitimized academic and political discourses" (Grosz, 1990, p. 148); and (c) the way in which his work demonstrates "the centrality of systems of meaning or signification to subjectivity and the social order" (Grosz, 1990, p. 148). As this book aims to illustrate, Lacan's critique of the Cartesian cogito aligns him with feminist critiques within the field of epistemology and ontology. Furthermore, the other two reasons provided by Grosz allow for the articulation of a feminist political philosophy ground on a feminist discursive mediation of Lacanian psychoanalysis.

Furthermore, Jessica Benjamin's book *The Bonds of Love* serves as a good starting point to engage with the difficult task of rethinking the framework of sexual difference in political terms. Jessica Benjamin affirms that

> [e]ven most radical Freudians left strangely untouched psychoanalysis's most profound and unexamined assumption about domination: the subordination of women to men. This assumption [...] provides, as we will see, the ultimate rationalization for accepting all authority.
>
> (Benjamin, 1988, p. 7)

Benjamin's observation is correct and extrapolable to the Lacanian Left, as this current has also evaded the discussion of domination, not only of men over women, but also of urbanity over the rural world, or whites over people of color. I maintain that there is a lack of intersectional and feminist analysis in the Lacanian approach to politics as there is a lack of intersectional analysis in the major works published by this set of authors (Laclau, 2007; Stavrakakis, 1999; Žižek, 2008), except for the theory developed by Judith Butler (Butler, 1997, 2004, 2009). This absence provides, as I will try to demonstrate in the book, the grounds upon which inequality springs. I share with Jessica Benjamin her primary concern:

The fundamental question we must consider is why these positions [master and slave] continue to shape the relationship between the sexes despite our society's formal commitment to equality; what explains their psychological persistence? I believe psychoanalytic theory can help illuminate what is formerly accepted: the genesis of the psychic structure in which one person plays subject and the other must serve as his object.

(1988, p. 7)

Nevertheless, I am not only interested in considering why man-woman relationships are articulated in the form of master-slave, but also in how the logics of master-slave and masculine-feminine mutate into the binomial we/they that governs political relations. That is to say; I intend to show how sexual differentiation is intimately related to how antagonistic political relations are constructed. Thus, this book will give an account of how antagonistic political logics result from a sexuation of Reality that produces the construction of feminine and masculine political subjectivities to whom socio-economic-political powers are unequally distributed. This book's central thesis is that a feminist and discursive mediation of Lacanian psychoanalysis can shed light on how discursive operations condition how a subject constructs their political subjectivity.

Which Lacan?

It is vital to highlight that this book does not purely rely on Lacanian psychoanalysis but relies on the Lacanian Left's discursive mediation to Lacan's work to develop a feminist discursive mediation. In this sense, this book heavily relies on the political translation that Laclau, Mouffe, and Stavrakakis develop of the Lacanian concepts of Reality and the Real into politics and the Political (Laclau, 2007; Laclau & Mouffe, 2001; Stavrakakis, 1999, 2007).

This book relies on the idea developed in Chapter 1 that affirms that Reality is a frame that establishes which elements and which lives are to count as political, as living, and existing, which is widely inspired by the works of Butler, Laclau, Mouffe, and Stavrakakis (Butler, 2004; Laclau, 2007; Mouffe, 2005; Stavrakakis, 1999). Furthermore, I argue that the discursive operation that establishes Reality acts upon the ontological level by creating two different spaces within it. These two differentiated spaces imply different ontological statuses: existence (existing inside the frame) and ex-sistence (existing outside the frame). Furthermore, this work offers a renovated and feminist reading of the idea of frames by developing a feminist discursive mediation that affirms that the discursive operations of political framing are processes of sexuation that construct Reality in an androcentric way.

To develop this feminist discursive mediation, this book analyzes some of Lacan's seminars from the 1970s to gain insights into how Lacan develops a reading on woman and analyzes the emergence of woman in the social world. As Yannis Stavrakakis (1999) and Dylan Evans (1996) point out, Lacan's work has been divided into several stages. These diverse chronological classifications may vary. One example is the division of his work in three different periods that Stavrakakis presents in his book *Lacan and the Political*:

> In his unpublished seminar on *Anxiety* (1962–3) he states, as if responding to a widely held conviction, that he does not believe that there were ever two distinct phases in his teaching, one focusing on his conception of the 'imaginary', on the 'mirror stage', and another articulated around his conception of the 'symbolic'. Today it would be possible to add one more phase, the one starting with his seminar on *The Four Fundamental Concepts of Psychoanalysis*, in which it is the concept of the 'real' that becomes the nodal point of his discourse—the 'imaginary', the 'symbolic' and the 'real' being the three most important categories, or registers, through which Lacan maps human experience.
>
> (1999, p. 6)

Each period is thus characterized by the focus and prioritization of one of these registers (Imaginary-Symbolic-Real). Thus, the work of Lacan focuses on the Real from 1964 with his seminar *The Four Fundamental Concepts of Psychoanalysis* (Lacan, 1998b).

However, since this book is deeply rooted in the discursive mediation that the Lacanian Left offers and a feminist turn to his political translations, this book focuses on seminars XVII to XXIII. The reason to approach these series of seminars is that the evolution and union of language and topology are visible in these seminars and, more importantly, in this set of seminars, Lacan's work focuses on how the feminine figure of woman emerges in the social world. As this book aims to demonstrate, it is not a coincidence that the prioritization of the Real and the focus on the feminine subject take place at the same time. As Bethany Morris pointed out, the Real is the register related to women (Morris, 2017). This book aims to illustrate how the Real—the radical alterity that threatens a Reality shaped for the masculine androcentric subject—is the excluded feminine principle. Furthermore, this book does not adhere to an orthodox reading of Lacan's body of work as it dwells in a discursive and feminist appropriation of his work.

Another question concerning how this book approaches Lacan's work relates to how it attempts to take Lacan to a broader audience. As Dylan Evans notes, Lacan's work

> has often been accused of being infuriatingly obscure and sometimes of constituting a totally incomprehensible 'psychotic' system. This obscurity has even been seen as a deliberate attempt to ensure that Lacanian discourse remains the exclusive property of a small intellectual elite, and to protect it from external criticism.
>
> (Evans, 1996, p. ix)

From a feminist perspective, the obscurantism and lack of criticism in the way in which knowledge is constructed must be overcome to lead to a feminist construction of knowledges. In this sense, this book heavily relies on Evans's book *An Introductory Dictionary of Lacanian Psychoanalysis*, as it can be seen as a successful exercise to disentangle and shed light on Lacan's ever-mutating concepts (1996).

Thus, the book approaches Lacan through a feminist discursive mediation heavily influenced by the Lacanian Left, specifically Judith Butler's work. This feminist discursive mediation focuses on the seminars that focus on the feminine subject and attempts to bring Lacanian notions to a broader feminist audience through a pedagogical reading.

The Lacanian Left

To develop a feminist approach to politics, this book departs from the affirmation that every historical time is articulated around different structures and elements that conform to an ontological discourse whose social bonds result in Reality. This Reality is the field upon which politics take place. As this introduction will show, the construction of Reality implies its delimitation. Such delimitation produces the emergence of a frame upon which politics, understood as the struggle for hegemony, takes place. This book adheres to the idea that Reality's delimitation is the product of the imposition of a Master Signifier. This Master Signifier cancels out any difference between the signifiers that inhabit the limits of Reality, while there is an imposition of a second Master Signifier in charge of establishing a chain of equivalences between the excluded signifiers. These two Master Signifiers have a double impact. They homogenize subjects that remain under each of these empty signifiers and inserts a radical heterogeneity between both groups of subjects. This double process produces the classical Schmittian antagonistic relation between enemy/friend, which functions as a political strategy that uses antagonism as an instrument to maintain Reality as the desirable option.

Although these ideas have been sketched and developed in different ways by several authors of the Lacanian Left (Butler, 1997, 2004, 2009; Laclau, 1990, 2007; Mouffe, 1993, 2005; Stavrakakis, 2007), this book aims to add a feminist dimension by developing an androcentric and ethnocentric critique to politics. Thus, by departing from the intricate relation between language, subjectivity, and discourse, I aim to show how the two Master Signifiers that define and give shape to dichotomic political relations correspond to the signifiers of masculine and feminine. Thus, Reality's framing operation is a process through which Reality is sexuated by the imposition of two sexual positions that correspond to two different ontological statuses. The signifier representing what inhabits Reality is the signifier masculine, while the signifier that represents what remains outside of Reality is feminine. To hold the masculine position allows the subject to enter politics; therefore, politics, as the struggle for hegemony, is an androcentric biased process. Furthermore, another main innovation this book introduces is that not every subject undergoes the same processes of subjectification, but the entrance of the subject in the Symbolic implies different dynamics depending on the sexual position they occupy.

The establishment and development of sexuated positions consist of two mechanisms. The first implies a hierarchization of sexual positions by praising the masculine position and stigmatizing the feminine position. Nevertheless, the second process implies the exclusion of the feminine from Reality. Furthermore, after this process of sexuation reaches its climax—there is a sexual position inside Reality and another outside—a further process starts, which corresponds to the controlled introduction of the excluded—feminine—sexual position within masculine Reality. Such inclusion takes place to feed the need for reproducibility of the frame (Butler, 2004); however, to secure the androcentric dimension of Reality, a hybrid political identity is produced to tame subjects with the feminine sexual position.

In chronological terms, this tamed and controlled inclusion of external agents takes place in Postmodernity, which does not refer to a time in which Modernity has been overcome but to the moment in which the masculine subject is the only subject that exists, condemning other subjects to the realm of ex-sistence, as existing outside the imposed frame. The beginning of this fourth stage is a moment in which neoliberal capitalism—the androcentric sociopolitical-economic system *par excellence*—seems to have established its hegemony and toppled any attempt for an alternative world system. Thus, Postmodernity starts with the fall of the Eurocommunist dream. As Chantal Mouffe and Ernesto Laclau noted, this fall was not articulated as a positive moment for the socialist strategy (2001). Socialism failed to take advantage of the fact that authoritarian socialism was a failure and take advantage of the necessary coalition between democracy and socialism. This book articulates the idea that this historical moment implies introducing the capitalist fantasy to the already established androcentric Reality, a fantasy in which consumerism becomes the primary process of identification for women. While this book agrees with Chantal Mouffe and Ernesto Laclau when they point out the fall of the Eurocommunist dream as a specific moment in which the alternative to capitalism seems to have disappeared (2001), this book looks at this moment from a different approach, the feminist approach, which allows analyzing it as the moment in which the androcentric man erects the totality of a structure of Reality.

This book's objective is to make visible how the androcentric man becomes the unique ontological identity that grants the status of existence, while precarious forms of life, those that differ from the androcentric identity, are given the ontological status of ex-sistence. Its main goal is to illustrate how specific discursive structures create different ontological spaces, and the contingency of the exclusion that later allows for an androcentrification of Reality. Nevertheless, this book does not develop an anthropological or historical study of how androcentrism is established in the form of patriarchy. Instead, it analyzes how politics—which concerns the grievable and the livable life—and the political—the excluded and not livable lives—are divided and sexuated, allowing for masculine hegemony, thus aiming at continuing Butler's theory of precarity (2004, 2009). Furthermore, this book attempts to be a feminist continuation of the theses presented by Chantal Mouffe and Ernesto Laclau in their book *Hegemony and Socialist Strategy: Towards a Radical Democratic Politics* (2001). In the preface to their second edition, they point out the necessity of clarifying both political moments in which the first and second edition appeared. A historical clarification needs to be made to circumscribe this book as a continuation of their work.

The political and theoretical moment that surrounds this book is a complex one. The idea that it *seems easier to imagine the end of the world than the end of capitalism*, first coined by Fredric Jameson and then wrongly ascribed to Slavoj Žižek, defines the current political and social horizon (Beaumont, 2014). This indestructibility of capitalism has been explicit in the pandemic times that surround this book. On the other hand, the theoretical moment of the political left from Central countries is characterized by a constant discussion between distributive politics and identity politics.[2] To divide or classify theoretical bodies between identity politics and distributive politics is just the result of the denial of androcentrism and the standardization of the masculine subject. To think of distributive politics out of the axis of identity is the result of alienation produced by the imaginary breach between structure and subject. To speak of structures as discursive products can overcome such alienation and speak of the social construction of structures without forgetting their material consequences.

Which Feminism?

The need to contextualize and locate this book within the Lacanian corpus is as crucial as the need to contextualize this book within the feminist tradition.

In the introduction to the book *Between Feminism & Psychoanalysis* (1989), Teresa Brennan makes a brief yet very useful introduction to the combination of psychoanalysis and feminism. This combination is articulated around the Lacanian concept of the Symbolic and how feminists respond to such a concept. Teresa Brennan defines the Lacanian Symbolic as follows:

> the symbolic places human beings in relation to others, and gives them a sense of their place in their world, and the ability to speak and be understood by others. It does this by enabling them to distinguish themselves from others, and through establishing a relation to language.
>
> (1989, p. 2)

From our perspective, the Symbolic corresponds to what traditionally has been understood as politics, as the register upon which the subject becomes a subject of politics and their needs are included within the political agenda. However, as Teresa Brenan also points out, this Symbolic is not neutral but patriarchal and adds that "the key to the patriarchal order is the fact that men are socially valuable" (1989, p. 3). The critique of the gendered base of politics has also been analyzed by Wendy Brown (1988), and several other authors have criticized how this bias is also present in the economy (Agenjo-Calderón & Gálvez-Muñoz, 2019; Barker & Kuiper, 2003; Nelson, 2003; Pérez Orozco, 2017; Valdés, 2019).

The dynamics and mechanisms that make men socially valuable place them as the standard or ideal, and prioritize the experience of men over other subjects when studying or defining social reality are mechanisms proper to what this book defines the process of *androcentrification*. Androcentrification can be defined as the process of centering men, the subject of androcentrism, within the Symbolic.

Traditional, hegemonic feminism defines androcentrism as the imposition of the masculine or the male as both the ideal and the standard (Fehr, 2018; Hibbs, 2014; Hundleby, 2011). This basic definition of the masculine as belonging to men suggests that gender is the unique axis around which oppression arises. However, this position evades questioning other axes of oppression, such as racism or ageism, as oppressions related to androcentrism. On the other hand, in decolonial feminism, the concept of androcentrism goes from a simple and lineal term to a broader and more complex concept that defines and characterizes the standard, not only as being male or masculine but includes certain key critical aspects such as being white, being adult, being abled, or being literate (Maffía, 2007; Trejo, 2006). In other words, the subjectivity of the person who occupies Reality's central position is not just characterized by its masculine dimension but articulated around other characteristics that transform women, indigenous people, or transgender people into exceptions. The present book endorses this complex conceptualization of androcentrism as the structure that defines the masculine as not only what belongs to maleness, but whiteness, ableness, literacy, and centrality, among others. Thus, the subject of economic theories, political theories, medicine, and other knowledge fields is this standardized and ideal man.

A considerable amount of literature focuses on the use of the terms patriarchy and androcentrism. One of the most relevant essays within this discussion is Gayle Rubin's foundational article, "The Traffic in Women: Notes for a 'Political Economy' of Sex", in which the author criticizes the use of the term patriarchy (1975). The author turns to the works of Claude Lévi-Strauss and Sigmund Freud to ask what the relationships that transform females into domesticated women are:

> The domestication of women, under other names, is discussed at length in both of their *ouvres*. In reading through these works, one begins to have a sense of a systematic social apparatus which takes up females as raw materials and fashions domesticated women as products.
>
> (1975, p. 158)

Rubin affirms that, when analyzing their work with a feminist perspective, "they provide conceptual tools with which one can build descriptions of the part of social life which is the locus of the oppression of women, of sexual minorities, and of certain aspects of human personality within individuals" (1975, p. 159). I believe that such a strategy is also valid and fruitful with Lacan's work because

Rubin, as Lacan did, reads Freud profoundly influenced by Lévi-Strauss. In this essay, Rubin introduces the term sex/gender system, which she defines as "the set of arrangements by which a society transforms biological sexuality into products of human activity, and in which these transformed sexual needs are satisfied" (1975, p. 159). Gayle Rubin counterposes this term to those of mode of repro- duction and patriarchy as she believes that the use of both terms misleads the central focus of feminism and argues for the term sex/gender system as "a neutral term which refers to the domain and indicates that oppression is not inevitable in that domain, but is the product of the specific social relations which organize it" (1975, p. 168). However, a significant problem with this theoretical articulation is that it does not leave room for an intersectional feminist theory that introduces variables such as ableism, urbanity, and literacy, among others.

This book's proposal is the articulation of a different feminist theoretical framework upon which to develop a critical analysis of how political subjects emerge. The proposed theoretical framework departs from three key elements: the Symbolic, intersectional feminism, and sexual position. Thus, the goal is to provide a conceptual, theoretical framework based on the Lacanian notion of sexual position that allows creating a wider frame for intersectional political fem- inism and continue the feminist campaign to create a theory that allows for the articulation of an inclusive political subject. Let me analyze these three central elements.

The Symbolic

This book endorses the idea that the European Symbolic's primary source of domination is androcentrism, an intricate structure formed by different systems of oppression that divides the whole into a valid and superior element and an invalid and inferior element. This division does not only imply a hierarchy but also implies the imposition of normativity, as it creates a frame that contains and limits.[3] However, although there are multiple axes of oppression that work as layers and arrows that transverse bodies, this book considers that this complex structure of domination should be denominated androcentrism from a holistic perspective. This account illustrates that it is under the feminine category that European ontology places dissident and non-normative agents and elements, while it is under the category of the masculine that it places the valid and success- ful. This sexuated differentiation legitimizes inequality and creates a hierarchy that goes beyond the European dichotomy of gender. This book develops the idea that forms of domination and oppression that form androcentrism, such as racism or ableism, tend to define or relate the inferior with the feminine. In the case of indigenous men, they undergo a process of femininization, becoming feminine/ femininized agents due to the imposition of alterity. In indigenous women, this femininization is double, exposing them to an even more precarious reality. In this sense, this book heavily relies on Judith Butler's work on precarity (2004, 2009).

Intersectionality

The adherence of this book to the more complex and broader concept of andro-centrism situates it under the umbrella term of intersectional feminism, which considers several axes of oppression besides gender.

As Kimberlé Crenshaw illustrates when speaking of violence against black women, these axes increase the risk for potential aggressions, oppressions, and exclusions of non-white women (1994). In her article "Mapping the Margins", Kimberlé Crenshaw affirms that intersectionality is invisible to feminist and anti-racist movements (1994). Although almost thirty years have passed since her article's publication, it seems that political feminist praxis is still unable, or unwilling, to see the importance of intersectionality. She points out that not considering a black woman's intersectionality leads to the marginalization of her experience. A brief introduction and definition of intersectionality could be that intersectionality is a theory that illustrates how different characteristics intersect and overlap, allowing for a broader and more complex analysis of the subject's position.

On the other hand, two different positions within feminism seem to oppose the postulates of intersectional feminism. I here refer to the traditional yet obsolete division between Anglo-American equality feminism and the French difference feminism. Teresa Brennan classifies some of the leading feminist, psychoana-lytical authors following such division (1989). On the one hand, Brenan situates Julliet Mitchell as one of the leading authors of equality feminism. On the other hand, she situates Luce Irigaray and Hélène Cixous within the current of differ-ence feminism (Brennan, 1989). This book does not endorse or adhere to any of these positions as they are.

On the one hand, to think of equality and difference in pure terms of gender (sometimes using biologicist arguments that link sex and gender) is a reductionist and non-intersectional reading of how political subjectivities are constructed in patriarchal/androcentric systems. Furthermore, to speak of equality and differ-ence in purely gendered terms implies the creation of woman as a homogeneous subject erase or what this subjectivity may imply. In this sense, this book divides feminisms into intersectional feminisms and gendered feminisms.

Gendered feminisms run over intersectionality, provoking the exclusion of the reality of millions of women and the exclusion of the reality of millions of men whose intersectionality pushes them to processes of feminization. Furthermore, there are three different positions toward intersectionality from the feminist approach.

• **Denial of intersectionality**: this position sees gender as the only crucial axis of oppression; it does not believe that cisgenderism or transmisogyny exist, but the main oppression results from the inequality of genders. Some currents may add other axes of oppression, such as the oppression lesbians suffer, but they still depart from the centrality of gender. Thus, their denial of intersec-tionality derives from the fact that the only system of oppression they observe is patriarchy—as the rule of males over females and its effect over reproduction—and heteropatriarchy—the heterosexual rule over females.

- **Intersectionality and oppression**: this positioning affirms the existence of a wider variety of systems of oppression such as racism, cisgenderism, ableism, and ageism, among others. Nevertheless, it considers gender as the primary source of inequality. Thus, it can observe intersectionality in women (whether cis or trans), but precarity and feminization are not analyzed in men. Therefore, the axis of gender is what identifies the intersectional subject as a subject of oppression.

- **Intersectionality, oppression, and privilege. Situated intersectionality**: this third position allows for a different conception of intersectionality. On the one hand, it analyzes different systems of oppression. Thus, patriarchy and heteropatriarchy are not the only systems of oppression that a subject must face. On the other hand, it analyzes these systems of oppression by the oppression they inscribe upon certain subjects and analyzes how other subjects are privileged within these oppression systems. Furthermore, its specificity is that it does not posit gender at the core of its analysis on inequality; instead, it departs from the idea that the central system of oppression depends on the context. In other words, and following the work of Donna Haraway, oppression is situated (1988). For example, in Europe, as it is the geographical context in which this book is placed, a cisgender lesbian or bisexual white woman may experience oppression in a different degree from that of a Moroccan gay cisgender male refugee. The crucial element that allows for a reading of situated intersectionality is the element of privilege. An intersectional reading of identities also needs to allow seeing how different dimensions of our identities may also privilege us in specific contexts. It is from this last point of view that we aim to analyze identities.

As I have affirmed in earlier articles (Fishel et. al., 2021; Valdés 2021), Kimberlé Crenshaw coined the concept of intersectionality as a worldview, as an active understanding of the world. However, some voices in gendered feminisms

> have appropriated the term and interpreted it as an ontological position characterized by the intersection of oppression. This appropriation brings along a crucial risk: by adopting intersectionality as a static ontological status – that is to say, avoiding questioning whether intersectionality is situated and therefore my oppression and privilege are dynamic and dependent on the context – we avoid analyzing how women, as an oppressed subject, may also deploy violence and become a threat to other subjects.
>
> (Fishel et al., 2021)

Identities are situated for two different reasons. Firstly, because subjects always occupy a specific position within the structure (Haraway, 1988) and, secondly, because identities are neither closed nor static, we engage in continuous identification processes. Furthermore, if identities are situated, intersectionality is also situated.

However, although gender is not the central axis of oppression, the ideal subject of European androcentrism is a man, since subjectivities are femininized or masculinized to fit in the dichotomic and hierarchized system of patriarchy. Thus the feminization of poverty and its subsequent distribution of precarious ontological statuses function in two different ways.

On the one hand, it defines the process through which women suffer more than men the consequences of economic crises and invisibility in political and economic agendas. On the other hand, the feminization of poverty is how low-income populations are dominated and infantilized in the same manner that women have suffered these processes from men over European history. Thus, to understand this double lecture, for a feminist political strategy, gender, sex, and sexual orientation are not enough variables to understand political processes. Instead, a new variable needs to be introduced: sexual position.

Sexual Position

Lacan introduced the concept of sexual position in his *Seminar XX* (1998a). The introduction of the concept of sexual position completely problematizes and poses fundamental questions for political feminism and functions as the main element to understand intersectional identities as situated. As Evans affirms in his Lacanian dictionary,

> For Lacan, masculinity and femininity are not biological essences but symbolic positions, and the assumption of one of these two positions is fundamental to the construction of subjectivity; the subject is essentially a sexed subject. 'Man' and 'woman' are signifiers that stand for these two subjective positions (S20, 34).
>
> (1996, p. 181)

Lacan's articulation of sexual positions is very interesting and fruitful for the understanding of situated intersectionality. He affirms that identification with masculinity or femininity depends on the subject's relation with the Symbolic (Lacan, 1998a). Departing from the affirmation that the European Symbolic implies specific systems of oppression such as racism, cisgenderism, sexism, ageism, and ableism, the sexual position of subjects, their femininity or masculinity, derives from their position within this intricate network of oppressive structures. Thus, from a situated theory of intersectionality that evaluates both oppression and privilege, a cis-hetero white upper-class urban woman possesses a masculine sexual position. In contrast, a black, gay male refugee occupies the feminine sexual position within the European sociopolitical context. In this sense, gender or assigned sex do not define vulnerability or life as livable, but the sexual position someone possesses concerning a Symbolic order.

The primary purpose of the following section is to introduce and contextualize my theory of sexual positions and feminist politics in the theoretical movement of the *Lacanian Left*. It will also examine how assigning sexual positions in politics is a discursive operation through which subjects and Reality are sexuated to construct a hierarchical political order with ontological consequences. However, before going any further into the hypothesis, a clarification needs to be made. The introduction of this new variable does not conceal neither intends to hide oppressions that spring from gender-related violence, homophobia, or sexual violence. Cisgender heterosexual women face higher rates of violence than cisgender heterosexual men, and they also face significant obstacles when they try to develop normative lives, i.e., having kids while developing their professional careers. Nevertheless, when facing the issue of developing feminist economics or politics, feminists need to look at political subjectivities by adding a new variable—sexual position.

Thus, by adhering to an intersectional commitment, this book illustrates that not every woman undergoes or suffers the same oppression. Furthermore, this commitment allows observing how social and gendered hierarchies go beyond the classical binomial man-woman and obliges to see how feminist theory must commit to the struggle of different subjects beyond the classical and homogeneous reading of woman. As Sandra Harding points out,

> Women need sciences and technologies that are *for* women and that are for woman in every *class, race and culture.* [...] Such sciences can and must benefit men, too—especially those marginalized by racism, imperialism and class exploitation; the new science are not to be only for women. [...] Moreover, it is time to examine critically the conflicting interests in science that women in opposing classes and races may well have; women's interests are not homogeneous.
>
> (1991, p. 5)

However, it is easy for the subject who can create shared knowledge to appropriate the location of the other. As Donna Haraway warns,

> Many currents in feminism attempt to theorize grounds for trusting especially the vantage points of the subjugated; here is good reason to believe vision is better from below the brilliant space platforms of the powerful. Building on that suspicion, this essay is an argument for situated and embodied knowledges and an argument against various forms of unlocatable, and so irresponsible, knowledge claims. Irresponsible means unable to be called into account. There is a premium on establishing the capacity to see from the peripheries and the depths. But here there also lies a serious danger of romanticizing and/or appropriating the vision of the less powerful while claiming to see from their positions.
>
> (1988, p. 583)

This book aims to unravel how the appropriation of the less powerful position and claiming their vision entails developing a discursive operation that implies the reproduction of the system that generates inequality. Thus, although women locate themselves in the place of a subjugated subject, woman, there are also subjects with ontological statuses that situate them under women within social and political hierarchies. Instead of applying the theoretical framework to the political and social situation of migrants and other subjectivities, this book applies its theoretical framework to the example of European women. Nevertheless, the proposed framework may work as a new starting point for a decolonial, feminist, and psychoanalytical analysis of political identities.

Lastly, as a way to conclude the contextualization of this book within feminism, I find it relevant to point out the classification of feminist positions that Elizabeth Wright develops following the work of Kristeva.

> In a recent critical assessment of the feminist struggle, Moi, following Kristeva, marks out three main positions for women: 1) demanding 'equal access to the symbolic order', a battle for equal rights; 2) rejecting the 'male symbolic order in the name of difference', an assertion of the uniqueness of their femininity; and 3) rejecting 'the dichotomy between masculine and feminine as metaphysical', a deconstructed from of feminism, which Kristeva sees as her own position.
>
> (1989, p. 141)

This book adheres to this third position as it allows for a questioning of the symbolic from an intersectional approach that goes beyond dichotomic binarism.

Toward a Feminist Lacanian Left

Chantal Mouffe and Ernesto Laclau spoke of the political differences between the early 1980s, in which Eurocommunism was still a viable project, and the early 2000s as a critical moment for the left, which, instead of taking advantage of the fall of a hostile political praxis of socialism, was defeated by it (2001). From a feminist standpoint, the analysis of the current state of the left in Europe cannot evade its androcentric bias.

From a feminist approach, the Eurocommunist project's fall implied the beginning of a new stage in Modernity. The defeat of Communism in Europe did not only strengthen the liberal promise, but it also affected how the European subject identified itself. The fall of the Berlin Wall was the historical point in which the Central subject's identification with Modernity and capitalism took place. This identification with the masculine subject started with the idea of the Cartesian subject (Bordo, 1986) and reached its climax with the identification of the capitalist subject as the masculine identity *par excellence*. Žižek already pointed out this idea in his book *The Ticklish Subject, the Hegemony of the Cartesian Subject* (2000). Nevertheless, while he introduces a defense on the idea of the Cartesian subject and ignores the feminist critique, from my point of view, the emergence of the Cartesian subject implied the beginning of identification with a specific and hegemonic masculine subjectivity at a macro level—an identification from which the left was not exempted.

It is precisely at this point that my analysis deviates from the one developed by Žižek. I aim to demonstrate how capitalism has depoliticized and commodified postmodern notions of identity by the logic of difference. That is to say, *capitalism has created different subjectivities that are differentiated by patterns of consumption and creates a sensation of heterogeneity and freedom to be whomever you want, without posing the ontological question of who can be.* However, I believe that to decline or reject difference does not necessarily imply a subversive answer to capitalism. This book seeks to illustrate how Reality is supported by the structure of fantasy. Fantasy is characterized by a void placed at the center of Reality that functions as its kernel. This void is filled by an *object petite a*, which functions as a portal through which Reality can reach and absorb the Real through the idea of *difference*.

I affirm that the left was not exempted from identifying with the masculine Cartesian subject and its evolution under capitalism. This affirmation situates me on the same path as Chantal Mouffe and Ernesto Laclau when they point out Marxism's incapability to articulate a theory able to dismantle capitalism (2001). For them, such incapability is due, among other reasons, to the incapability of Marxism to admit the inadequacy of its categories to operate upon the ever-mutating reality that capitalism offers. When they speak of the impasse of Marxist theorization in the mid-1970s, they affirm that "[t]here was an increasing gap between the realities of contemporary capitalism and what Marxism could legitimately subsume under its own categories" (2001, p. viii). Capitalism mutated faster than Marxist theory did, creating dimensions of capitalism that Marx had never imagined. However, this book considers that this incapability is still active, as there is still an impossibility to give an alternative, a Marxist response—understanding Marxist as anti-capitalist—to capitalist crises and Reality.

Nevertheless, from this book's perspective, Marxism's impossibility to conceptualize the Reality of capitalism does not come from the breach between capitalist reality and Marxist theory but springs from the fact that capitalism and Marxism share an androcentric bias that reinforces an economic and political system based on alienation. Thus, Marxism is incapable of offering a proper theoretical and practical answer to capitalism because capitalism and Marxism share an androcentric ontological theory. This androcentric root makes alienation possible. While alienation is visible in capitalist production, as Marx analyzed (1992), alienation is also a necessary element in orthodox Marxism as in the idea of state-centrism and in the absence of a proper analysis of reproductive work (Mies, 2001). I believe that Marxism, and a considerable part of the hegemonic Central left, cannot give a proper response to the constant capitalist challenge as they both rely on a masculine—androcentric and ethnocentric—conception of Reality. Following the line of argumentation that they develop in their prologue to the second edition, I also use their redefinition of Husserlian sedimentation and reactivation.

> Sedimented theoretical categories are those which conceal the acts of their original institutions, while the reactivating moment makes those acts visible again. For us—as opposed to Husserl—that reactivation had to show the original contingency of the synthesis that the Marxian categories attempted to establish.
>
> (2001, p. viii)

Mouffe and Laclau develop a strategy based on the reactivation of the preconditions that make discursive operations possible. Furthermore, in the introduction to the book *The Rhetorical Foundation of Society*, Ernesto Laclau again defines these terms as follows, "[s]edimented ideas are those crystallized form that have broken their link with the original intuition from which they proceeded, while reactivation is the revelation of that forgotten link" (2014, p. 3). This book aims to reactivate the ontological concepts that exclude what it defines as feminine identities. Thus, the book does not examine concepts such as gender, race, or the problems derived from them. Instead, it aims to examine the contingency of the exclusion of subjects based on such identity dimensions. Thus, this book could be placed in what Laclau and Mouffe call post-Marxism, but feminist post-Marxism since it analyzes the contingency of political exclusion with a feminist approach.

Before developing a further analysis of how Laclau and Mouffe reactivate the category of hegemony, a definition of the concept is needed. Mouffe and Laclau understand that hegemony is the central category of political analysis (2001); nevertheless, this book affirms that hegemony is the central category of analysis of *politics* and not of the *political* itself. Departing from Yannis Stavrakakis's distinction between politics and the political, politics is defined as "[…] constituting a separate system, the political system, and is expected to stay within the boundaries of this system […] and also expect it to be performed by the accordingly sanctioned agents" (Beck, 1997:98) (1999, p. 71); while the political is found

> not in what we call political activity, but in the double movement whereby the mode of institution of society appears and is obscured. It appears in the sense that the process whereby society is ordered and unified across its divisions becomes.
>
> (1999, p. 72)

To speak of politics from a critical and feminist point of view leads to understanding politics as a separate system in which only masculine subjects, the accordingly sanctioned agents, can engage. Thus, to reactivate the exclusion that generates the breach between masculine and feminine subjects, the analysis cannot focus on hegemony, as it occurs on an already biased Reality, but needs to dig into the political. The analysis must focus on the preconditions of the emergence of the element that institutes the breach between subjects. As this book attempts to illustrate, this occurs when the signifier of exclusion is imposed, and the gap between politics and the political emerges. While for Mouffe and Laclau, hegemony responds to a political moment in which "a *particular* social force assumes the representation of a *totality* that is radically incommensurable with it" (2001, p. x). To speak of universality, the discussion must first focus on the finitude of a system that allows speaking of a totality that allows for a hegemony. This thought is also present in Mouffe and Laclau, who speak of universality as political universality that depends on frontiers, internal frontiers that represent antagonisms (2001). These antagonisms are the limits of society. However, this book affirms that there is an original antagonism that allows for the internal differences found in politics. Again, their analysis of the role of the empty signifier when studying hegemony is also valid for this book's purpose, as they affirm that

> the category of point de capiton (nodal point, in our terminology) or master-signifier involves the notion of a particular element assuming a 'universal' structuring function within a certain discursive field—actually, whatever organization that field has is only the result of that function—without the particularity of the element per se predetermining such a function.
>
> (2001, p. xi)

This book relies on the idea that there is a discursive operation in which two central Master Signifiers (masculine and feminine) are imposed. These two Master Signifiers allow separating the political (the Real, feminine) from politics (Reality, masculine). Nevertheless, before speaking of how the separation occurs, the analysis must begin by focusing on the separated elements.

On the one hand, this book differs with the two authors and considers politics in the way in which Mouffe and Laclau consider the political: "we conceive the political not as a superstructure but as having the status of an ontology of the social" (2001, p. xiv). Thus, following Mouffe and Laclau's conception of the social "as a discursive space" (2001, p. x), this book understands that politics is the product of a discursive operation with ontological consequences that delimits what the social can be. Thus, it is ontological in the sense that it also sets limits to *who* can *be*. Understanding discourse as a structure, as Lacan does, allows imagining a topology of discourse and to develop a cognitive map in which to illustrate how signifiers and signifieds are articulated to make both, exclusion and hegemony, possible.

This book refers to Lacan's seminar *The Other Side of Psychoanalysis* (2007) to speak of discourse as a structure. It is here where Lacan defines discourse "as a necessary structure that goes beyond speech" being able to subsist without words as it "subsists in fundamental relations which would literally not be able to be maintained without language" (2007, p. 12). Thus, language is relational and establishes the fundamental relation of one signifier to another; it is within this relationship that "results the emergence of what we call the subject" (Lacan, 2007,

p. 13). Signifiers are the critical element when analyzing language and discourse in Lacan. As the Master's Discourse structure shows, the Master Signifier S_1 is the point of departure of discourse. Nevertheless, while this book will analyze Lacanian discourse theory in upcoming chapters, it is necessary to stress how Master Signifiers function by establishing both the limits and the content of the politics as an ontological discursive structure.

First, the ontological consequences of the discursive operation that founds Reality—the Master's Discourse—are the conditioning and limitation of subjects' capacity to become subjects of politics. The Master Signifier (S_1) that intervenes upon the battery of signifiers (S_2) conditions the subject that emerges from the discursive structure ($\$$), thus, conditioning how subjects that may not relate to $\$$ emerge. When analysis focuses on why a specific S_1 intervenes instead of others, it focuses on hegemony issues. Hegemony is defined by Mouffe and Laclau as the relation

> by which a certain particularity assumes the representation of a universality entirely incommensurable with it, is what we call a hegemonic relation. As a result, its universality is a contaminated universality: (1) it lives in this unresolvable tension between universality and particularity; (2) its function of hegemonic universality is not acquired for good but is, on the contrary, always reversible.
>
> (2001, p. xiii)

Therefore, politics can be defined as the grounds upon which the struggle for hegemony occurs and the result of an ontological discursive operation that delimits Reality. Nevertheless, for the analysis of hegemony, the book aims to analyze a previous stage, the stage in which an exclusion emerges to create a finite ground for hegemonic struggle. As Laclau points out in his book *Emancipations*, for a Master Signifier to intervene over a battery of signifiers, this battery needs to have its own limits; it must form a totality that can only be acquired by the separation between the inside and the outside of the battery (2007, p. 19).

It is at this very theoretical moment that the book is situated. It aims to demonstrate that the Master Signifier that intervenes upon the battery of signifiers is the signifier masculine. Masculine subjects depart from a favorable position when constructing their subjectivity, but what about feminine subjectivities? How have feminine subjectivities been built in a masculine modern Reality? Who are to be included in the categories of the masculine and the feminine? Moreover, how can we start thinking about the subversion and feminization of politics? This book aims to respond to these questions.

Summing up, Reality is the product of a series of discursive operations that occur through the Master's Discourse structure. These discursive operations take place at two different levels: the ontic and the ontological level. Ontological discursive operations are paradoxical. On the one hand, they produce a division that creates radical alterity. This radical alterity is introduced by the opposition of two dichotomic terms: masculine and feminine. However, such radical alterity needs to be concealed to provoke a sense of heterogeneity, harmony, and universality among the elements that rest under the Master Signifier masculine. This is done by taming the feminine through the construction of a weak, fragile, and dependent subjectivity. While the ideal subjectivity in androcentric reality is man, this secondary subjectivity is woman. In this sense, as masculine and feminine principles may not interact due to the threat that the Real poses to Reality, two complementary and hierarchical genders are created to justify androcentrism. In this sense, love, as the relation between man and woman, makes up for the lack of relation between the feminine and masculine principles: "[w]hat makes up for the sexual relationship is, quite precisely, love" (Lacan, 1998a, p. 45).

Structure of This Book

This book's overall structure takes the form of two different parts to address such a complex topic. The first part develops a theoretical framework, and the second part applies it to the analysis of the construction of woman's identity in European politics and economy.

Part I, "Toward a Feminist Lacanian Left", starts with a brief introduction to central elements and ideas of Lacanian psychoanalysis and develops a feminist and critical reading based on the discursive mediation offered by the Lacanian Left. Furthermore, it aims to develop a Lacanian theory of discourse from a feminist perspective. This first part aims to illustrate how the exclusion of the feminine is necessary to create a masculine finite Reality within which the hegemony of the masculine is established. This first part is divided into different chapters to simplify and make accessible the understanding of Lacanian theory. It develops the idea that a specific discursive structuring operation founds reality and that such operation relies on establishing two main Master Signifiers (masculine and feminine) that separate the Real from Reality to set the grounds for the hegemonic struggle. Along these sections, the book affirms that Reality's framing operation operates at two different levels; by preparing the grounds for hegemony—at an ontic level—and by delimiting the subjects that may engage in such a hegemonic struggle—at an ontological level. The feminist turn here corresponds to the idea that these Master Signifiers correspond to the signifiers masculine and feminine, which transform the construction of Reality into a process of sexuation. Thus, this part focuses on how spaces for inhabitancy are created and how the inhabitancy of different spaces implies an unequal distribution of political ontological statuses. On the other hand, after analyzing the ontological consequences of discursive operations, part one focuses on explaining how hegemonic struggles occur at a discursive level. Thus, the book analyzes how Reality possesses the Borromean knot structure and how discursive operations locate different signifiers to create an illusion of finitude and harmony to shield Reality from the possible threats that the Real may pose.

Part II, "Some Notes for a Genealogy of Sexuation", applies the theoretical framework and illustrates how the imposition of the Master Signifier masculine implies a process of androcentrification through which the masculine subject is placed as the standard and ideal until it becomes the hegemonic and unique subjectivity. On the other hand, the imposition of the Master Signifier feminine implies the progressive exclusion of feminine elements and subjectivities from Reality and, therefore, from politics. This second part departs from the feminist critique to the Aristotelian division between matter and form, a division that operates excluding women from Reality. It aims to illustrate how the feminine—understood as elements that have been socially constructed not belonging to the masculine—has been stigmatized as non-valid and excluded from Reality. This part also analyzes how the liberal and the orthodox Marxist discourses share an androcentric ontological base that supposes the definition of centrality as the valid and masculine, and the periphery as the non-valid and non-masculine. Furthermore, this second part finishes by analyzing how women's introduction to Reality occurs through the imposition of a capitalist fantasy and subjectification that allow women to think of themselves as active agents within the hegemonic struggle.

Lastly, the book ends with a brief concluding chapter that offers some notes for a feminist political and economic praxis through community currencies and municipalism.

Notes

1 I hope that the clarification of the approach to the Lacanian Left as the central element for a Lacanian feminist reading of politics illustrates the reason why the central axis of this book is the work of the Lacanian Left and not the feminist reading of Lacan. Nevertheless, we are aware of the potential of feminist psychoanalysis for our theoretical framework and we hope to engage in further publications.
2 The terms Central and Peripherical countries will substitute the terms West and East.
3 This is easily observable in the way in which binary sex works. By the imposition of two unique sexes (male/female) the complex reality of intersexuality is obviated.

References

Agenjo-Calderón, A., & Gálvez-Muñoz, L. (2019). Feminist Economics: Theoretical and Political Dimensions. *American Journal of Economics and Sociology*, 78(1), 137–166.

Barker, D. K., & Kuiper, E. (Eds.) (2003). *Toward a Feminist Philosophy of Economics.* Routledge.

Beaumont, M. (2014). Imagining the End Times: Ideology, the Contemporary Disaster Movie, Contagion. En M. Flisfeder & L.-P. Willis (Eds.), *Žižek and Media Studies: A Reader* (pp. 79–89). Palgrave Macmillan US. https://doi.org/10.1057/9781137361516_7

Beck, U. (1997). *The Reinvention of Politics*, trans. M. Ritter, Cambridge: Polity.

Benjamin, J. (1988). *Bonds of Love. Psychoanalysis, Feminism, and the Problem of Domination.* Pantheon Books.

Bordo, S. (1986). The Cartesian Masculinization of Thought. *Signs*, 11(3), 439–456.

Brennan, T. (1989). Introduction. En T. Brennan (Ed.), *Between Feminism & Psychoanalysis* (pp. 1–23). Routledge.

Brown, W. (1988). *Manhood and Politics. A Feminist Reading in Political Theory.* Rowman & Littlefield International.

Butler, J. (1997). *The Psychic Life of Power. Theories in Subjection.* Stanford University Press.

Butler, J. (2004). *Precarious Life: The Powers of Mourning and Violence.* Verso.

Butler, J. (2009). *Frames of War: When is Life Grievable?* Verso.

Crenshaw, K. (1994). Mapping the Margins: Intersectionality, Identity Politics, and Violence Against Women of Color. En M. Albertson Fineman, & R. Mykitiuk (Eds.), *The Public Nature of Private Violence* (pp. 93–118). Routledge.

Evans, D. (1996). *Introductory Dictionary of Lacanian Psychoanalysis.* Routledge.

Fehr, C. (2018). Feminist Philosophy of Biology. En E. N. Zalta (Ed.), *The Stanford Encyclopedia of Philosophy (Fall 2018).* Metaphysics Research Lab, Stanford University. https://plato.stanford.edu/archives/fall2018/entries/feminist-philosophy-biology/

Fishel, S. R., Fletcher, A., Krishna, S., McKnight, U., du Plessis, G., Shomura, C., Valdés, A., & Voelkner, N. (2021). Politics in the Time of COVID. *Contemporary Political Theory.* https://doi.org/10.1057/s41296-021-00500-1

Grosz, E. (1990). *Jacques Lacan. A Feminist Introduction.* Routledge.

Haraway, D. (1988). Situated Knowledges: The Science Question in Feminism and the Privilege of Partial Perspective. *Feminist Studies, 14*(3), 574–599. https://doi.org/10.2307/3178066

Harding, S. G. (1991). *Whose Science? Whose Knowledge? Thinking from Women's Lives.* Cornell University Press.

Hibbs, C. (2014). Androcentrism. En T. Teo (Ed.), *Encyclopedia of Critical Psychology* (pp. 94–101). Springer New York. https://doi.org/10.1007/978-1-4614-5583-7_16

Hundleby, C. (2011). *Androcentrism as a Fallacy of Argumentation* (p. 13). University of Windsor. https://scholar.uwindsor.ca/cgi/viewcontent.cgi?article=1013&context=ossaarchive&httpsredir=1&referer=#:~:text=ABSTRACT%3A%20The%20deep%20operation%20of,as%20a%20form%20of%20fallacy.&text=Androcentrism%20is%20related%20to%20other,%E2%80%9Cappeal%20to%20the%20standard.%E2%80%9D

Lacan, J. (1998a). *On Feminine Sexuality: The Limits of Love and Knowledge.* Norton.

Lacan, J. (1998b). *The Four Fundamental Concepts of Psychoanalysis (Reiss).* Norton.

Lacan, J. (2007). *The Other Side of Psychoanalysis* (R. Grigg, Trad.). Norton and Company.

Laclau, E. (1990). *New Reflections on The Revolution of Our Time.* Verso.

Laclau, E. (2007). *Emancipations.* Verso.

Laclau, E. (2014). *The Rhetorical Foundation of Society.* Verso.

Laclau, E., & Mouffe, C. (2001). *Hegemony and Socialist Strategy: Towards a Radical Democratic Politics* (2nd ed.). Verso.

Maffía, D. (2007). Epistemología feminista: La subversión semiótica de las mujeres en la ciencia. *Revista venezolana de estudios de la mujer, 12*(28), 63–98.

Marx, K. (1992). *Capital_ Critique of Political Economy Volume 1.* Penguin Classics.

Mies, M. (2001). *Patriarchy and Accumulation on a World Scale: Women in the International División of Labour.* Zed.

Morris, B. (2017). We've Always Been Borderline: Understanding the Site of a Radical Subjectivity. *Free Associations: Psychoanalysis and Culture, Media, Groups, Politics, 71*, 51–64.

Mouffe, C. (1993). *The Return of the Political*. Verso.

Mouffe, C. (2005). *On the Political*. Routledge.

Nelson, J. A. (2003). How Did "The Moral" Get Split from "The Economic"? En *Toward a Feminist Philosophy of Economics* (pp. 134–141). Routledge.

Pérez Orozco, A. (2017). *Subversión feminista de la economía. Aportes para un debate sobre el conflicto capital-vida* (3.a ed.). Traficnates de Sueños.

Rubin, G. (1975). The Traffic in Women: Notes on the "Political Economy" of Sex. En R. R. Retier (Ed.), *Toward an Anthropology of Women* (pp. 157–210). Monthly Review Press.

Stavrakakis, Y. (1999). *Lacan and the Political*. Routledge.

Stavrakakis, Y. (2007). *The Lacanian Left: Psychoanalysis in Contemporary Political Theory*. Edinburgh Univ. Press.

Trejo, M. R. (2006). Aproximaciones a los estudios críticos feministas de las ciencias sociales en México y Centroamérica. *Revista Clepsydra*, *15*, 11–33.

Valdés, A. (2019). Can erotic Capital Subvert Masculine Economy? Aesthetic Work and the Post-Feminist Approach to Economics. *Recerca: revista de pensament i analisi*, *24* (2), 87–108.

Valdés, A. (2021). The Facemask Paradigm: Symptoms and Non-neutral Limits during Coronavirus. *Free Associations: Psychoanalysis and Culture, Media, Groups, Politics*, *81–82*, 18–30. https://doi.org/10.1234/fa.v0i81-82.380

Wright, E. (1989). Thoroughly Postmodern Feminist Criticism. En T. Brennan (Ed.), *Between Feminism and Psychoanalysis* (pp. 141–152). Routledge.

Zizek, S. (2000). *The Ticklish Subject. The Absent Centre of Political Ontology*. Verso.

Žižek, S. (2008). *The Sublime Object of Ideology (Nachdr.)*. Verso.

Part I

Toward a Feminist Lacanian Left

Chapter 1

Reality as a Discursive Operation

Before engaging in a feminist reading of Lacan, certain fundamental Lacanian theoretical notions need to be explained. Nevertheless, this introduction does not deepen into the different and multiple appropriations of specific Lacanian notions by the authors of the Lacanian Left. Instead, this introduction aims to clarify certain notions from Lacanian psychoanalysis applicable to the analysis of Reality. However, central concepts that are missing in this introduction are explained in the upcoming chapters.

Toward a Lacanian Discourse Analysis

One of Lacan's most famous theoretical articulations is his study on language and discourse, which can be described as a theoretical corpus with a high potential for political philosophy. Nevertheless, and as Callum Neill affirms, "Lacan was not a discourse analyst and there is not already a clearly demarcated and established approach to analysing discourse which would claim to the name Lacanian Discourse Analysis" (2013, p. 334). However, several attempts have been made to develop such a theoretical body. While many authors of the Lacanian Left have managed to start building a theoretical body from Lacanian thought applicable to politics, the first and leading development of a potential Lacanian Discourse Analysis applicable to the field of political theory was developed by Chantal Mouffe and Ernesto Laclau in their book *Hegemony and Social Strategy* (2001). A book in which they show the importance of signifiers, in the form of nodal points, for constructing political discourse. Nevertheless, it is vital to highlight that, as well as a Lacanian Discourse Analysis does not exist as such, the idea of a Lacanian Left, as Stavrakakis points out, does not embrace a homogenous group that shares an exact and unique position or approach toward politics (2007).

In this sense, this book attempts to grasp the formulation of a theoretical corpus that will analyze how Reality is constructed through a political discursive operation departing from Ernesto Laclau's work. However, while the book shares fundamental conceptualizations developed by Laclau in discourse analysis, it differs from other formulations of his work, such as his conceptualization of the Real

DOI: 10.4324/9781003167587-3

and *jouissance*. Furthermore, the feminist approach of this book also implies a renovation of his work.

Discourse and Reality

The relation between discourse and Reality in Lacan's work is easily observable. In his *Seminar XX*, Lacan affirms that "[t]here's no such thing as pre-discursive reality. Every reality is founded and determined by a discourse" (1998, p. 32). Thus, Reality can be seen as a product of a specific discursive operation. In this sense, Lacan defines ontology as a worldview discourse, a philosophical discourse that attempts to embrace Reality as *what it is*. In this sense, ontology results problematic.

On the one hand, ontology defines Reality, not the Real, because Reality exists and can be deciphered by language. On the other hand, the Real has the status of ex-sistence, which impedes deciphering the Real using language. Lacan also points out the problem that ontology brings by dwelling on the verb to be: "a verb that is not even, in the complete field of the diversity of languages, employed in a way we could qualify as universal—to produce it as such is a highly risky enterprise" (1998, p. 31). As Yannis Stavrakakis puts it, "Lacan suggests that social reality is not a stable referent, a depository of identity, but a semblance created by the play of symbolization and fantasmatic coherence [...] Reality is always constructed at the level of meaning and discourse" (1999, p. 54). In his *Seminar XVII. The Other Side of Psychoanalysis*, Lacan manages to define discourse "as a necessary structure that goes beyond speech" (2007, p. 12). It is important to clarify here that, as Lacan affirms, "discourse can clearly subsist without words. It subsists in certain fundamental relations which would literally not be able to be maintained without language. Through the instrument of language, a number of stable relations are established" (2007, p. 13). The *fundamental relation* between signifiers thus forms language. The result of the relations between signifiers is the production of signifying chains, which are characterized by two different properties:

- Metonymy: which is the connection of one word to another; this property gives language a sense of continuity.
- Metaphor: which is the exchange of one word by another and gives the sense of combination.

These two properties, as Stavrakakis points out, give signification (1999). Nevertheless, the process of signification is limited; therefore, metonymy and metaphor are not infinite. As Stavrakakis notes, when analyzing the development of the *point de capiton* in the seminar *The Psychoses*, signification is stopped by the role of specific signifiers that Lacan calls *points de capiton* (1999). A similar description is given by Lacan in his *Seminar XVII* when he says that S_1, the Master Signifier, "intervenes in a signifying battery [...] forming a network of what is called knowledge" (2007, p. 13). Thus, from these two theorizations, *points de capiton* are Master Signifiers that limit signifying chains and provide meaning, forming knowledge. The role of *points de capiton* is to link signifiers to signifiers.

> The *point de capiton* fixes the signifier to a signifying knot and not to an object [...] the existence of points de capiton never produces an eternally stable meaning, only a relative and temporary—albeit necessary—fixation; nevertheless, this fixation, most of the time, mythically invested with the properties of a final one.
>
> (Stavrakakis, 1999, p. 60)

Two main ideas emerge from this affirmation. First, Master Signifiers that work as *points de capiton* can change; they are not eternal. Second, *points de capiton* establish a close connection to an illusionary, *fantasmatic* object that provides these Master Signifiers with the image of eternity and completeness. It is in this theoretical frame that Laclau sets his work, as Yannis Stavrakakis and Jason Glynos affirm, "[c]learly, Laclau's work aims at showing the discursive nature of social objectivity: it understands human reality as socially constructed and articulated in discourse" (2004, p. 203). Reality, as Bruce Fink also affirms while analyzing Lacan's work, is a creation of the Symbolic as a discourse,

> is that which is named by language and can thus be thought and talked about. The social construction of reality implies a world that can be designated and discussed with the words provided by a social group's (or subgroup's) language. What cannot be said in its language is not part of its reality; it does not exist, strictly speaking.
>
> (1995, p. 25)

Two different ideas spring from the above extract. Firstly, that which cannot be said does not properly exist. What leads to the issue of power relations and language: *Caesar dominus et supra grammaticam* (the emperor is ruler over grammar as well). As this part aims to illustrate, subjectivities are also distributed by discursive mechanisms, as Lacan illustrates in his *Seminar XX* with the sexuation formulas (1998, p. 78). Thus, discourse operates in an ontic way by establishing what can be talked about and, in an ontological way, by establishing who may, or may not, speak. Thus, both the ontic and the ontological are results of discursive operations. However, this chapter focuses on the ontological level of discourse as political issues of unequal distribution spring from an unequal distribution of political subjectivities. Thus, it is necessary to analyze who the subjects that enter discursive operations are. As Lacan says, discourse is

> a mode of functioning or a utilization of language qua link [...] is a link between those who speak. You can immediately see where we are headed— it's not just anyone who speaks, of course; it's beings, beings we are used to

qualifying as 'living', and it would, perhaps, be rather difficult to exclude the dimension of life from those who speak.

(1998, p. 30)

Therefore, the capacity to speak does not imply a subject's entrance into the link of discourse. By referring to beings and life itself, an ontological differentiation between subjects determines whether a subject enters the signifying chain as a speaker. Therefore, those who speak, who enter into discourse, understood as a signifying chain, are specific beings that are qualified as living. This ontological differentiation is also present in the theoretical work developed by Judith Butler on grievable and livable lives (2004, 2009). It is necessary to note here the main ideas that can be extracted from the relation between Butler and Lacan for the analysis of reality as a discursive operation. Firstly, as Butler observed, not every life is conceptualized as livable nor living (2009). This unequal conceptualization takes back to the already mentioned idea that the production of discourse is relational and takes place within unequal power relations. Since not every subject is conceived as living, not every subject can enter the signifying chain by producing signification, in other words, as speakers. We suppose that Lacan is aware of this disparity when he affirms that

Every dimension of being is produced in the wake of the master's discourse— the discourse of he who, proffering the signifier, expects therefrom one of its link effects that must not be neglected, which is related to the fact that the signifier commands. The signifier is, first and foremost, imperative.

(1998, p. 32)

In the quote above, Lacan refers to a specific relational structure that discourse can take, the Master's Discourse. In this structure, there is the operation of introducing the (Master) signifier that functions fixating the signifying chain—precariously and temporarily. As a second idea from the relation between Butler and Lacan, for a subject to impose this intervening Master Signifier, the first condition is for the subject to be living. Furthermore, the Master's Discourse structure is not a temporal stage in the construction of Reality as a discursive operation but a form of discourse that operates continuously and prohibits the entrance of certain subjects categorized as non-living. In other words, there is a constant struggle to be able to impose the Master Signifier, a struggle that is commonly known as the struggle for hegemony.

Summing up, by introducing Butler to Lacan, Lacan's words can be radicalized through the idea that not only the establishment of *points de capiton* is reduced to power relations, but every relational operation in discourse responds to a struggle for power to control and govern inclusion and exclusion from the Symbolic. Thus, not only does discourse have its limits, as limits of the signifying chain itself, but they also set limits to who can produce signification and meaning. Therefore, discourse operates in two different levels, establishing the limits of what can be spoken about—ontic—and the limits of who can speak—ontological.

Discourse establishes what exists and who exists, which leads to speaking of that and those who are not part of the signifying chain as speakers, leading to the Heideggerian differentiation between existence and ex-sistence analyzed by Bruce Fink (1995). As Fink affirms, ex-sistence

> was first introduced into French in translations of Heidegger (e.g., *Being and Time*), as a translation for the Greek *ekstasis* and the German *Ekstase*. The root meaning of the term in Greek is 'standing outside of' or 'standing apart from' something [...] Lacan uses it to talk about 'an existence which stands apart from,' which insists as it were from the outside; something not included on the inside, something which, rather than being intimate, is 'extimate'.
>
> (1995, p. 122)

Thus, the translation and shifting of the Lacanian theoretical corpus toward an analysis of social reality in political terms need to embrace the discussion of subjects that enter or are excluded from processes, mechanisms, and institutions. Thus, those who are not seen as living, as speaking, only ex-sist. Ex-sistence refers to a different ontological status characterized by the fact that the subject stands outside of something. In the Lacanian analysis this book proposes, subjects stand out of Reality; in other words, it stands out of a specific relational discursive operation that founds Reality through the imposition of a Master Signifier. On the other hand, and opposing ex-sistence to existence, existence refers to the ontological status of the subject that stands inside the discursive relation proper of the Master's Discourse. In this sense, if existence refers to the ontological status of beings that inhabit Reality, ex-sistence, as there is no pre-discursive Reality, refers to the ontological status of the beings that inhabit the Real, "[t]he real is perhaps best understood as that which has not yet been symbolized, remains to be symbolized, or even resists symbolization; and it may perfectly well exist 'alongside' and in spite of a speaker's considerable linguistic capabilities" (Fink, 1995, p. 25). The political approach this book endorses is thus interested in analyzing specific questions about the Real. Does every subject that inhabits the Real resist symbolization? How is it decided, or who is to decide whether the Real must remain unsymbolized? These questions necessarily take to the conception of hegemony developed by Mouffe and Laclau in *Hegemony and Social Strategy* (2001).

From a political perspective, discursive operations are developed to hegemonize Reality. Although, as Fink affirms, "[e]very person's reality differs from the mere fact that every cultural and religious group, subculture, family, and set of friends develops its own words, expressions, and idiosyncratic meanings" (1995, p. 25), since a partial fixation is necessary for the production of meaning, there is also a hegemonic conception of reality, called Reality. Reality is the ground where antagonistic relations among subjects struggling to impose their hegemony occur. From this perspective, and as this book will examine further in later chapters, antagonism is a relational struggle to achieve hegemony in which only subjects who exist can take part. While dislocation, as Laclau names it from *New Reflections on the Revolution of Our Time* onward, refers to the moment in which the Real can be observed by the Symbolic's inability to represent it (1990).

Summing up, some core ideas of our theoretical body need to be emphasized:

- A specific discursive operation founds Reality by the intervention of a Master Signifier upon a battery of signifiers and imposes a specific order.
- A Master Signifier also works as a *point de capiton*, whose function is to fix the meaning of the signifying chain.
- The relational discursive operation that founds Reality consists and results in unequal relations of power.
- What/who inhabits Reality has existence, while that which is outside is relegated to ex-sistence.
- The struggle that takes place among existing subjects to impose the *points de capiton* is called a hegemonic struggle.

Nevertheless, the Reality that results from these discursive operations is fragile as the fixation that produces the Master Signifier is always partial and precarious. This precariousness adds another dimension to the hegemonic struggle; it is not enough to impose the Master Signifier but is also necessary to assure its continuity as a *point de capiton*. This continuity can be assured by providing the Reality of coherence and harmony, legitimating the status quo that such hegemony establishes. The imposition of a fantasy achieves this coherence; this is what Stavrakakis names the 'fantasmagoric coherence' (1999, p. 54). Certain notions about the subject's conception in Lacan need to be developed to speak of the fantasy that supports Reality.

The Lacanian Subject

Why do humans keep developing discursive operations that aim to establish a closed system to confine everything that exists? Before dwelling on such a question, it is necessary to analyze certain elemental aspects of the Lacanian subject.

As Stavrakakis points out, Lacan articulates his notion of the subject by addressing the Freudian idea of the split subject, "[t]he roots of this conception of subjectivity can be traced to the Freudian idea of *Spaltung* (splitting)" (2008, p. 1041). This Freudian turn implies a fundamental rupture with the androcentric liberal individualist conception of the subject that emerged with the Cartesian revolution of thought (Bordo, 1986; Grosz, 1990). As Lacan himself affirms, the conceptualization of the subject in psychoanalysis "is an experience that leads us to oppose any philosophy directly issuing from the Cogito" (2001, p. 1). More politically, Stavrakakis notes that

According to Lacan the subject of psychoanalysis is not the self-sufficient, 'autonomous' subject as it is constructed in the tradition of philosophy, that is to say, as corresponding to consciousness, to the conscious cogito, but the ex-centric subject, one structured around a radical split, a radical lack.

(2008, p. 1041)

Lacan radicalizes Freud by maintaining that the conscious subject, the ego, "is clearly not an active agent, the agent of interest being the unconscious. Rather than qualifying as a seat of agency of activity, the ego is, in Lacan's view, the sear of fixation and narcissistic attachment" (Fink, 1995, p. 37). The ego is an imaginary representation that emerges in what Lacan calls the Mirror Stage; at this stage, the child acquires an imaginary unity of their identity by the image that the mirror reflects. Nevertheless, this image is never a reliable one but distorted in size and direction, which "prefigures its alienating destination" (Lacan, 2001, p. 2). This first identification results in alienation and the failure to construct a stable identity in the Imaginary register; this takes the child to attempt to construct their identity in the Symbolic register, the signifying chain discursive relation. Stavrakakis defines the passage from the Imaginary to the Symbolic as follows:

instead of transgressing alienation in the direction of acquiring a solid iden-tity, the subject of the signifier, the subject constituted on the basis of the acceptance of the laws of language, is uncovered as the subject of lack *par excellence* [...] This lack can only be thought as a trace of the ineliminable act of power at the root of the formation of subjectivity, as the trace of an *ex nihilo* decision entailing the loss of certain possibilities or psychic states (the imaginary relation with the mother, for example) and the formation of new ones.

(1999, p. 20)

The passage to the Symbolic register—Reality—implies the submission of the subject to the Symbolic, the Signifier, also called the Other (A). Interestingly and smartly, Butler, although she is not referring to Lacan, but Foucault and Althusser, maintains that such submission is a condition *sine qua non* for the pro-cess of subjectification that takes place in the entrance of the subject to discourse (1997). Butler denominates this process 'subjection' which refers to the process of submission and the process of developing the subject: "'Subjection' consists precisely in this fundamental dependency on a discourse we never chose but that, paradoxically, initiates and sustains our agency" (1997, p. 2). It is interesting to see here that there are two different processes: subjectification and subjection.

On the one hand, subjection is the process through which any subject is depend-ent on a discourse. On the other hand, the process of subjectification appears once the subject is introduced in the signifying chain, thus producing or reproducing discourse. In this sense, the process of 'subjection' is common for subjects that are to be found inside and outside the discursive operation that founds Reality. Both subjects are dependent on discourse, as Butler admits in the quote above, but only the subject who enters the signifying chain can undergo the process of subjectification. In other words, *subjection assures ex-sistence, while the process of subjectification provides existence.* What are the mechanisms that allow or prohibit the subject from entering the production of existence? The structure of the Master's Discourse that founds Reality also allows for the emergence of the subject that is to inhabit such Reality. In this sense, as Reality responds to interests and unequal relations of power, the subject that emerges through the Master's Discourse is also an ideal subject representing specific interests. As Lacan himself affirms,

> There is, according to analytic discourse, an animal that happens to be endowed with the ability to speak (*qui se trouve parlant*) and who, because he inhabits the signifier, is thus a subject of it. Henceforth, everything is played out for him at the level of fantasy, but at the level of a fantasy that can be perfectly disarticulated in a way that accounts for the following – that he knows a lot more about things than he thinks when he acts.
>
> (1998, p. 88)

Although Lacan does not seem to refer to a specific speaking animal among the ones that can speak, I maintain that the emergence of the subject that inhabits the signifier is the emergence of an ideal subject. Such an ideal subjectivity is not reachable by every subject. Thus, politics should be read as identity politics, as the first step to engage in politics relates to affection and identification toward the subject offered by discourse for the continuous process of identification. The entrance in the Symbolic is alienating since it obliges the subject to reject specific dimensions that do not fit in the identification process offered by the Symbolic.

The Lacanian subject emerges into his work as a revolutionary category, as a subject constituted by a split between consciousness, the ego as the imago, and unconsciousness, "between an ineluctably false sense of self and the automatic functioning of the language (the signifying chain) in the unconscious" (Fink, 1995, p. 45). Thus, Lacan turns to discourse to dwell on the agency of the subject who has been marked by alienation in the first identification in the Imaginary register and who will undergo a second alienation in identification in the Symbolic register. In this second alienating identification, the lack appears as what must be lost to enter the Symbolic. Going back to Butler, she asks why the subject renders to submission. Far from agreeing with the idea that the subject is responsible for their submission, Butler affirms that "the attachment to subjection is produced through the workings of power, and that part of the operation of power is made clear in this psychic effect, one of the most insidious of its productions" (1997, p. 6). Butler mentions Foucault and the passionate attachment that a child develops toward whom they depend on and adds that

> Although the dependency of the child is not political subordination in any usual sense, the formation of primary passion in dependency renders the child

vulnerable to subordination and exploitation, a topic that has become a pre-occupation of recent political discourse. Moreover, this situation of primary dependency conditions the political formation and regulation of subjects and becomes the means of their subjection. If there is no formation of the subject without a passionate attachment to those by whom she or he is subordinated, then subordination proves central to the becoming of the subject. As the condition of becoming a subject, subordination implies being in a mandatory submission. Moreover, the desire to survive, 'to be,' is a pervasively exploitable desire.

(1997, p. 7)

Furthermore, by transferring these thoughts to the analysis of politics, I maintain that political identification is an affective attachment toward a specific narrative offered by discourse once the subject has undergone a previous subordination process (subjection). Furthermore, this affective attachment is unidirectional; the person who aims to undergo subjectification needs to establish affective bonds toward an ideal subject that may or may not represent them.

For Lacan, a unique subject emerges from the structure of the Master's Discourse; from this book's perspective, this discursive operation results in the emergence of different subjects. Subjects with existence are those that successfully enter the signifying chain. This is due to their resemblance, or potential resemblance, with the ideal subject of the Symbolic and their adequation to the rules of the Symbolic. However, the success of symbolic identification does not imply the achievement of a complete identity, as the lack of the subject makes it an impossible campaign. Instead, it only assures the entrance in the continuous process of identification that can occur once the subject enters the Symbolic register. Success is the affective attachment that certain subjects can develop toward the ideal subject that emerges from a specific discursive operation. The failure to engage Symbolic identification is the rejection certain subjects receive when attempting an identification, whether it is a result of their rejection of the Symbolic order or a result of their imposed incompatibility with the subject offered in the Symbolic register. The critical element of the process of subjectification—successful symbolic identification—is thus affection, affection toward the ideal proposed by the Symbolic order. Consequently, different political subjects emerge from the process of subjectification.

- **Subjects with existence**: subjects with a constitutive lack that impedes their achievement of a full identity but that, nevertheless, have a successful symbolic identification as they can enter the signifying chain and develop affective attachments toward a specific narrative within discourse and the ideal subject it proposes. These subjects inhabit the space of Reality.
- **Subjects with ex-sistence**: subjects with a double lack. They possess the constitutive lack and a second constituted lack that results from their resistance or prohibited entrance toward the ideal or the normativity that offers the Symbolic order. These subjects inhabit the Real.

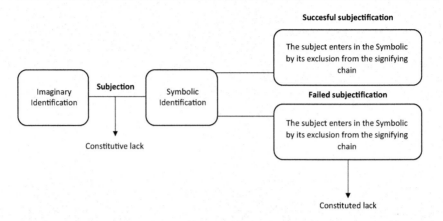

Figure 1.1 Illustrates the Process of Identification.

This classification of subjects (Figure 1.1) is only possible when referring to Reality's political dimension, as it allows us to think in terms of hegemony, power, and antagonism. Although there is an unequal distribution of the ability to become a subject from a political perspective, there is a common element in every subject, the constitutive lack. However, what is the subject lacking?

Lack and Desire

Lack is the product of the multiple attempts of identification by the subject. The constitutive lack of the Lacanian subject precludes its identity as positive, as complete. However, at the same time, this impossibility is precisely what makes possible the constant identification process. In this infinite process of identification, the subject turns to whatever social reality offers them as the instrument to suture their consistently failed identity. Thus, the Lacanian subject becomes an element to consider in political theory, since, as Stavrakakis affirms, "the objects of identification in adult life include political ideologies and other socially constructed objects, the process of identification is revealed as constitutive of socio-political life" (1999, p. 30).

As seen in the previous section, there are two different identifications in Lacan, imaginary and symbolic. Both identifications imply an alienating dimension and a split. The constant failure of identification processes makes the lack emerge due to the impossibility of achieving a total identity of completeness. This lack is inserted in a play of possibility and impossibility. The lack is a result of the impossibility of identity. Simultaneously, due to the rejection of certain elements to submit to the Signifier, it allows the subject to enter into the Symbolic register to introduce itself into new identification processes. Nevertheless, I have added a double result of this entrance on the Symbolic; a subject can enter the Symbolic register through inclusion—the subject enters the signifying chain—or through exclusion—the subject cannot enter the signifying chain and remains in the space of the Real.

The constitutive lack connects to the idea of an original loss, a sacrifice the subject makes, the loss of completeness. On the other hand, the constituted lack is a lack produced by the resistance or the prohibition to enter the signifying chain. While the constitutive lack is an inherent one, the constituted lack comes from outside the subject, and it is the result of an explicit imposition of power. If the lack is constitutive, if the subject never achieves an entirely satisfactory identity, why does the subject remain in a constant and infinite identification process? Why does not the subject give up identity? The root of such an insistency is to be found in desire.

Roger Horrocks affirms that "[d]esire itself flows from loss" (1997, p. 68). More politically, Stavrakakis affirms that "[l]ack stimulates desire and thus necessitates the constitution of every identity through processes of identification with socially available objects of identification" (2008, p. 1041). Thus, desire is the by-product, along with lack, of the necessary rejection to enter the Symbolic. Nevertheless, the entrance in the Symbolic is not a process allowed for every subject. Therefore, there must also be different forms of desire for different political identities. Thus, desire needs to be defined in constitutive lack and constituted lack. As Stavrakakis affirms when speaking of the relationship between lack and desire, "this is what creates the symbiotic relation between subjectivity and power" (2008, p. 1041). Nevertheless, to differentiate between the process of subjection and that of subjectification implies that there must also be two different relations between subjectivity and power. However, before I focus on how subjects who ex-sist relate to power, I will focus on how the subject who exists establishes the relationship between lack and desire.

Lack stimulates the desire for identification; these identifications rely on the organized Other (A). The Other

> designates radical alterity, an otherness which transcends the illusory otherness of the imaginary because it cannot be assimilated through identification. Lacan equates the big Other with language and the law, and hence the big Other is inscribed in the symbolic order. Indeed, the big Other is the symbolic insofar as it is particularized for each subject. Thus, the Other is both another subject in its radical alterity and unassimilable uniqueness and also the symbolic order which mediates the relationship with that subject.
>
> (*Other – No Subject – Encyclopedia of*
> *Psychoanalysis – Encyclopedia of Lacanian*
> *Psychoanalysis*, s.f.)

The Other can thus be read as the Symbolic, the Law, which imposes rejection to enter the process of subjectification. Therefore, the submission to the Symbolic, whether it ends up in mere subjection by exclusion or subjectification by inclusion, is the submission to the Other. Although there are different conceptions of the Other in Lacan's work, the focus here is on the Other as the Symbolic. However, in the upcoming chapters, I will also develop later reading of the Other as the Other sex.

As seen before, such submission implies alienation, "[a]lienation is essentially characterized by a 'forced' choice which rules out being for the subject, instituting instead the symbolic order and relegating the subject to mere existence as a place-holder therein" (Fink, 1995, p. 53). Nevertheless, I add here the double outcome of existence and ex-sistence.

On the one hand, the Symbolic only provides existence to those who enter the Symbolic by their inclusion in the signifying chain. On the other hand, those who do not enter the signifying chain enter the Symbolic through a process of exclusion that provides them with mere ex-sistence. This affirmation is closely related to the idea of the space of being and non-being developed by Frantz Fanon (2008). For Fanon, "[t]here is a zone of nonbeing, an extraordinarily sterile and arid region, an utterly naked declivity where an authentic upheaval can be born" (2008, p. 2). In Lacanian terms, the zone of non-being relates to the Real. However, in both possible outcomes of the subjection to the Other, alienation implies choosing our own disappearance, "*[a]lienation gives rise to a pure possibility of being*" (Fink, 1995, p. 52). Bruce Fink adds that the process of separation follows the operation of alienation:

> Lacan's second operation, *separation, involves the alienated subject's con-frontation with the Other, not as language but as desire* [...] separation con-sists in the attempt by the alienated subject to come to grips with that Other's desire as it manifests itself in the subject's world.
>
> (1995, p. 50)

In this process, the Other and the subject are separated, which pushes the subject to realize the Other is not complete. In more general and political terms, when the subject enters the Symbolic searching and attempting a full identity, it real-izes that such a fullness cannot be achieved through the Other. The Other cannot provide the subject with the full identity as the Symbolic order, Reality, cannot embrace the wholeness. As Stavrakakis affirms, "[t]he field of representation is itself revealed as lacking because it attempts the impossible, that is to say, the representation of something ultimately unrepresentable"(1999, p. 38). The Real escapes its symbolization. The Other also has a lack. If the subject has a lack that takes him to the Symbolic, but the Other is also lacking, the subject must appeal to a third element: "[t]he subject's *being* must come, in a sense, from 'outside,' from something *other* than the subject and the Other, something that is neither exactly one nor the other" (Fink, 1995, p. 53). This third element is fantasy; "[n]othing in the symbolic can provide us with a solution for our division, a way out from this frustrating state. Thus, we are led to bring something in from another register, the quasi-imaginary *objet petit a*, the field of fantasy" (Stavrakakis, 1999, p. 45).

Fantasy is the ultimate mechanism to solve the lack in the Other and also connects to desire; "[f]antasy is a construction that stimulates, that causes desire, exactly because it promises to cover over the lack in the Other, the lack created by the loss of *jouissance*" (Stavrakakis, 1999, p. 46).

Jouissance, Fantasy, and Objet petit a

The recognition of the lack of the Other implies the emergence of three new elements into the analysis: *objet petit a*, fantasy, and *jouissance*. The obscurantism of Lacanian thought is even more palpable in the articulation of the terms *objet petit a* and *jouissance*, which makes their analysis and study complex. However, these two terms are central elements of Lacanian theory.

The entrance of the subject in the Symbolic implies, as stated above, submission, which requires that the subject must leave specific desires behind. However, the lack produced by the subject's entrance in the Symbolic results in creating new desires related to the subject's constant identification processes. Lacan calls the prohibited desire *jouissance*. As Lacan affirms, "*jouissance* is forbidden to him who speaks as such" (2001, p. 243). What the subject may get from the fulfilled desires in the Symbolic is thus pleasure, and what the subject may get from *jouissance* is pain. In purely psychoanalytical terms, Oedipus must abandon the dream of having his mother, which was already impossible. Thus, Oedipus enters the Symbolic with this prohibition. This prohibition makes possible the formation of a desire acceptable in the Symbolic, by the Law, in this case, the father. Thus, *jouissance* is the price that must be paid to enter the Symbolic.

However, what happens with this lost *jouissance*? *Jouissance*, far from disappearing, haunts the subject. As stated above, fantasy is the element to which the subject turns once the subject is aware of the lack of the Other. Since there cannot be an Other of the Other, fantasy works as the mechanism that allows the constant identification process. Lacan illustrates fantasy with the matheme $\$\lozenge a$. In this matheme, there is the split subject, a subject that cannot solve their split through the Other as the Other is also lacking. Fantasy offers the subject the elimination of the lack by articulating the subject around the *objet petit a*, which works as a lure of the lost *jouissance*, as Stavrakakis affirms,

> If the human condition is marked by a quest for a lost/impossible enjoyment, fantasy offers the promise of an encounter with this precious *jouissance*, an encounter that is fantasised as covering over the lack in the Other and, consequently, as filling the lack in the subject.
>
> (1999, p. 46)

Although Lacan's articulation and definition of *objet petit a* vary over time, as it happens with the majority of his most complicated ideas, his last definition of *objet petit a* offers an interesting addition for political implementation. The status of the *objet petit a* is singular. It plays, moves, and stands on top of the line that divides the Symbolic and the Real. As Evans points out, "[i]n the seminars of 1962–3 and of 1964, *objet petit a* is defined as the leftover, the remainder (Fr. *reste*), the remnant left behind by the introduction of the symbolic in the real" (1996, p. 129). However, it is also important to point out that, while *jouissance* is conceptualized as a negative dimension of the Real, the creation of the *objet petit a* as a lure of such *jouissance* is also a process through which the Real is positivized. As Glynos and Stavrakakis note, "the lack of the real is usually positivized (imaginarized) and presented in fantasy as an object of desire – what Lacan calls the *objet petit a*, the object-cause of desire" (2004, p. 207). In *Seminar XVII*, Lacan affirms that in the Master's Discourse, *objet petit a* emerges as the loss in the formation of knowledge (2007). Thus, in the Master's Discourse, a Master Signifier interferes in a given battery of signifiers producing a loss, the loss of *jouissance* represented—positivized, imaginarized—in the *objet petit a*.

Summing up, the loss of *jouissance* is bearable by the subject as long as its renunciation assures the relation with the Other and allows the subject to enter in continuous identification processes. After the subject realizes the Other is also lacking and that the promise of fullness is empty, the subject appeals to fantasy. Fantasy articulates the split subject around *object petit a*, which functions as a lure of the lost *jouissance*, which is the result of the impossible operation by the Symbolic to embrace the Real. However, these generally accepted conceptualizations of the Lacanian subject lack a feminist dimension of analysis. Let me develop them.

Objet petit a or the Non-androcentric Subject

The relevance of this book is the introduction of a feminist turn to the Lacanian Left. Such innovation rests on the affirmation that not every subject undergoes the same process of subjectification. As affirmed before, the entrance in the Symbolic has two different outcomes: subjection and subjectification. Although the subject that inhabits Reality can be analyzed through different theorizations offered by Lacan, I believe that a different theorization is needed to analyze subjects who inhabit the Real. Consequently, there needs to be a new way of describing the relation that such ex-sisting subjects maintain with the Other, *objet petit a*, fantasy and *jouissance*.

In the process of exclusion, I argued that the subject, after being appealed by the Other and its '*Che vuoi?*', finds itself unable to speak. In other words, the subject cannot enter the signifying chain as a speaker, as being able to produce or reproduce knowledge. More politically, it could be said that, although everyone must render submission to the Law, the Law does not necessarily imply justice or recognition to everyone. In other words, they are not able to speak. Such a question was already addressed by Gayatri Spivak when she asked whether the subaltern could speak (1988). Thus, although the subject rejects *jouissance* as the condition *sine qua non* to enter the Symbolic, such rejection is not validated by the Other. This failed acceptance by the Other can have two different outcomes:

(a) the subject offers more submission to the Other, making it impossible for the subject to see the lack in the Other; or (b) the subject denies the Other and accepts *jouissance* as the condition of ex-sistence.

These different outcomes are observable in different political identifications. Frantz Fanon analyzes how the black man wishes to be white (2008). In this sense, the subject offers an unconditional submission to the Other and cannot see its lack since the process of identification is impossible due to its negation by the Other. Another example is visible in how women attempt to become the ideal (masculine) subject of capitalism. On the other hand, the subject can also deny the Law, the Other, thus becoming a hysteric subject that embraces *jouissance*. Examples of this negation or denial of the law of the Other as the Symbolic are the dislocation that different native tribes in Abya Yala and transgender identities pose over normativity. While the first outcome, the total submission to the Other that impedes the observation of the lack in the Other, does not posit a risk to the Symbolic—*jouissance* is still out of the picture and does not even need to be positivized by the *objet petit a* for their desire to be articulated. The second outcome posits a risk to the Symbolic order as there is a subject closely related to the untamed Real. This encounter with the Real is observed as unfavorable by the Other as it is not controlled by fantasy.

Therefore, I argue that we face three different subjects. Three classes of subjects are characterized by the relation between lack, desire, *jouissance* each of them represents.

- The desiring subject: it refers to the subject that enters in subjectification. This subject can create affective bonds toward the ideal subject proposed by the founding discourse of Reality. Thus, this subject is entirely able to reject *jouissance* and to articulate its desire around the *objet petit a*. Summing up, the desiring subject is the subject of politics. This subject has rejected *jouissance*, sees the lack in the Other, and articulates desire around the *objet petit a* through the structure of fantasy.

- The anxious subject: it refers to the subject that undergoes subjection and can enter in the process of subjectification, but the ideal subject does not represent it. The process of subjectification is thus incomplete. The anxious subject rejects *jouissance* and expects to achieve a complete identity; nevertheless, such identity is not offered to the anxious subject. This lack of offering makes it impossible for the anxious subject to see that a complete identity is impossible. In contrast to the desiring subject, the anxious subject cannot see the lack in the Other, which makes it impossible for the anxious subject to enter in fantasy and articulate desire around the *objet petit a*. The subject has anxiety as Lacan defines it in his Seminar X; anxiety is provoked by a situation characterized by *the lack of the lack* (2014, p. 53). The subject does not see the lack in the Other and is not able to separate from it. It is through anxiety that a new form of desire appears. As Evans affirms, quoting Lacan,

[i]n the seminar of 1960–1 Lacan stresses the relationship of anxiety to desire; anxiety is a way of sustaining desire when the object is missing and, conversely, desire is a remedy for anxiety, something easier to bear than anxiety itself (S8, 430).

(1996, p. 11)

Thus, by not engaging in fantasy, the anxious subject finds themselves in a situation in which the object is missing and turns to desire as the remedy for the anxiety provoked by the incapability to see the lack in the Other. In anxiety, the subject does not articulate desire around *objet petit a*, but around an object put in such place. The anxious subject does not articulate desire around a lure of *jouissance* but around any object. The main characteristic of anxiety concerning the relation of the subject toward the Other is that the anxious subject does not know what they represent to the Other. This is because the only identity presented to them is the identity of an ideal subject that does not represent them, a subject toward which the anxious subject cannot establish the same affection as the desiring subject.

• The hysteric subject: the subject that, being subjected to the Symbolic, is not accepted by the Other. The lack of acceptance provokes the rejection of the Other by the subject and the decision to embrace *jouissance* as the central element of their ex-sistence. The relation between hysteria and desire is more complicated than the ones presented above. As Evans defines, "the hysteric is precisely someone who appropriates another's desire by identifying with them" (1996, p. 80). As with the anxious subject, the hysteric finds itself not recognized by the Other. Nevertheless, while the anxious struggles for acceptance by continuous submission, the hysteric feels that the father forces the rejection of *jouissance* to enter the Symbolic so the father can monopolize the enjoyment of *jouissance* and decides to go against him by embracing *jouissance*. In a Lacanian description, the hysteric is the one that embraces *jouissance* by identifying itself with the father, with that who grazes *jouissance*.

Summing up, this introduction suggests that these three subjects inhabit different spaces that invest them with unequal and different political capabilities. Such spaces of inhabitancy are:

• Reality: space inhabited by the desiring subject and the anxious subject. The desiring subject enters Reality by producing and reproducing meaning within the signifying chain's pre-given limits. The anxious subject cannot produce new meaning as it is not recognized by the Other; nevertheless, by not seeing the lack in the Other, this subject constantly reproduces the meaning already structured by the signifying chain. As I analyze in the following section, Reality, as a frame in which politics takes place, needs reproducibility that implies the production and reproduction of the frames, a task undertaken by these two subjects.

• The Real: the hysteric subject, the subject that embraces *jouissance*, inhabits the Real. The hysteric poses a constant risk to Reality as it does not accept the signifying chain's meaning. The hysteric cannot bear to become the object of desire, which makes the subject reject what has been established in the Symbolic, defying the reproduction of the frames of Reality.

References

Bordo, S. (1986). The Cartesian Masculinization of Thought. *Signs*, *11*(3), 439–456.

Butler, J. (1997). *The Psychic Life of Power. Theories in Subjection*. Stanford University Press.

Butler, J. (2004). *Precarious Life: The Powers of Mourning and Violence*. Verso.

Butler, J. (2009). *Frames of War: When is Life Grievable?* Verso.

Evans, D. (1996). *Introductory Dictionary of Lacanian Psychoanalysis*. Routledge.

Fanon, F. (2008). *Black Skin, White Masks* (New ed.). Pluto-Press.

Fink, B. (1995). *The Lacanian Subject. Between Language and Jouissance*. Princeton University Press.

Glynos, J., & Stavrakakis, Y. (2004). Encounters of the Real Kind: Sussing Out the Limits of Laclau's Embrace of Lacan. En S. Critchley & O. Marchart (Eds.), *Laclau: A Critical Reader* (pp. 201–216). Routledge.

Grosz, E. (1990). *Jacques Lacan. A Feminist Introduction*. Routledge.

Horrocks, R. (1997). *An Introduction to the Study of Sexuality* (J. Campling, Ed.). Palgrave Macmillan UK. https://doi.org/10.1057/9780230390140

Lacan, J. (1998). *On Feminine Sexuality: The Limits of Love and Knowledge*. Norton.

Lacan, J. (2001). *Ecrits: A Selection* (A. Sheridan, Trad.). Routledge. https://www.taylorfrancis.com/books/e/9780203995839

Lacan, J. (2007). *The Other Side of Psychoanalysis* (R. Grigg, Trad.). Norton and Company.

Lacan, J. (2014). *Anxiety* (J.-A. Miller, Ed.; English edition). Polity.

Laclau, E. (1990). *New Reflections on The Revolution of OurTime*. Verso.

Laclau, E., & Mouffe, C. (2001). *Hegemony and Socialist strategy: Towards a Radical Democratic Politics* (2nd ed.). Verso.

Neill, C. (2013). Breaking the Text: An Introduction to Lacanian Discourse Analysis. *Theory & Psychology*, *23*(3), 334–350. https://doi.org/10.1177/0959354312473520

Other—No Subject—Encyclopedia of Psychoanalysis—Encyclopedia of Lacanian Psychoanalysis. (s. f.). Recuperado 7 de septiembre de 2019, dehttps://nosubject.com/Other#cite_note-4

Spivak, G. (1988). Can the subaltern speak? En C. Nelson (Ed.), *Marxism and the Interpretation of Culture* (pp. 271–313). Macmillan Education.

Stavrakakis, Y. (1999). *Lacan and the Political*. Routledge.

Stavrakakis, Y. (2007). *The Lacanian Left: Psychoanalysis in Contemporary Political Theory*. Edinburgh Univ. Press.

Stavrakakis, Y. (2008). Peripheral Vision: Subjectivity and the Organized Other: Between Symbolic Authority and Fantasmatic Enjoyment. *Organization Studies*, *29*(7), 1037–1059. https://doi.org/10.1177/0170840608094848

Chapter 2

The Topology of Reality

The Space of Existence the Space of Ex-sistence

Why have not technological advances, civil and human rights, economic development, and other advances made equality a universal fact? Why does it seem that equality is a status only reachable by achieving the white cisgender male's socioeconomic position? Why does it have to be a Latina sweeping the floor every time a white woman breaks the glass ceiling? Why did Marxism fail to achieve real equality for women? I believe these and other questions can be answered by analyzing how different subjectivities are constructed and the place they inhabit in the structure of Reality.

Furthermore, subjectivities and the place they inhabit are results of discursive operations. By departing from the discursive mediation the Lacanian Left offers of Lacan's theoretical corpus and adding a critical feminist reading of their work, this chapter aims to develop a topology that illustrates how subjects emerge through discourse and how such an emergence locates them in a specific space of inhabitancy. Topology illustrates how constituent parts are interrelated or arranged. Evans analyzes what topology implies in the work of Lacan and points out that

> Lacan's interest in topology arises, then, because he sees it as providing a non-intuitive, purely intellectual means of expressing the concept of STRUCTURE that is so important to his focus on the symbolic order. It is thus the task of Lacan's topological models 'to forbid imaginary capture' (E, 333). Unlike intuitive images, in which 'perception eclipses structure', in Lacan's topology 'there is no occultation of the symbolic' (E, 333).
>
> (1996, p. 210)

Lacan's interest in topology can be observed in his use of the figures of the cross-tap, the torus, and the Borromean knot, among others. I agree with Evan's interpretation of Lacan's interest in topology and agree with the idea that topology can help analyze and visualize how structures are articulated and built. Thus, topology

DOI: 10.4324/9781003167587-4

is an interesting tool to create a cognitive map that illustrates political discourse and the spaces for inhabitancy it creates.

However, some clarifications are needed to briefly introduce the topic that concerns this first part of the book. This book relies on the idea developed in Chapter 1 that affirms that Reality is a frame that establishes which elements and which lives are to count as political, as living, and existing. The processes that give shape to this frame are discursive operations. This chapter aims to analyze how Reality, as a frame of existence, functions and is constructed. This analysis involves studying the structure of discourse and attempts to offer a topology of this frame. Lastly, this analysis aims to function as the grounds for a feminist reading that affirms that the discursive operations of political framing are processes of sexuation that construct Reality in an androcentric way. In other words, the frame of existence of Reality is a frame that situates the androcentric existence at the center.

Reality

Although reality is subjective, every one of us can read reality differently; *there are as many realities as people that analyze it*. The truth is that such reading is conditioned by what we could name the hegemonic reading of Reality. To speak of Reality and not of realities attends to the fact that legislation, regulations, norms, and other symbolic elements are thought and applied by embracing a particular reading of reality. This capitalized Reality has a political root as the hegemonic reading of Reality results from the exercise of power proper of politics. In other words, (Political) Reality denominates what counts as existing from the standpoint of politics. Such Reality is the result of a discursive operation that works in two different manners. First, by establishing the signifying chain, it delimits that which can be talked about. Second, it delimits which subjects can produce, and not only reproduce, new meanings in the signifying chain.

This chapter's thesis is that these discursive operations work in two different planes or levels. One of them corresponds to what Heidegger named the ontic, while the other corresponds to the ontological (Figure 2.1). Michael Inwoods describes in a very concise and clear manner the difference between ontic and ontological, quoting Heidegger:

> Ontology is the 'study of beings as such', but it can be a 'regional' ontology, concerned with the BEING or nature of e.g. numbers, space, or a work of literature (XXII, 8). In contrast to such ontological, *ontologisch(e)*, inquiry, the inquiry and findings of unphilosophical mathematicians, geometers or philologists are *ontisch(e)*, concerned with beings, not with their being. [...] But 'ontology', like its near equivalent, 'metaphysics', usually indicates a general study of beings (Nil,209/niv, 155).
>
> (2000, p. 147)

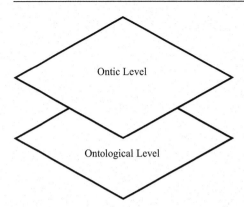

Figure 2.1 Topology of Political Reality.

In her book *On The Political*, Chantal Mouffe translates these Heideggerian terms to political analysis and affirms that

> we could, borrowing the vocabulary of Heidegger, say that politics refers to the 'ontic level' while 'the political' has to do with the ontological one. This means that the ontic has to do with the manifold practices of conventional politics, while ontological concerns the very way in which society is instituted.
>
> (2005, pp. 8–9)

More specifically, Mouffe defines politics as "the set of practices and institutions through which an order is created, organizing human coexistence in the context of conflictuality provided by the political" (2005, p. 9). Moreover, as Stavrakakis points out, she also defines the Political as "what is related to what generates society, the different forms of society" (1999, p. 73). On the other hand, as seen in the introduction, Stavrakakis, who also uses the opposition between politics and the Political, defines politics as a separate system that possesses boundaries, unique spaces where politics are performed by specific agents sanctioned to do so. Moreover, Stavrakakis also connects the notions of politics and the Political to the notions of Reality and the Real (1999). Thus, politics responds to a framed Reality that is exceeded by the Real as the Political. Therefore, Stavrakakis appeals to Beck and Laclau and their notions of the Political and defines it as that which excesses politics and needs to be repressed by politics for politics to be (1999, p. 71).

However, I slightly differ from Mouffe's translation of the Heideggerian terms of ontic and ontological to political usage. While I believe that there is an evident opposition between politics as Reality and the Political as the Real, I do not believe that such opposition can be translated into the terms of ontic and ontological.

Thus, Reality, politics, does not only consist of an ontic level, that is to say, related to the question of beings; but it also consists of an ontological plane in the sense that, although politics may not be interested with the being of its beings, it is interested in controlling of their not being. That is to say, *it controls the way in which the existence of the beings comes to be.* This way, politics acts upon the two different levels in which Reality consists. On the other hand, the Political understood as the Real that exceeds Reality and can suppose a threat to Reality needs to be excluded from the ontic and, more importantly, from the ontological to assure a non-threatening being of the beings. In this sense, the Political inhabits the outside, the periphery, of the ontological level imposed by discourse (Figure 2.2).

Thus, the discursive operation that establishes Reality acts upon the ontological level by creating two different spaces within it. These two differentiated spaces imply different ontological statuses: existence and ex-sistence. Let me analyze these ideas more profoundly.

The ontic level of politics establishes which elements, issues, demands, or interests are worth entering politics. It is the level concerned with beings, their needs, and desires. The ontic level of politics is responsible for limiting the signifying chain of political discourses, i.e., what are the things that can be distributed through taxes and what are the limits of freedom of speech. The ontological level of politics establishes who can intervene in politics. It is here where this book differs the most from Mouffe. At the ontological level, I argue that a framing operation establishes limits between the space for existence and the space for ex-sistence. Those who produce and reproduce the signifying chain of political discourse inhabit the place for existence. I call that place the Basic Political Community. The place of ex-sistence is where the Real, as the Political, inhabits. In other words, the ontological level of politics sets limits to the being of beings that accede to the ontic. Consequently, the Political is something that exceeds the clearly delimited ontic and ontological levels of politics. The Political is the ontological space where subjects that are not allowed to enter the Basic Political Community inhabit. Another way to express the differentiation between the ontic and the ontological level is to compare Foucault's theory of discourse and Lacan's theory of discourse. While Foucault

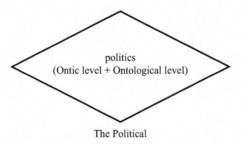

Figure 2.2 Politics and the Political.

works with the concrete material of the signifier, which puts the accent on the content of a discourse. Lacan, on the contrary, works beyond the content and places the accent on the formal relationships that each discourse draws through the act of speaking.

(Verhaeghe, 1995, p. 4)

In other words, the ontic is related to the content of discourse and the struggle to hegemonize knowledge by the imposition of a given S_1, while the ontological is related to the form, the social bonds that result, and the subjects that emerge from discursive relations. Nevertheless, how do the discursive operations work and construct the ontic and the ontological level?

The Ontological Level and the Basic Political Community

While the distinction between politics and the Political offers an interesting and promising horizon for social movements, I believe that to speak of the ontological level of Reality without addressing different ontological statuses has impeded the left to articulate a proper praxis to confront capitalism. Furthermore, recognizing different kinds of existences would allow European political theory and praxis to include subaltern agents in their agendas.

Every field of knowledge is susceptible to possessing an androcentric bias. This bias is visible in political praxis and theory as there are still struggles for identification, recognition of needs and desires, and issues of representation. To invoke a political proposal that only involves or puts the accent on the ontic does not result in the incorporation of new agents to politics. Neither does the addition of the ontological level without questioning the place that everyone inhabits and how such spaces invest the agent with different political subjectivities. I argue that the Lacanian Left, except for Judith Butler's work, has not been able to construct and offer a solution for the inclusion of every agent in politics due to its reduction of politics' ontological level to normative existences. The problem is not that different authors have not appealed the ontological, but the problem is that prominent authors have located the Real, the Political, in what we consider the wrong space and, therefore, in the wrong bodies.

Generally, political theory and philosophy are written from privileged positions. Just as policies do not focus on subjects in regular administrative situations (unless these policies are anti-immigration policies), political theory seems to speak of subjects who are already a part of a political community (Reality). Furthermore, several counterpower movements that have been going on all around Europe have been signalized for relying on different biases. For example, first-wave feminism has been pointed out as racist (Valverde, 1992); certain branches of white European ecologism that prioritize veganism over food sovereignty have been pointed out because of their profound urban and racist biases, and certain currents of white feminism have been criticized for their transphobia. In other words, even movements that could be read as threats to the prevailing ontological frame end up reproducing specific patterns that derive from the normativity of the ontological level of politics.

This section of the book analyzes the results of discursive operations occurring at the ontological level, which create different subjectivities and spaces of inhabitancy. As stated before, the ontological level of Reality delimits and differentiates subjects that can speak of politics—that can produce or reproduce the signifying chain—and those that cannot. Thus, the ontological level is produced by two different, yet not separated, processes: the processes of inclusion and exclusion of the signifying chain. From a political analysis, I affirm that the subject's inclusion in the signifying chain implies its inclusion in the Basic Political Community (BPC) (Figure 2.3).

Thus, I agree when Chantal Mouffe affirms that "Schmitt is right to insist on the specificity of the political association" (1993, p. 131). However, I diverge from her conception and from Schmitt's conception of what a political community is. For me, the definition of the public sphere developed by Judith Butler is an accurate definition of the BPC as the grounds upon which a subject is seen as living:

> The public sphere is constituted in part by what can appear, and the regulation of the sphere of appearance is one way to establish what will count as reality, and what will not. It is also a way of establishing whose lives can be marked as lives, and whose deaths will count as deaths.
>
> (2004, pp. xx–xxi)

Butler's definition is intimately connected to the one offered by Alexander Kluge when he defines the public sphere as "the site where struggles are decided by other means than war" (Negt & Kluge, 2016, p. ix). These definitions allow observing how political inhabitancy, ontological statuses, and the safety and livability of a life are deeply interrelated, which is a core idea in Butler's work. Following these definitions, those who inhabit the BPC are considered living, who, as Judith Butler analyzes, can be injured and grieved; those who do not suffer conflicts of violence and death (2009). From the approach of discursive mediation, the lives that can speak inhabit the BPC as the signifying chain that political discourse

Figure 2.3 Topology of the Ontological Level.

establishes. It is in the BPC that we find the desiring subject and the anxious subject. On the other hand, the space of ex-sistence is where the hysteric subject remains.

Thus, I believe that politics has an ontic dimension and an ontological level that serves as the legitimization of the ontic. This construction is intimately related to the construction of the political fantasy. Speaking of the political delimitation of the ontological level allows speaking of subjectivities that are not producing or reproducing the Symbolic and do not articulate a relation with the fantasy that supports Reality. At the ontic level, the struggle for hegemony occurs, but such a struggle is a privilege that only belongs to specific subjects that inhabit the BPC. Political discourses are potentially hegemonic because they appeal to a finite, definite, and delimited political community (BPC). Thus, the hegemonic struggle can only occur in a space that affirms the possibility of universality.

Universality depends on two central conditions in liberal democracies. On the one hand, universality cannot exist in an infinite space; if something is not finite, we may not embrace its fullness. On the other hand, universality is impossible in liberal democracies if they do not embrace the right to be different. This second point is the necessary heterogeneity. Universalism in liberal democracies needs finitude and heterogeneity; it is here where the anxious subject plays a central role. Universality is considered as taking place because the same agent that marks the limit is also the one that illustrates the heterogeneous nature of such democracy.

If heterogeneity is an essential characteristic of the BPC, how is the difference between the BPC and what remains outside defined? As affirmed in the introduction, a signifying system is only possible through a framing process that establishes non-neutral limits. The limits of a signifying process, as Ernesto Laclau affirms, imply an interruption with that which is outside. Thus, "true limits can never be neutral limits but presuppose an exclusion. A neutral limit would be one which is essentially continuous with what is at its two sides, and the two sides are simply different from each other" (Laclau, 2007, p. 37). Thus true limits, those that presuppose exclusion, are not derived from heterogeneity but radical alterity. This radical alterity imposes an antagonistic relation between what is inside the BPC and what remains outside. Thus, the BPC framing process is based on the basic *differentia especifica* principle developed by Carl Schmitt in his relational dichotomy friend/enemy, a relational and discursive process placed at the very basic notion of the political community (2007). Friends are placed inside the frames of Reality (the BPC); they are worthy of entering into the struggle of hegemony—remember that an inevitable heterogeneity is needed for the notion of universality. On the other hand, real enemies are placed outside, rejected, and left in the Real, out of the BPC. Nevertheless, before introducing ourselves to the analysis of hegemonic struggles, I must analyze how political discourse operates at the ontological level and articulates the BPC as an exclusive and excluding space.

Ontology as a Discourse

To think of the BPC as the result of a political discursive operation with ontological consequences reflects Judith Butler's work and her theory of framing (2009). For Butler, framing is an operation that works differentiating the lives that we can apprehend from those we cannot apprehend, "[t]he 'frames' that work to differentiate the lives we can apprehend from those we cannot (or that produce lives across a continuum of life) not only organize visual experience but also generate specific ontologies of the subject" (2009, p. 3). Butler also differentiates between apprehending a life and recognizing such life; to apprehend "can imply marking, registering, acknowledging without full cognition" (2009, p. 5), while to recognize a life implies the entrance of the subject into a frame that fully recognizes them.

The Butlerian reading of framing and her differentiation between apprehending and recognizing a life can be shifted into our terms of existence and ex-sistence. Apprehension only grants ex-sistence as being marked as the threat, as being registered as existing from outside, as dependent on a Symbolic that does not necessarily imply recognition. On the other hand, full recognition is only granted with existence once the subject has been allowed to enter the BPC. Furthermore, the issue of framing, as Butler notes, is a political process:

> the frames through which we apprehend or, indeed fail to apprehend the lives of others as lost or injured (lose-able or injurable) are politically saturated. They are themselves operations of power. They do not unilaterally decide the conditions of appearance, but their aim is nevertheless to delimit the sphere of appearance itself.
>
> (2009, p. 1)

Thus, framing is a discursive operation of power that originates from political interests and has political consequences. Furthermore, the question of unequal distribution of political subjectivities that opens this chapter has to be responded analyzing "the specific mechanisms of power through which life is produced" (Butler, 2009, p. 1). I believe that such power mechanisms can be analyzed through a *Lacanian theory of discursive ontology* translated to political analysis.

References

Butler, J. (2004). *Precarious Life: The Powers of Mourning and Violence*. Verso.
Butler, J. (2009). *Frames of War: When Is Life Grievable?* Verso.
Evans, D. (1996). *Introductory Dictionary of Lacanian Psychoanalysis*. Routledge.
Inwood, M. J. (2000). *A Heidegger Dictionary*. Blackwell Publishers.
Laclau, E. (2007). *Emancipations*. Verso.
Mouffe, C. (1993). *The Return of the Political*. Verso.
Mouffe, C. (2005). *On The Political*. Routledge.
Negt, O., & Kluge, A. (2016). *Public Sphere of Experience. Analysis of the Bourgeois and Proletarian Public Sphere*. Verso.

Schmitt, C. (2007). *The Concept of the Political* (Expanded ed.). University of Chicago Press.

Stavrakakis, Y. (1999). *Lacan and the Political*. Routledge.

Valverde, M. (1992). When the Mother of the Race is Free: Race, Reproduction, and Sexuality in First-Wave Feminism. En Franca Iacovetta and Mariana Valverde (eds.) *Gender Conflicts. New Essays in Women's History* (pp. 3–26). University of Toronto Press.

Verhaeghe, P. (1995). From Impossibility to Inability: Lacan's theory on the four discourses. *The Letter. Lacanian Perspectives on Psychoanalysis*, *3*(Spring), 91–108.

Chapter 3

A Lacanian Theory of Discursive Ontology

In *Seminar XI*, Lacan narrates when Jacques-Alain Millers asked him what his ontology was (1998b). Lacan answers that when speaking of the gap, the structuring function of the lack, "one is dealing with an ontological function" (1998b, p. 29). Nevertheless, "[t]he gap of the unconscious may be said to be pre-ontological" (Lacan, 1998b, p. 29). In his article "The Question of Lacanian Ontology: Badiou and Žižek as Responses to Seminar XI", Michael Austin suggests that Miller's question to Lacan about what his ontology is should be answered reading the texts of Badiou and Žižek (2016, p. 14). Austin notes that

> *Seminar XI* marks the beginnings of Lacan's famously difficult later work with its focus on diagrammatics, knots and locks. What his later work signifies is a move beyond language towards topology and structure-as-such, but it begins in this seminar, with its focus on the Real in opposition to the Symbolic.
>
> (2016, p. 14)

Nevertheless, although I agree with the observation of the importance of *Seminar XI* in a possible development for a Lacanian ontology, I believe that it is the constant tension between the ontological, the pre-ontological, the gap, and the Real what should be analyzed as the point of departure of a Lacanian ontology that focuses on the structuring function of the lack. Furthermore, Lacanian ontology is best developed by Lacan himself on *Seminar XVII* and his discourse theory (2007). This chapter aims to illustrate how Lacanian discourse theory, specifically his work on the structure of the Master's Discourse, gives the key for a Lacanian ontology. Therefore, we do not just speak of a possible Lacanian ontology but a Lacanian *discursive* ontology that embraces and continues the Butlerian theory of performativity. Thus, although Austin is right when he points out Badiou's ontology of the event and Žižek's emphasis of the Real as two essential articulations for a Lacanian ontology (2016), I believe that the discursive mediation to Lacanian theory that the Lacanian Left articulates paves the path for a political translation of a Lacanian ontology.

DOI: 10.4324/9781003167587-5

Far from aiming to develop a philosophical treaty on ontology, this chapter focuses on analyzing the power and influence that discourse has over the classification of lives as living and how *Reality, as a place where we exist, is the result of a political discursive operation with ontological consequences.* Therefore, instead of concentrating on the debate of whether we can speak of ontology and social ontology, or just social ontology, I will concentrate on how the classification between what ex-sists and exists occurs. Consequently, I will not argue whether water exists or not and if, therefore, we can speak of a pure or natural ontology. Instead, I will argue that ontology is a dominant discourse that establishes which lives are to be apprehended as living by developing a feminist discursive mediation to Lacan's *Seminar XVII* (2007). *Thus, ontology is always social, not because of its study's object, but because of ontology's discursive origin.*

The Master's Discourse as the Foundation of Political Reality

Lacan articulates his theory of the four discourses in his *Seminar XVII, The Other Side of Psychoanalysis* (2007). In this seminar, Lacan explains that words are not a condition *sine qua non* for discourse and that the core of discourse is relations that cannot subsist without language. Lacan also defines this fundamental relation "as the relation of one signifier to another. And from this there results the emergence of what we call the subject—via the signifier which, as it happens, here functions as representing this subject with respect to another signifier" (2007, p. 13). Thus, the subject is in need of a signifier that can represent them to another signifier.

In the case of the desiring subject, there is a signifier representing the desiring subject as it exists. That is to say, as introduced in earlier sections, the subject's successful subjectification springs from the affective attachment toward the ideal subject that emerges from a specific discursive operation. This discursive operation is precisely the Master's Discourse. The desiring subject enjoys a signifier representing it as it exists because there is a specific signifier for the ideal subject with whom the desiring subject identifies. On the other hand, the signifier in charge of representing the anxious subject to another signifier has been excluded from the signifying chain; the anxious subject, as the following section will show, is a sign that represents a signifier that has been excluded. This produces anxiety for this subject; the anxious subject attempts a constant (failed) identification with the desiring subject's signifier. Nevertheless, before dwelling on the construction of the subjectivity of the anxious subject, let us analyze Lacan's considerations on discourse through a feminist discursive mediation.

First, discourse consists of four different elements: (a) S_1: the Master Signifier: "the one that is the point of departure for the definition of discourse" (Lacan, 2007, p. 13), thus, the one that originates knowledge and meaning; (b) S_2: the battery of signifiers upon which S_1 intervenes; (c) $: the barred subject, the split subject; and (d) *a*: *objet petit a*. At the same time, these four elements can occupy four different positions (Figure 3.1).

The agent: it is the source of discourse. The horizontal arrow illustrates how the agent addresses the other.

The other: it is which or whom the agent addresses.

The truth: from this book's approach, the line that separates agent and truth illustrates that these two elements inhabit different levels. While the agent inhabits the ontic level, truth is at the ontological level. The agent relies or supports itself on a truth that legitimizes its existence at the ontic. The arrow that points upwards illustrates how truth is the original source of the agent's addressing operations.

The product/loss: from the addressing operation developed by the agent, there is a product of discourse. Nevertheless, the result can also be read in terms of loss, as what is lost in the agent's trajectory to the other. However, the loss does not fall to the ontological level. Loss is expelled from the structure of discourse while the product is what *falls* in the ontological. The arrow pointing downwards illustrates this fall. This idea is further developed in upcoming sections.

Furthermore, two arrows intersect in the middle of our schema. One of the arrows goes from product/loss back to the agent, which represents the process of communication. This process fails; the other does not receive the message as the agent intended it. This is why there is no direct relation between product and truth. This lack of relation is also expressed by a double bar (//) in other representations. The fact that the original message (truth) is not the same as the result of its reception (product) represents the failure of communication, which makes the agent engage in another addressing operation to develop another attempt to communicate the truth. On the other hand, the arrow that goes from truth to the other represents that, although the addressing operation's product is not the truth, truth still impacts the other.

From the positioning of the four different elements in these four positions, Lacan arrives at four different structures.[1] Lacan starts his *Seminar XVII* by describing the Master's Discourse structure due to its historical importance (2007). As Fink affirms, this discourse represents "the fundamental matrix of the coming to be of the subject through alienation" (1995, p. 130). Furthermore, Lacan affirms that "it is at the very instant at which S_1 intervenes in the already constituted field of the

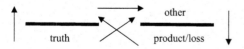

Figure 3.1 Positions in Discourse.

other signifiers [...that...] the subject as divided, emerges" (2007, p. 15). If, as this book affirms, the possibility of becoming a subject and not remaining a mere living individual is a matter of power, there must be an unequal distribution of subjectivities that must spring from this discursive structure (Figure 3.2).

Lacan described that the subject emerges from this structure. However, we claim that when Lacan speaks of the emergence of *the subject*, he refers to a specific subject. Lacan focuses his analysis on the desiring subject, which is the androcentric subject from a feminist perspective. Let us analyze the emergence of the desiring subject.

In this structure, a Master Signifier, S_1, intervenes in a battery of signifiers, S_2, which, as Lacan describes, "we have no right, ever, to take as dispersed, as not already forming a network of what is called knowledge [*savoir*]" (2007, p. 12). However, Lacan goes on and affirms that "[k]nowledge initially arises at the moment at which S_1 comes to represent something, through its intervention in the field defined" (2007, p. 13). From this paradox, I assume that the batteries of signifiers upon which S_1 intervenes are already formed by different signifiers, including a Master Signifier. Thus, there can be a constant substitution of Master Signifiers, which leads to assuming that the Master's Discourse is not a punctual form of discourse, but constant, which allows thinking of the struggle for hegemony as the struggle to conform and impose an S_1 that takes the place of the agent. This struggle takes place at the level of the ontic. On the other hand, at the lower level of the Master's Discourse structure, the other main result from this discourse occurs, the distribution of unequal ontological statuses: the emergence of subjects. Thus, if the struggle for hegemony is placed at the ontic level, the relational struggle to become a subject that can strive for hegemony takes place at the ontological level. Thus, the Master's Discourse and the structure of Reality have an ontological and an ontic dimension (Figure 3.3). Thus, such discourse's structure illustrates Reality's construction as a discursive operation.

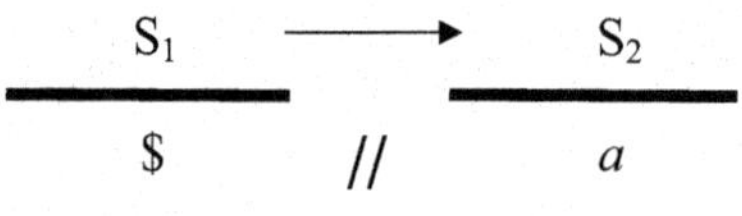

$$\frac{S_1 \longrightarrow S_2}{\$ \quad // \quad a}$$

Figure 3.2 Master's Discourse.

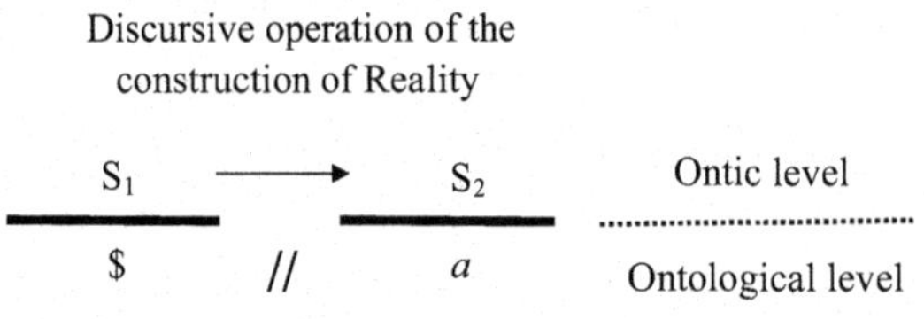

Discursive operation of the
construction of Reality

$$\frac{S_1 \longrightarrow S_2}{\$ \quad // \quad a} \qquad \begin{array}{l} \text{Ontic level} \\ \cdots\cdots\cdots\cdots\cdots\cdots \\ \text{Ontological level} \end{array}$$

Figure 3.3 Discursive Operation of the Construction of Reality.

At the ontic level, discursive dynamics constitute the signifying chain that governs the Symbolic, which decides what can be talked about. At the lower level, I find the ontological dimension of such a chain; the subjects that can talk. The dynamic of the ontic level—the intervention of S_1 over S_2—makes the split subject emerge ($). Thus, the ontic determines which type of subject will be able to control or reproduce the signifying chain, which leads us to think that the struggle for hegemony can be defined as the struggle to decide which S_1 will intervene in S_2, not just to create knowledge, but also to determine which individual can be thought of as a subject. However, this chapter first focuses on the ontological level.

This feminist discursive mediation allows for a different reading on Lacan's claim that *a signifier is what represents a subject to another signifier*. From this perspective, in the Master's Discourse, the relation is visible between the split subject ($) and the Master Signifier. Thus, departing from the Butlerian idea of performativity, there is a subject represented by a Master Signifier that precisely emanates from such a subject. This subject occupies in Lacan's schema the position of the truth; thus, S_1 relies on the existence of $ to hold its power at the same time that makes $ appear. The subject emerges as barred in relation to the other, to which he or she needs to be represented by a signifier. What is specific to the Master's Discourse is that $, the subject that emerges, is precisely represented as a subject of power. In other words, the Master's Discourse illustrates how a master subject, a desiring subject, appears. In this sense, it is interesting to see how, before the agent's location in the top left corner, Lacan placed desire. The dimension of the power of this discourse is visible at the upper level. S_1 intervenes over S_2 and creates meaning. Such meaning emanates from the condition of master of the subject represented by S_1. In other words, and as a way to clarify, the battery of signifiers is ordered around the master/desiring subject. From a feminist and antiracist perspective, this is easy to understand as our current battery of signifiers is androcentric and ethnocentric, that is to say, ordered around the European white male subject's experiences.

In the intervention of S_1 over S_2, $ emerges and is represented by S_1 to another signifier. Nevertheless, other elements result from the intervention of S_1 over S_2. Lacan affirms that when the subject emerges by entering into the Symbolic, he or she is commanded to reject *jouissance*. From a discursive mediation of his work, there can be a separation between loss and product in the structure in the Master's Discourse. On the one hand, *jouissance*, as the loss, is pushed out of the structure. On the other hand, what remains in the structure as the product of the intervention over S_2 is a new element that derives from the rejection of *jouissance*, *objet petit a* (Figure 3.4).

Jouissance, as the loss, as what needs to be rejected in order to emerge as a subject, is represented by $\neg S_1$. *Jouissance* is recreated as the Master Signifier of negativity that does not form part of the signifying chain; it is the Signifier of Pure Threat. It is created in opposition to the Master Signifier to establish de classical Schmittian political relationship of friend/enemy (Schmitt, 2007). Furthermore,

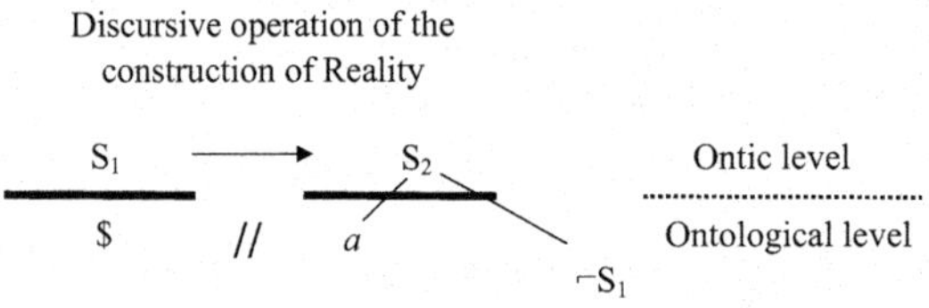

Discursive operation of the
construction of Reality

$$S_1 \longrightarrow S_2 \qquad \text{Ontic level}$$
$$\rule{2cm}{0.4pt}$$
$$\$ \quad // \quad a \qquad \text{Ontological level}$$
$$\qquad\qquad {}^{\neg}S_1$$

Figure 3.4 Distribution of Master Signifiers at the Level of the Ontological.

and as analyzed later on, this signifier also represents a subject to another signifier. In the case of the Signifier of Pure Threat, it represents the hysteric subject. On the other hand, what remains inside the Master's Discourse structure is a, the *object petite a*; the lure of *jouissance* that functions as the fuel of this construction of Reality. The unreachability of *jouissance* through the Master's Discourse, the constant loss, makes S_1 continuously intervene in S_2. *The impossibility of communication is precisely what makes communication possible.* Finally, the *hypokeimenon* of the Master's Discourse is not the anxious or the hysteric subject, but the desiring one, as it is the only subject that can articulate desire around the a that fantasy offers. The specificity of this subject is also pointed out by Lacan when he affirms that this subject "represents the specific trait of being distinguished from the living individual" (2007, p. 13).

Summing up, from a feminist discursive mediation, the Master's Discourse illustrates how the barred subject, as the quilting point of knowledge, as the androcentric subject, emerges. With his emergence, the anxious and the hysteric subject also appear. The emergence of these unequally distributed subjectivities also implies the apparition of spaces of inhabitancy. Thus, from this perspective, the Master's Discourse shows how Reality is constructed as a place for the desiring subject's existence and how the Real is constructed as the space of ex-sistence for those that may deny or threaten its mastery.

I believe that the Master's Discourse structure does not allow for the apparition of the Hysteric's Discourse, as the space of the hysteric's inhabitancy is the Real. The construction of Reality needs to delimit and obviate the Real and to be able to frame an S_2 in which S_1 can intervene. Thus, this leads to believe that, while S_1 governs Reality, it establishes an S_1 for the Real, which I name Signifier of Pure Threat ($\neg S_1$). The signifying chain works establishing true and antagonistic limits through two dichotomic Master Signifiers that define Reality and the Real following the Schimittian usage of the signifier we/they (2007).

To think of the Master's Discourse as the structure of the discursive operation that results in the imposition of Reality combined with the feminist critique allows articulating a different reading of the Master's Discourse. In an orthodox reading of this structure, we would conclude that S_1 is "the signifier, the signifier function, that the essence of the master relies upon" (Lacan, 2007, p. 21), and it addresses S_2 as the slave and the slave's knowledge. In the addressing operation, the master steals the knowledge from the slave, resulting in the product of a certain surplus.

What remains hidden is the master's split. The master has also undergone castration as the needed rejection to enter in the Symbolic. However, from the feminist, political discursive mediation, this discursive operation implies a sexuation. This sexuation is visible in the imposition of Master Signifiers S_1 (masculine) and $\neg S_1$ (feminine). Let us develop such reading.

The desiring subject, as the agent in Reality's discursive production, can create Master Signifiers. In the structure of the Master's Discourse, the desiring subject produces a Master Signifier that imposes limits to the signifying chain—it intervenes upon S_2 creating a knowledge and therefore its limits—and conditions who can enter in the signifying chain—the desiring subject is used by the same signifier that will enable its emergence as a subject. From the feminist and discursive mediation, this operation illustrates how the androcentric subject imposes the S_1 masculine as the signifier representing man and imposes a specific order upon S_2. Furthermore, the knowledge it creates is androcentric. The Basic Political Community (BPC), as the ontological result of this discursive operation, is also androcentric. As seen, the idea of the BPC relies on the idea of belonging to a specific signifying chain. Within this chain, a Master Signifier establishes a particular relatedness between those inside. On the other hand, $\neg S_1$ is excluded. If S_1 is masculine as the signifier representing the androcentric subject to another signifier, $\neg S_1$ is its dichotomic term; it corresponds to the signifier feminine. These two Master Signifiers work then as *points de capiton*. The function of *points de capiton* is key to constructing and establishing limits of discourse and, therefore, the BPC limits. Yannis Stavrakakis affirms the importance of the *points de capiton* within the analysis of discourse within Lacanian theory:

> In his seminar on The Psychoses it is clear that the *point de capiton*, the quilting point, is the point with which all concrete analysis of discourse must operate (III:267) [...] Thus meaning is produced in the relations between signifiers through the establishment of certain points de capiton. Since it is indeed impossible to attach a definite signification to a signifier, what the point de capiton does is link signifiers to signifiers. The point de capiton fixes the signifier to a signifying knot and not to an object.
>
> (1999, pp. 61–62)

The function of the *point de capiton* is to provide the political discourse with an element of the universal, of the image of wholeness. This completeness is achieved by constructing a BPC that creates the image of a universal community. As seen before, this universality is achieved by constructing a feeling of finitude and heterogeneity: the anxious subject is different from the desiring one; thus, it can contribute with heterogeneity. On the other hand, Master Signifiers provide the signifying chain with a sense of finitude.

However, it is not enough to create a sense of finitude or heterogeneity. More importantly, these two elements need to produce a sense of wholeness or harmony, which is also sustained by creating a dichotomic structure. In other words, if a closed system has a supposed heterogeneity but does not possess a harmonic relation between subjects, any social issue can be understood as not having a solution. On the other hand, the system can assure its continuity if it offers perfect harmony among its subjects. The threat to this imaginary and the desired situation is represented by the opposition of two dichotomic Master Signifiers; a harmonic one representing the BPC and one representing the threat to achieve such harmony. Thus, the fantasy is created, "[t]he social fantasy of a harmonious social or natural order can only be sustained if all the persisting disorders can be attributed to an alien intruder" (Stavrakakis, 1999, p. 66). Thus, $\neg S_1$ captures the Real, positivizes it—imaginarizes it—and enacts an exclusion of those considered intruders, who will become scapegoats of the ideological discourse.

Thus, this book endorses the idea that the ontological level of Political Reality—in its completeness, BPC, and the Real—is structured like a language because it is part of a signifying system. Nevertheless, the Real and the BPC play different roles in this signifying system. As Laclau affirms referring to Saussure, language, as well as all signifying systems

> is a system of differences, that linguistic identities—values—are purely relational and that, as a result, the totality of language is involved in each act of signification. Now, in that case it is clear that the totality is essentially required—if the differences did not constitute a system, no signification at all would be possible.
>
> (2007, p. 37)

Thus, the BPC works as the relational network upon which a language is structured. Different values constitute it, there are different types of subjects and individuals, but they all rest under an equivalence relationship based on difference—heterogeneity. Furthermore, going back to the Master's Discourse, we can see how the signifying system is constructed. The relational network can be seen as the knowledge obtained in the very moment in which S_1 intervenes in S_2 (ontic level). Thus, the element that can impose an equivalent relationship between $ and a (ontological level) is S_1, what Laclau calls the Signifier of Pure Being (2007, p. 38). This Signifier of Pure Being acts upon the battery of Signifier and cancels out every possible difference within signifiers, elements, and subjects. Thus, the differences between different desiring subjects and even the differences between desiring and anxious subjects are canceled out; they are part of the same whole; part of a universal.

Nevertheless, a Master Signifier is not enough to frame the ontological for a later struggle for hegemony. Moreover, completeness and universality need a second Master Signifier that sets limits between what is inside and outside the BPC. Totality can only be achieved in a closed system. Again, going back to Laclau, he affirms that the limits of a signifying system

> cannot be themselves signified, but have to show themselves as the interruption or breakdown of the process of signification [...] true limits can never

be neutral limits but presuppose an exclusion.[…] In the case of an exclusion we have[…] authentic limits because the actualization of what is beyond the limit of exclusion would involve the impossibility of what is this side of the limit.

(2007, p. 37)

Therefore, the positivization of the Real constructs true limits through its partial fixation by the imposition of a Master Signifier as the nodal point that quilts the meaning of what remains outside the BPC, $\neg S_1$ (Signifier of Pure Threat). Thus, the ontological level consists of two Master Signifiers that maintain a relationship of true antagonism. They represent a non-neutral limit; the relation between both Master Signifiers is the Schmittian one. Thus, social bonds that take place within the BPC are inscribed in terms of relations between friends. However, the relation between the BPC and the Real is to be read as the classical Schmittian relationship friend/enemy. Thus, two objectives are achieved for the constitution of Reality: a sensation of finitude and control over Reality and delegitimization of what remains outside for their potential as threats.

Summing up, the ontological level consists of two spaces separated by a true limit constructed by establishing two opposite Master Signifiers. These two Master Signifiers relate to each other in the same way that friend and enemy relate in the classical Schmittian relation characterized by an impossibility to establish a union between the two spaces and the political subjects that inhabit each of them. Upon the ontological space of 'friend', 'we', the ontic is constructed as every significant difference is concealed for constructing an arena for politics (BPC). On the other hand, the ontological space of 'enemy', 'they', is constructed as a threat to the BPC's harmony.

The Impossibility of Society and the Impossibility of the Sexual Relationship

This book endorses Mouffe's affirmation that, when speaking of collective identities, we always deal with relations articulated around a 'we' and a 'they' (2005, p. 11). She also notes that this relation does not necessarily result in a friend/enemy relation. For her, the classical Schmittian relation takes place when 'they' are seen as a threat (2005, p. 16). Besides the antagonistic Schmittian relationship, for Mouffe, the political relation compatible with a pluralist democracy is the one that she defines as agonistic. For Mouffe, the agonistic relation is a

we/they relation where the conflicting parties, although acknowledging that there is no rational solution to their conflict, nevertheless recognize the legitimacy of their opponents. They are 'adversaries' not enemies. This means that, while in conflict, they see themselves as belonging to the same political association, as sharing a common symbolic space within which the conflict takes place.

(2005, p. 20)

From this book's perspective, agonistic relationships occur within the BPC, while the Schmittian occurs where true limits are. This shift from Mouffe involves a different conception of the political and the social. While Mouffe affirms that "[t]he political is linked to the acts of hegemonic institution" (2005, p. 17), I believe that this struggle is characteristic of politics. On the other hand, when Mouffe affirms that "[t]he social is the realm of sedimented practices, that is, practices that conceal the original acts of their contingent political institution and which are taken for granted, as if they were self-grounded" (1993, p. 17), I believe that the social that she refers to is homologous of the BPC. Furthermore, what the BPC conceals is precisely the original impossibility that characterizes the ontological level; it conceals what Laclau understands as *the impossibility of society* (1991).

From a feminist point of view, the construction of the social through the imposition of Master Signifiers as nodal points that quilt meaning constitutes a process of androcentrification. Androcentrification is a term that results from the union of gentrification and androcentrism. A notion that makes direct reference to a movement through which the masculine is placed at the center—of the ontological level through the BPC's constitution—while the feminine is relegated to the periphery that remains excluded—by the delimitation of such BPC. Thus, Reality's construction responds to a process of sexuation that results in two ontological spaces and statuses that create two differentiated political subjects.

Although some elements for a feminist reading of a discursive ontology have already been pointed out, let us put those elements together and dwell more profound on the hypothesis.

The process of sexuation rests on creating two Master Signifiers that order the ontological level: S_1 and $\neg S_1$. Nevertheless, these two Master Signifiers perform different functions. S_1, masculine, intervenes upon a given battery of signifiers and governs it producing knowledge. On the other hand, $\neg S_1$, feminine is the loss that such intervention produces. The discursive operation of the Master's Discourse is that of sexuation as it excludes feminine from the signifying chain as a valid signifier. From the intervention of the Master Signifier masculine over the battery of signifiers, androcentric knowledge is obtained; furthermore, the subject that emerges is the androcentric subject, man. On the other hand, *a* also emerges at the ontological level. In the excluding process of the feminine, something is produced. I claim that what is produced is a lure of the rejected *jouissance*—the lure of the feminine, supposedly connected to the feminine, woman. Before going further into the ontological relation between man and woman, let us point out specific central dimensions of what subjectivities imply in political terms. As Judith Butler points out,

> Some lives are grievable, and others are not; the differential allocation of grievability that decides what kind of subject is and must be grieved, and which kind of subject must not, operates to produce and maintain certain exclusionary conceptions of who is normatively human: what counts as a livable life and a grievable death?
>
> (2004, pp. xiv–xv)

This book relies on this *differential allocation of grievability* and aims to illustrate how it is the product of the already mentioned unequal redistribution of political subjectivities. As shown above, the specific mechanisms that define which lives are normatively human and therefore produce lives are discursive. Thus, when Judith Butler affirms that "[t]he 'frames' that work to differentiate the lives we can apprehend from those we cannot (or that produce lives across a continuum of life) not only organize visual experience but also generate specific ontologies of the subject" (2004, p. 3), discursive operations, such as the creation of Master Signifiers, are the ones that create different political subjectivities.

Thus, I identify two main political ontologies; subjects of politics—in the BPC—and subjects of the political—under the Signifier of Pure Threat. Furthermore, when she affirms that "[t]hese normative conditions for the production of the subject produce a historically contingent ontology, such that our very capacity to discern and name the 'being' of the subject is dependent on norms that facilitate that recognition" (2004, p. 4), I understand that the inclusion or exclusion of specific subjectivities is related to contingent political interests. That is to say, the reproducibility of the frame, as Butler calls it (2004), implies the expansion and contraction of the BPC that takes place through the feminization or masculinization of the subject in specific moments.

The Master's Discourse makes man emerge as a predilect subject; the emergence of the subject is accompanied by the construction of a Reality articulated around the predilect subject's ($) needs and desires. Therefore, the role of MS masculine is to validate as real, as existing, everything that produces interest or benefit to man, while feminine is the signifier that represents that which may imply a risk or a threat to man's interests. Nevertheless, to avoid possible revolts or disruptions, this radical dichotomy is tamed by the translation of *jouissance* into an *objet petit a*. Thus, the feminine, *jouissance*, is tamed by the idea of woman.

This feminist reading of S_1 as masculine and $\neg S_1$ as feminine allows a new reading on Laclau's impossibility of society and Lacan's impossibility of the sexual relationship. From this new perspective, the impossibility of the *rapport sexuelle, of the sexual relationship*, refers to the impossibility to unite the two ontological dichotomic spaces necessary for exclusionary politics.

As Evans points out when analyzing the idea of sexual difference in Lacan, "masculinity and femininity are not biological essences but symbolic positions, and the assumption of one of these two positions is fundamental to the construction of subjectivity; the subject is essentially a sexed subject" (1996, p. 181). From the feminist discursive mediation that this book offers, masculinity and femininity are positions derived from discursive operations through which political subjectivities emerge. As previously stated, the primary discursive process in the construction of Reality is the one that corresponds to the Master's Discourse. At the lower level of this discourse's structure, the impossibility of the direct relation between $ and *a* ($// *a*) can be observed. Nevertheless, as previously mentioned, such impossibility needs to be concealed to provoke a feeling of fullness and harmony in the signifying chain. Thus, although an androcentric system does not allow for a direct relationship between masculine and feminine, it manages to create an imaginary relationship, a fantasy, where the feminine and masculine seem to get together by the articulation of $ and *a*, which, unsurprisingly, is represented by the *matheme* that Lacan used to describe fantasy: $\$ \Diamond a$.

From Impossibility to Fantasy

How is the subject sexuated? How is political subjectivity distributed? As Evans points out, sexual position depends on the relationship of the subject with respect to the Oedipus Complex in both Freud and Lacan:

> For Freud, the subject's sexual position is determined by the sex of the parent with whom the subject identifies in the Oedipus complex (if the subject identifies with the father, he takes up a masculine position; identification with the mother entails the assumption of a feminine position). For Lacan, however, the Oedipus complex always involves symbolic identification with the Father, and hence Oedipal identification cannot determine sexual position. According to Lacan, then, it is not identification but the subject's relationship with the PHALLUS which determines sexual position.
>
> (1996, p. 181)

As Bethany Morris puts it, "Lacanian sexual difference can come to be understood as radically different from contemporary conceptualizations of gender identity and or sexuality" (2020, p. 15). From a feminist political perspective, Lacan's different approach to the Oedipus Complex allows reading sexuation as the process that distributes unequal political subjectivities and is intimately linked to language and discourse. However, as Teresa Brennan notes, although sexual position and the Symbolic are helpful notions for the feminist political appropriation of Lacan, "[t]he real problem is that Lacan's symbolic makes patriarchy seem inevitable" (1989b, p. 3). However, as many of the authors included in the book *Between Feminism and Psychoanalysis* (Brennan, 1989a), this book aims to subvert these notions through a feminist discursive mediation.

In his *Seminar XX*, Lacan draws for the first time the formulas of sexuation (1998a). Lacan points out that these formulas address speaking beings, "[e]very speaking being situates itself on one side or the other" (Lacan, 1998a, p. 79). Furthermore, for Lacan, these two sides correspond to man and woman. From a feminist discursive mediation, it is impossible to affirm that every human being is a speaking being since to be read as a speaking being is to refer to someone as being part of the BPC as a subject of the signifying chain. Thus, the condition *sine qua non* to be considered man or woman—a speaking being—is to go through the processes of subjection and subjectification that the entrance in the BPC implies. In other words, sexuated/speaking beings, what Lacan calls man and woman, are two different statuses of existing in Reality. Let us dwell in the process of sexuation.

For Lacan, what differences man and woman as sexuated beings is their relationship toward the phallic function. The phallus, for Lacan, does not designate a biological element, he does not refer to the penis as such, but phallus refers to "the signifier that has no signified" (2007, p. 81). However, feminist critiques have been articulated around the usage and conception of the idea of the phallus in the Lacanian Symbolic. As Teresa Brennan points out, although "Lacanians never tire of insisting that the penis and the phallus are not the same thing, and they are right, this visual significance is none the less a point at which the penis and phallus converge" (1989b, p. 4). Furthermore, Elizabeth Wright notes that "[p]sychoanalysis is a double-edged weapon [...] on the one hand it enables feminists to demonstrate that gender is symbolic and not biological; on the other hand it constructs around the phallic sign" (1989, p. 142). Moreover, Margaret Whitford, in her reading on Irigaray, although referring to Freud's girl-child, emphasizes the consequence of this phallic-governed Symbolic:

> It is not simply, as a psychoanalyst might say, that because women lack a penis it is more difficult for them to symbolize lack. The boy-child, with his penis *but also* with a system of representations which is phallic, can more readily symbolize the loss of origin. The girl-child has available to her no adequate representations of 'what she might fear to lose', since 'what she might ...lose, has no value'.
>
> (1989, p. 116)

As this book will analyze in later chapters, this lack of representation has essential consequences on women's political subjectivity. For Lacan, the phallic function refers to the relation of the subject toward castration. In discursive terms, the phallic function refers to how S_1 acts upon the subject, allowing him or her to enter the Symbolic after rejecting the Real, *jouissance*. However, by establishing a phallic Symbolic, women can never reach a finite and whole subjectivity. This is visible in Lacan's sexual equations.

In the case of man, the equations that represent this subject are $\forall x \Phi x$ and $\exists x \overline{\Phi} x$. Lacan explains these equations as follows:

> $\forall x \Phi x$ indicates that it is through the phallic function that man as whole acquires his inscription (prend son inscription), with the proviso that this function is limited due to the existence of an x by which the function Φx is negated (niée): $\exists x \overline{\Phi} x$. That is what is known as the father function [...] the whole here is thus based on the exception posited as the end-point (*terme*), that is, on that which altogether negates Φx.
>
> (2007, pp. 79–80)

Some elements in the above paragraph need to be analyzed for an alternative comparison between man, woman, and non-speaking subjects. Man is essentially a whole, a subject with finitude, with limits. In a more psychoanalytical way, this finitude, these limits correspond to the fact that the father function limits man's desire: you must reject incest. More politically, man is limited by S_1, by the Master Signifier that establishes the signifying chain—the Symbolic—upon which man inscribes his identity as a political subject. This is also present in the above paragraph; man is whole because there is something that delimits him. Fink illustrates man's relation, as a whole, with the father functions by inscribing man into a closed circle related by a line to the Father (1995, p. 109). Man's essence as whole implies the existence of the father. This affirmation by Bruce Fink connects man's sexuation formulas with the Master's Discourse. When S_1, the Master Signifier masculine—the father function—is created, man appears, the subject $ emerges. Bruce Fink translates into discursive functions the idea of man as whole by replacing the encircled word man with S_2, and the word Father with S_1: "S_2 corresponds to $\forall x \Phi x$ and stands for the son here, while S_1 corresponds to and stands for the father $\exists x \overline{\Phi x}$" (1995, p. 112). However, I believe that Fink's observation misses the fact that the father's emergence and that of the son are intimately related and conditioned by each other, as S_1 and $. If we look at the structure of the Master's Discourse as the structure through which the political subject emerges and Reality is instituted, we cannot analyze man as S_2 but as $, as the predilect subject of an androcentric Symbolic governed by a masculine rule. In this sense, this book proposes a different representation (Figure 3.5).

Thus, $ is a product of the establishment of S_1. *Man is man because a man established the Master Signifier masculine and defined what a man is. Man gives birth to the father in order for the son to emerge.* In this sense, the equation of $\dfrac{S_1}{\$}$

in which $ is the truth of S_1 illustrates how the performativity of language works. It is precisely the construction and use of S_1 by $ that allows $ to emerge. S_1 acts and intervenes upon S_2 creating knowledge and producing the loss of what is conceived as antagonistic, $\neg S_1$, the Real. Thus, I differ from Fink because I disagree with the idea that S_2 represents the son as the product of the intervention of S_1. For me, the result of the intervention of S_1 is precisely $, "[t]he signified is the effect of the signifier" (Lacan, 1998a, p. 33).

Summing up, in order to be sexuated, to be constructed as man or woman, the subject needs to be part of the BPC; the subject needs to speak. While Lacan affirmed that, to be sexuated, the subject needs to be able to speak, Fink goes further and suggests that Lacan's formulas of sexuation concern "only neurotic subjects: the men and women defined in these formulas are neurotic, clinically speaking; neurotic men differ from neurotic women in the way in which they are alienated by/within the symbolic order" (1995, p. 106).

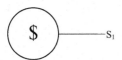

Figure 3.5 Man as a Product of a Discursive Operation.

It is now interesting to combine this book's proposed classification of political identities—desiring subject, anxious subject, and hysteric subject—with Lacanian nosology. Lacanian nosology is an interesting way to analyze how different political identities emerge from the relation of the subject with Reality's founding discourse. As Evans affirms,

> Lacanian nosology identifies three clinical structures: neurosis, psychosis and perversion, in which there is no position of 'mental health' which could be called normal (S8, 374–5; but see E, 163). The normal structure, in the sense of that which is found in the statistical majority of the population, is neurosis, and 'mental health' is an illusory ideal of wholeness which can never be attained because the subject is essentially split.
>
> (1996, p. 126)

Furthermore, Evans goes on and affirms that

> According to Lacan, 'the structure of a neurosis is essentially a question' (S3, 174). Neurosis 'is a question that being poses for the subject' (E, 168). The two forms of neurosis (HYSTERIA and OBSESSIONAL NEUROSIS) are distinguished by the content of the question. The question of the hysteric ('Am I a man or a woman?') relates to one's sex, whereas the question of the obsessional neurotic ('To be or not to be?') relates to the contingency of one's own existence. These two questions (the hysterical question about sexual identity, and the obsessional question about death/existence) 'are as it happens the two ultimate questions that have precisely no solution in the signifier. This is what gives neurotics their existential value' (S3, 190).
>
> (1996, p. 126)

According to the classification between the desiring subject, the anxious subject, and the hysteric subject, the normative status, neurosis, corresponds to those subjected to the Symbolic. Furthermore, as Evan points out, there are two forms of neurosis: hysteria and obsessional neurosis. For Lacan, obsessional neurosis corresponds to man's structure, and hysteria refers to woman's structure. However, I argue that the feminine form of neurosis cannot correspond to woman as she holds a masculine sexual position.

If man and woman are found in the Symbolic as subjects of the process of subjectification, under the S_1 masculine, both subjects possess a masculine structure. Thus, man and woman are characterized by obsessional neurosis. Nevertheless, there is a radical difference between these two positions because of the different affective ties they develop toward the ideal subject. Woman's affect is characterized by anxiety, anxiety as the product of the impossibility to separate from the Other as the Other does not recognize her position, and thus, she is unable to separate from the Other. On the other hand, the true hysteric, characterized by a feminine structure of neurosis, remains outside, under the $\neg S_1$ feminine. Thus, subjects with masculine structure, masculine sexual position inhabit Reality, while subjects with feminine sexual positions inhabit the Real (Figure 3.6).

There is no such thing as sexual relationship because there cannot be a direct relation between the two sexes, between the two sexual positions ($S_1//\neg S_1$). The impossibility of society relies on the very impossibility to embrace the Real. However, this impossibility is concealed by the possibility of the social; relations that occur within Reality. There cannot be a direct relationship between the two sexual positions due to the political strategy of framing and the Schmittian antagonistic relationship between we and they. However, there can be a direct relationship between two sanctioned political subjectivities, between the desiring subject and the anxious subject. This relationship can be represented by the same *matheme* of fantasy ($\$ \lozenge a$).

Let us now focus on woman's formulas. In the intervention of S_1 upon S_2, $\$$ emerges as a subject, and $\neg S_1$ is the loss produced in such an intervention. On the other hand, as seen previously, there is another product of such an intervention, *a*, the surplus *jouissance*. To differentiate the loss and the remaining products of the intervention of the Master Signifier is what allows us to observe how the imposition of the masculine Master Signifier implies a paradoxical division and exclusion of the feminine. When the Master Signifier masculine acts upon the battery of signifiers, among which there is the signifier feminine, the Master Signifier masculine creates a relation of radical alterity with another Master Signifier ($\neg S_1$), in this case, feminine. Nevertheless, as affirmed in previous sections, although the play of signifiers occurs at the ontic level, there is an ontological correspondence of such play at the lower level.

I believe that the ontological counterpart of the emergence of man, the androcentric subject, is the emergence of *a*, woman, as the subject forced to remain in Reality to complete the heterosexual fantasy that would assure the continuity of an androcentric reality ($\$ \lozenge a$).

In psychoanalytical terms of desire, man stays within the boundaries of the desire of the signifying chain, and does not try to reach *jouissance* as that which remains out of his hand. Man profoundly obeys the father; in this sense, man is neurotic. In their neuroses, "[m]en's fantasies are tied to that aspect of the real that under-writes, as it were, the symbolic order: object (*a*). Object (*a*) keeps the

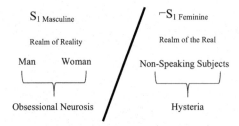

Figure 3.6 Sexual Positions.

symbolic moving in the same circuitous paths, in constant *avoidance* of the real" (Fink, 1995, p. 107). The *matheme* of fantasy is again present as the mechanism through which the system of signification prevails. Due to their rejection of *jouissance*, something is offered to men that something is not only power but fantasy. On the other hand, women

> are defined as not being wholly hemmed in [...] though alienated, she is not altogether subject to the symbolic order. The phallic function, while operative in her case, does not reign absolutely. With respect to the symbolic order, a woman is not whole, bounded, or limited.
>
> (Fink, 1995, p. 107)

This coincides with my earlier readings of the feminine subject, woman, as the anxious subject. The anxious subject is characterized by undergoing the process of subjection but not reaching the process of subjectification. Thus, and going back again to a translation into psychoanalytical terms of desire, while the signifier limits masculine desire, feminine desire is only partially fixed. What characterizes feminine desire is its potentiality to experience the Other's *jouissance*. As Bethany Morris puts it, being the relationship toward the Symbolic the first distinguishing factor of Lacanian sexuation, "[t]he second distinguishing factor in Lacan's understanding of sexuation is the relation to jouissance, or how one enjoys" (2020, p. 16). For Fink, that Other's *jouissance* is connected to S_1, and that relationship is what makes the other the Other,

> the unary signifier, the signifier that remains radically Other, radically different from all other signifiers. Whereas S_1 (the father's 'No!') functions for a man as a limit to this range of motion and pleasures, S_1 is an elective 'partner' for a woman, her relationship to it allowing her to step beyond the boundaries set by language and beyond the pittance of pleasure language allows. An endpoint for men, S_1 serves as an open door for women.
>
> (1995, p. 107)

I slightly differ from Fink's view, if each sex is constructed around a third element, I agree that S_1 might be the element for man, but woman relates to $\neg S_1$. That is why the Master Signifier implies different relations for these two subjects. This is why I also believe that woman, as the connection between Reality and the Real, is to be represented with *a* due to her relationship with a surplus *jouissance*.

Again, from the feminist discursive mediation this book proposes, there is no such thing as sexual relationship and can thus be translated as *there cannot be a direct relation between S_1 and $\neg S_1$*. The Real, the feminine, needs to be tamed to enter the Symbolic. The feminine is thus tamed by different historical, contingent, and normative conceptions of woman. When Lacan situates "a certain Other between man and woman that certainly seemed like the good old God of time immemorial" (1998a, p. 68), I believe that he is speaking about the conversion of the normative idea of woman in the lure of the feminine, of the Real. In this sense, woman is the *objet petit a* that pins Reality to the Real. Thus, as Evans affirms when analyzing Lacan, "heterosexuality is not natural but normative" (1996, p. 184). Heterosexuality is the base of the fantasy that supports an androcentric Reality. Man, $, must articulate ($\lozenge$) his desire around woman, *a*, and woman needs to remain in a constant anxious state creating the structure of fantasy. As Elizabeth Wright puts it, "[w]oman in patriarchy is condemned to occupy the place of signifier for the male other, who can give free reign to his fantasies and obsessions, and, what is more, implicate her in them" (1989, p. 142).

If the male obsessional neurosis question remains "To be or not be", the question that haunts the female obsessional neurosis is "What am I to him?" referring to an Other that is incarnated by man as $. In this sense, in androcentric heterosexuality, the existential question of woman is what she is to Him. On the other hand, the question posed by the hysteric "Am I a woman or a man?" describes the ex-sistence of the subject's feminine structure that depends on discourse as it establishes relations of power but that threats such discourse by the very posing of that question.

Summing up, Reality is the product of a series of discursive operations that occur through the Master's Discourse structure. These discursive operations take place at two different levels: the ontic and the ontological level. Ontological discursive operations are paradoxical. On the one hand, they produce a division that creates radical alterity. This radical alterity is introduced by the opposition of two dichotomic terms: masculine and feminine. However, such radical alterity needs to be concealed to provoke a sense of heterogeneity, harmony, and universality among the elements that rest under the Master Signifier masculine. This is done by taming the feminine through the construction of a weak, fragile, and dependent subjectivity. While the ideal subjectivity in androcentric reality is man, this secondary subjectivity is woman. In this sense, as masculine and feminine principles may not interact due to the threat that the Real poses to Reality, two complementary and hierarchical genders are created to justify androcentrism. In this sense, love, as the relation between man and woman, makes up for the lack of relation between the feminine and masculine principles "[w]hat makes up for the sexual relationship is, quite precisely, love" (Lacan, 1998a, p. 45).

Note

1 In his *Seminar XVII* Lacan arrives to four different structures: Master's Discourse; however, he adds a fifth structure in his Rome Discourse, which he names the capitalist discourse.

References

Austin, M. (2016). The Question of Lacanian Ontology: Badiou and Zizek as Responses to Seminar XI. *International Journal of Zizek Studies*, 5(2), 14.

Brennan, T. (Ed.) (1989a). *Between Feminism & Psychoanalysis*. Routledge.

Brennan, T. (1989b). Introduction. In T. Brennan (Ed.), *Between Feminism & Psychoanalysis* (pp. 1–23). Routledge.

Butler, J. (2004). *Precarious Life: The Powers of Mourning and Violence*. Verso.

Evans, D. (1996). *Introductory Dictionary of Lacanian Psychoanalysis*. Routledge.

Fink, B. (1995). *The Lacanian Subject. Between Language and Jouissance*. Princeton University Press.

Lacan, J. (1998a). *On feminine Sexuality: The Limits of Love and Knowledge*. Norton.

Lacan, J. (1998b). *The Four Fundamental Concepts of Psychoanalysis (Reiss)*. Norton.

Lacan, J. (2007). *The Other Side of Psychoanalysis* (R. Grigg, Trans.). Norton and Company.

Laclau, E. (1991). The Impossibility of Society. In A. Kroker & M. Kroker (Eds.), *Ideology and Power in the Age of Lenin in Ruins* (pp. 24–27). Macmillan Education UK. https://doi.org/10.1007/978-1-349-22346-6_3

Laclau, E. (2007). *Emancipations*. Verso.

Morris, B. (2020). *Sexual Difference, Abjection and Liminal Spaces. A Psychoanalytic Approach to the Abhorrence of the Femine*. Routledge.

Mouffe, C. (1993). *The Return of the Political*. Verso.

Mouffe, C. (2005). *On the Political*. Routledge.

Schmitt, C. (2007). *The Concept of the Political* (Expanded ed.). University of Chicago Press.

Stavrakakis, Y. (1999). *Lacan and the Political*. Routledge.

Whitford, M. (1989). Rereading Irigaray. In T. Brennan (Ed.), *Between Feminism and Psychoanalysis* (pp. 106–126). Routledge.

Wright, E. (1989). Thoroughly Postmodern Feminist Criticism. In T. Brennan (Ed.), *Between Feminism and Psychoanalysis* (pp. 141–152). Routledge.

Chapter 4

Traversing Fantasy

Let me now analyze how the three political identities introduced in the previous chapter relate to the fantasy that love presents.

Love, for Lacan, is related to the idea of the One. At the beginning of his *Seminar XX* Lacan posits a question to this respect, "is love about making one (*faire un*)? Is Eros a tension towards the One?" (1998, p. 5). Right after these questions, Lacan affirms that "[t]here's such a thing as One" (1998, p. 5). Through the feminist discursive mediation, this One is conceived as the relationship between the two sexes, the two opposite principles earlier formulated as S_1 and $\neg S_1$. A relationship that is impossible $S_1//\neg S_1$. Nevertheless, love is the fantasy that makes up for such an impossible sexual relation by creating a relationship between two sanctioned political subjectivities, two genders constructed to conceal the lack of relationship between sexual positions. On the one hand, man is the subjectivity that emerges with the imposition of S_1 masculine; on the other hand, woman, as gender, results from the taming of the feminine principle. Love thus begins with the idea of One, the idea that both sexes can establish a relationship, "'[w]e are but one' [...] The idea of love begins with that" (Lacan, 1998, p. 47). Nevertheless,

> Love is impotent, though mutual, because it is not aware that it is but the desire to be the One, which leads us to the impossibility of establishing the relationship between 'them-two' (*la relation d'eux*). The relationship between them-two what?—them-two sexes.
>
> (Lacan, 1998, p. 6)

Paradoxically, the idea of love as conforming a One does not imply the disappearance of the 'parts' that conform this one, "[i]t could affect anyone, moreover, couldn't it, to realize that love, while it is true that it has a relationship with the One, never makes anyone leave himself behind" (Lacan, 1998, p. 47). In this sense, the One is the prolongation, projection of the parts, "[t]he One everyone talks about all the time is, first of all, a kind of mirage of the One you believe yourself to be" (Lacan, 1998, p. 47). I believe that these two last quotes perfectly define love as narcissistic and make visible how love is an intersubjective situation through which the subject tries to define their existence. In man's case,

DOI: 10.4324/9781003167587-6

heterosexual and androcentric love reaffirms his existence as $ by having an *a* around which to articulate desire. In the case of woman, woman defines her existence by defining herself as the *a* in the gaze of the Other.

Lacan analyzes the logic of intersubjectivity in his article "Logical Time and the Assertion of Anticipated Certainty" (2006). In this article, Lacan sets the situation in which three prisoners face a logical problem; they must find out, by logical and not statistical means, the object given to them as their representation. The prize for the prisoner that discovers the given object is freedom. There are two different objects: a black disk or a white disk placed in their backs, so they cannot see it. Nevertheless, they are allowed to observe the object of representation of their mates. It is interesting to analyze this situation in existential terms. Somehow, the question they are posing in this logical problem is "What am I?", which is the question that the anxious woman formulates about her political existence as seen before. "What am I to Him?" becomes here "What am I to them?", which, in both senses, is the question of trying to define our existence to the Other. As Lacan states:

> In that article, I highlighted the fact that something like intersubjectivity can lead to a salutary solution (*issue*). But what warrants a closer look is what each of the subjects sustains (*supporte*), not insofar as he is one among others, but in so far as he is, in relation to the two others, what is at stake in their thinking. Each intervenes in this ternary only as the object *a* that he is in the gaze of the others.
>
> (1998, p. 49)

From the feminist discursive mediation of Lacan, I differ from Lacan in a certain sense. On the one hand, while I believe that certain desiring subjects ($) can find themselves in the place of object *a*, we believe that this only happens in particular and punctual situations, as Lacan presents in his article. On the other hand, intersubjectivity implies a salutary solution for those subjects that, belonging to the $\neg S_1$, are tamed by intervening in the ternary relation as *objet a*. In other words, this ternary intersubjectivity is the salutary solution for the emergence of the feminine as a woman, as the *objet a* in the other's gaze.

The fantasy of love as an intersubjective identification process imposes a third element between man and woman (between subjects that inhabit Reality). As Lacan affirms, "[w]ell-intentioned people—who are far worse than ill-intentioned ones—were surprised when they heard that I situated a certain Other between man and woman that certainly seemed like the good old God of time immemorial" (1998, p. 68). From a feminist perspective, Lacan mistakes sex and gender. Man and woman are not different sexes; they do not hold different sexual positions; they are two different genders that depart from the same sexual structure, the masculine structure. *La femme does not exist* as she does not exist unless Master Signifiers related to sexual difference are imposed as central categories of existence and ex-sistence. The certain Other that stands between the two sexes is precisely woman as a gender, woman, as the Other sex.

This certain Other is the One, and not the Other as language or the Other sex as Lacan also names woman. Nevertheless, the ternary intersubjectivity that love offers does not imply the same resolution or process for man or woman. Man and woman have a masculine structure; it is the hysterical subject who possesses the feminine structure; nevertheless, woman's masculine structure is not successful. In this sense, I affirm that between masculine—man—and feminine—the hysteric—there is an Other, an Other that is woman. Woman is the *objet petit a* around which man can articulate desire. As Lacan affirms, the two do not become the One:

> there are three of them, but in reality, there are two plus *a*. This two plus *a*, from the standpoint of *a*, can be reduced, not to the two others, but to a One plus *a*. You know, moreover, that I have already used these functions to try to represent to you the inadequacy of the relationship between the One and the Other, and that I have already provided as a basis for this little *a* the irrational number known as the golden number. It is insofar as, starting from little *a*, the two others are taken as One plus *a*, that what can lead to an exit in haste functions.
>
> This identification, which is produced in a ternary articulation, is grounded in the fact that in no case can two as such serve as a basis. Between two, whatever they may be, there is always the One and the Other, the One and the *a*, and the Other cannot in anyway be taken as the One.
>
> (1998, p. 49)

When Lacan affirms that departing from the position of *a* what we see is not the two others, but precisely a One plus *a*, I believe, from the feminist discursive mediation, that it refers to what woman observes from her position. In an androcentric Reality, woman sees man as One, as a complete subject. Her position toward this One is precisely *a*, as she is there to allow man, the One, to articulate his desire in the fantasy that has been constructed around genders. On the other hand, this One plus *a* is the relationship that conceals the real relationship, two plus *a*. This two-plus-*a* relationship is the definition of the relationship between masculine sexual position, feminine sexual position, and woman. Masculine sexual position and feminine sexual position are the two that can never be One ($S_1 // \neg S_1$). To affirm the direct relationship between the two sexual positions or structures would imply the disintegration of the idea of man as a whole. Androcentric Reality avoids the direct relation between the sexual positions by excluding the feminine from Reality. Woman as gender is constructed as the element that allows the One to be separated in two, as the central element of the two plus *a*. Love as a ternary articulation allows for the identification of woman with *a*.

This leads to rethinking the idea that *la femme does not exist*. Woman comes into being as the product of an identification that results from a ternary articulation.

La femme does not exist because woman emerges in a ternary articulation that constructs woman as a gender to which we can identify. In other words, *la femme* does not exist as she is not a signifier. This affirmation rests on the grounds of the differentiation that Lacan develops between signifier and sign:

> The signifier, as I have said, is characterized by the fact that it represents a subject to another signifier. What is involved in the sign? The cosmic theory of knowledge or world view has always made a big deal of the famous example of smoke cannot exist without fire. So why shouldn't I put forward what I think about it? Smoke can just as easily be the sign of a smoker. Everyone knows that, if you see smoke when you approach a desert island, you immediately say to yourself that there is a good chance there is someone there who knows how to make fire. Until things change considerably, it will be another man. Thus, a sign is not the sign of some thing, but an effect that is what is presumed as such by a functioning of the signifier.
>
> (1998, p. 49)

This idea is also present in Monique Wittig's work. Wittig affirms that "the category of 'woman' as well as the category of 'man' are political and economic categories not eternal ones" (1993, p. 106). I agree with Wittig in the idea of man and woman as contingent political and economic categories. Furthermore, from the discursive mediation of Lacan, it could be added that those categories result from discursive operations. Additionally, Wittig also rejects the idea of woman. Woman does not exist for Wittig:

> For "woman" does not exist for us: it is only an imaginary formation, while "women" is the product of a social relationship. [...] "Woman" is not each one of us, but the political and ideological formation which negates "women" (the product of a relation of exploitation).
>
> (Wittig, 1993, p. 106)

For Wittig and Simone de Beauvoir, woman is a myth. However, for us, as we will attempt to illustrate, woman is the symptom.

Woman is a political subject constructed from the taming of the feminine sexual position. The Master's Discourse creates a political subject denominated woman; woman is not a signifier but a manipulated sign. The ultimate mistake of gendered feminism was to take women as a signifier and not as a sign. Woman is the smoke that cannot exist without what makes fire; without the signifier feminine. Androcentrism and *machismo* have constructed a lure, a tamed sign called gender, and have structured woman around it. As it has been constructed in Europe over the last centuries, woman is the *objet petit a* around which man articulates his desire. Woman as heterosexual and reproductive has been constructed as a sign, as the central element of the heterosexual fantasy of love that serves as the main grounds and lock of an androcentric system that does not allow for feminine subjects. Woman is thus the remainder of a hypothetical unity between S_1 and $\neg S_1$; the One exists because the construction of a has been done to make it possible to think of the prior status of the One. This is also visible in psychoanalysis when speaking of the hypothetical unity motherchild, as Bruce Fink points out:

> Object a can be understood here as the *remainder* produced when that hypothetical unity breaks down, as a last trace of that unity, a last *reminder* thereof. By cleaving to that rem(a)inder, the split subject, though expulsed from the Other, can sustain the illusion of wholeness; by clinging to object a, the subject is able to ignore his or her division. That is precisely what Lacan means by fantasy.
>
> (1995, p. 59)

Can the feminine enter Reality? Can woman be constructed beyond the structure of heterosexual androcentric love? How can we introduce the feminine beyond the *objet a*? *By traversing and transgressing fantasy.* Bruce Fink scrutinizes what traversing the fantasy implies:

> By seminars XIV and XV, the term 'alienation' comes to signify both alienation and separation as elaborated in 1960-64, and a new dynamic notion is added: *la traversée du fantasme*, the crossing over, traversal, or traversing of the fundamental fantasy.
>
> (1995, p. 61)

Fink also notes that the reformulation of the term alienation has to do with how Lacan defines the analyst's role in the analysis. The analyst must escape from the construction that the analysand has for him or her. The analyst cannot take the place of the Other supposed to know, of a person to whom the analyst must imitate and confirm their values. Instead, the analyst must adopt the form of the *objet a*. Thus, the role of the Lacanian analyst is not "modeling the analysand's desire on his or her own, but rather at shaking up the configuration of the analysand's fantasy, changing the subject's relation to the cause of desire: object a" (Fink, 1995, p. 62). In Lacanian psychoanalysis, the traversing of fantasy implies for the split subject to adopt the place of the *objet a* in the structure of fantasy (Figure 4.1).

Nevertheless, in Reality, the construction of subjectivities is unequal. Therefore, the traversing of fantasy defers from one political subjectivity to the other. Fantasy affects man, woman, and non-speaking subjects in very different

Figure 4.1 Traversing Fantasy.

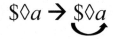

$\$ \Diamond a \rightarrow \$ \Diamond a$

Figure 4.2 Man's fantasy.

manners. The desiring subject holds the most comfortable position in the structure of fantasy. As pointed out in earlier sections, the only subject that can cor-
rectly enter in fantasy is the subject who can see the lack in the Other. Thus,
only the desiring subject can articulate fantasy as Lacan defines it. On the other
hand, although they occupy the position of submission, the anxious subject can
articulate fantasy from a different position, which implies a different traversing of
fantasy. Lastly, in the position of the hysteric subject, those who hold a feminine
sexual position are subject to a Symbolic that denies them; they are also subject to
an alien fantasy that, again, denies them by introducing obje*ct a*. Thus, there are
different relations with fantasy; there must be different ways to traverse it.

Man's Fantasy

In the traversing of fantasy (Figure 4.2), the desiring subject moves and places
themselves in the position of *a*. Fink defines this movement as the one that
attempts "to invest or inhabit that which brought him or her to existence as split
subject, to become that which *caused* him or her" (1995, p. 62). Nevertheless, if
as stated before, each sex is articulated around a different third element, and what
the fantasy of love does is to introduce a third element which is *a* as woman—as
the element that makes up for the impossible relation between the two sexual
positions. Thus, from the feminist discursive mediations, the traversing of fantasy
for man cannot culminate with man inhabiting the place of *a*, but developing
a new discursive operation. In this sense, the subject, by acquiring the position
of *a* needs to set in motion the Analyst's Discourse. Nevertheless, to take the
place of the other, as an exercise of political empathy, does not necessarily imply
this discourse's production. While Bruce Fink defines the process of traversing
the fantasy in psychoanalysis as "the process by which the subject subjectifies
trauma, takes the traumatic event upon him or herself, and assumes responsibility for that *jouissance*" (1995, p. 63), the feminist discursive mediation implies
that the traversing of political fantasy, the assumption of political responsibility,
implies the questioning of $. From this perspective, I slightly transform the clas-
sical structure of the Analyst's Discourse and substitute the S_2 place in truth for
the $\neg S_1$ (Figure 4.3).

This new form should be read as follows. *Objet a* questions the privileged
position of the desiring subject, the product of this questioning is S_1 as the signifier that provokes the split in a specific political manner that allows the desiring
subject to hold and use power. The visibilization of S_1 produces the $\neg S_1$, which
is the truth upon which the idea of *a* relies. In other words, by questioning the

Ontic Level	$a \longrightarrow$	$\$$
Ontological Level	$\neg S_1$	S_1

Figure 4.3 Analyst's Discourse.

privileged position of the desiring subject, we find the identity dimension that provides power; we observe that a dichotomy is created to support a hierarchy. This discursive operation is situated; it allows seeing what the privilege may be in different situations and how different S_1 may interconnect. More politically, traversing fantasy requires a political reflection that has to do with intersectionality, privilege, and oppression. There may be multiple S_1 and $\neg S_1$ and to observe them, the privileged subject must put themselves in the place of the Other by understanding the threat that their privileged identity may pose to the others.

Another remarkable aspect of this feminist discursive revision of the Political Analyst's Discourse is how it allows seeing what and who inhabits different spaces of Reality. At the level of the ontic, there are man and woman, the subjects produced by heteronormativity. On the other hand, S_1 appears at the ontological level with $\neg S_1$ as the two only possible ontological positions, one that assures existence at the ontic level and another that remains in ex-sistence and cannot enter the struggle—play—of signifiers—hegemony.

Woman's Fantasy

The anxious subject traverses fantasy in the same manner as the desiring subject. Nevertheless, the process of traversing the fantasy is more paradoxical in this case. Woman needs to address $\$$ not as the other but as herself, woman as a political subject needs to question her political identity and realize that her identity, like that of the desiring subject, relies on a masculine sexual position that grants her existence. Thus, woman can observe that the S_1 that grants her power and existence is masculine and that her identity relies on the paradoxical status of negating $\neg S_1$ and representing it in a tamed form. This way, the anxious subject understands that her anxiety springs from the necessity to construct her political identity as that of object *a*. It is only through this deconstructive path that the anxious subject will observe their privilege behind the submission that *objet a* imposes them. This may be clarified by explaining a political situation in which several forms of oppression are present.

A white cisgender woman is herself subject to many oppressions by specific structures, she must face higher rates of sexual violence, and she is also subject to several other forms of gender violence. Moreover, if her sexual orientation is not straight, she will also face homophobia. The oppressions she faces in a heteronormative Reality must have hindered the achievement of a full political subject's status—that of the desiring subject. Nevertheless, following this hypothetical scenario, this woman can enter the Spanish Parliament as a deputy. If this woman is not aware or does not understand her oppressions as the core of her political subjectivity, this woman may not develop her political career by considering the specificities that woman as *objet a* face in Political Reality. In other words, this woman, by not identifying herself with *a* cannot develop the Analyst's Discourse. On the other hand, if this woman is aware of the specificity of woman (*a*) as a political subject, she may take one of these two paths. First, she may understand that her status as *a* is given through an only axis of oppression, multiple oppressions, or she may prioritize specific oppressions over the others. Therefore, she may get into the Analyst's Discourse by addressing $ as the key of the opposition to her identified oppressions. By identifying her political identity only through oppression, the Analyst's Discourse does not take place. Instead, the discourse that takes place is that of the university (Figure 4.4).

The feminist discursive mediation has also intervened in this structure. Thus S_2 does not appear, but $\neg S_1$ does. In this discursive operation, the agent believes she is $\neg S_1$ and addresses *a* as others that hold similar oppressed political subjectivities. What results from this operation is $, and the truth that moves the agent is precisely S_1. In other words, by addressing herself as $\neg S_1$, a political subject with masculine structure is only reproducing the emergence of desiring subjects; this hypothetical deputy is not deconstructing her political subjectivity but helping in the reproduction of desiring subjects of power by not addressing the radical alterity. She is developing Mouffe's agonistic relationship analyzed in earlier chapters.

On the other hand, this hypothetical deputy can develop the Analyst's Discourse. When she enters the Spanish Parliament, she may see only one black man. In this sense, the deputy is aware of her subjectivity as *a*, but she must also be aware that identity is relational and that, although she is *a*, she may also be $ for other political subjectivities that may not be represented at all in the Spanish Parliament, such as black trans women. Thus, by taking both facts into account, the Analyst's Discourse is implemented. This woman asks $, herself as a white person, in other words, herself as a situated desiring subject, why there are white people in parliament, and why only one man represents black people. She finds S_1, the signifier that grants her political identity here, is whiteness, whiteness related to a masculine sexual position. The same addressing operation develops when she asks herself, as a cisgender woman, why trans women are not in parliament. Thus, to implement the Analyst's Discourse, central requirements need to be met. First, the subject needs to understand that static identities do not exist. Second, the subject also needs to understand that identification is a relational process. Third,

Ontic Level	$\neg S_1 \longrightarrow$	*a*
Ontological Level	S_1	$

Figure 4.4 University's Discourse.

the subject needs to understand that what she considers her identity is temporal, contingent, and formed by axes of oppression and privilege.

In this sense, this feminist discursive mediation offers a renovation of the classical Schmittian political relation between friend/enemy. I agree with Mouffe and Schmitt when they pose antagonism as the central element of political relations. Nevertheless, Mouffe's agonistic relation as a solution for inequality is not enough in a Reality where not every subject holds existence. From this book's perspective, feminist politics, as the politics that try to traverse fantasy by unveiling the Signifier of Exclusion and provide every subject with existence, needs to embrace the idea of reverse antagonism (Fishel et al., 2021; Valdés, 2021). The idea of reverse antagonisms departs from the affirmation that political relations rely on antagonism. Nevertheless, by acquiring the inversed position, that is to say, if feminist agents are aware of both their identity as a and as subjects that hold masculine sexual positions $, they will be able to articulate a political theory and praxis that does not leave anyone behind. If feminist economics and politics are characterized by their desire to pose life at the center of both politics and economics, feminists are obliged to ask themselves which lives are they putting at the center. Is it the white cisgender life? Feminists need to get to the root of the sexuation of Reality.

It is indispensable to assume identity as essentially impossible due to the original split of the subject to analyze such sexuation; something needs to be rejected by every subject to achieve the desired subject's full status. Androcentrism denies femininity—as sexual position—in anxious subjects and in desiring subjects. As stated earlier, the feminist discursive mediation affirms that the desiring subject ($) is a social construction that results from a discursive operation in which S_1, masculine as the negation of feminine, is imposed as the only valid sexual position in Reality. Thus, following, there is no identity but continuous processes of identification. Such identification processes are situated; your position as $ or a may derive from structures of oppression that operate in a specific space for a specific time. In other words, *man and woman are contingent*. Thus, to understand identification, one needs to go beyond the ontic level and reach the ontological. Only by reaching the ontological can the subject arrive to S_1 and $\neg S_1$, observe ontological statuses, and see the privilege of existence through the analyst's discursive operation.

Hysteric's Fantasy

The feminist discursive mediation affirms that S_1 is constructed; from the intervention of S_1 there is a product and a loss; the loss is $\neg S_1$ which functions as the signifier that is created to give harmony and completeness to the system that S_1 now governs. The product of the intervention is a, as the necessary element to assure that $\neg S_1$ is not desirable. Furthermore, a also functions as the element that gives a sense of heterogeneity to the system. Thus, $\neg S_1$ is a threat to an already heterogeneous system. The system S_1 constructs relies on the idea that the

Ontological Level	$\neg$\$ $\longrightarrow$	S_1
Ontic Level	a	$\neg S_1$

Figure 4.5 The Hysteric's Discourse.

sexual relationship is impossible ($S_1 // \neg S_1$), on the *differentia specifica* principle. Nevertheless, the system now creates the fantasy of heterosexual love to make up for such an impossible direct relationship between sexual positions. This fantasy ties \$ and a but does not include $\neg S_1$ in any form. The hysteric ($\neg$\$) as the ultimate negation of the desiring subject (\$) cannot be in the picture. Thus, by not being part of the fantasy, the hysteric cannot traverse it but can transgress it. The transgression of fantasy implies a different discursive operation, the Hysteric's Discourse. The structure of the hysteric discourse—again intervened by the feminist discursive mediation—is explained as follows (Figure 4.5):

The hysteric is the agent of an unintelligible discourse. Its unintelligibility springs from two central facts. First, this discourse does not start at the ontic but the ontological level. A subject not supposed to speak becomes the agent of a discourse. In this sense, this discourse is unintelligible. Second, this discourse does not address another agent but directly questions a signifier and, therefore, a structure. Furthermore, nobody seems responsible for creating the signifier, neither the system it governs, so the Hysteric's Discourse seems illogical. Another factor of this discourse's unintelligibility is that it does not follow the analyst or the master's structure. This discursive structure can be read as follows: a non-speaking subject questions and addresses the signifier that governs the signifying chain that excludes them. This addressing operation makes $\neg S_1$ appear as the product; in other words, by questioning the Master Signifier of Pure Being, we can observe that $\neg S_1$ has been constructed to deny specific subjects' existence. Nevertheless, the lower level is characterized by an impossibility; in this case, the impossibility is $\neg S_1 // a$. This impossibility shows that this discourse may not be appealing to the anxious woman as they hold the idea that they are the real $\neg S_1$. In other words, intersectional coalitions that oblige anxious subjects to recognize their privileged position may fail due to the incapacity of a to see their privileged and relational intersectionality. Thus, the Hysteric's Discourse fails when feminist politics and economics cannot develop the Analyst's Discourse.

Dislocating Reality, Transgressing Fantasy

Reality's structure, the signifying chain, works by establishing a system. Thus, and following Butler's theorizations on frames, this framing operation needs reproducibility (2009). Frames are not static; they respond to political and economic interests and needs and may be forced to expand or contract themselves to include and exclude subjects. As Judith Butler states when defining frames, the conditions of reproducibility of frames are purely dynamic processes in which this very reproducibility entails a constant breaking from context, a constant delimitation of new context, which means that the "frame" does not quite contain what it conveys, but breaks apart every time it seeks to give definitive organization to its content.

(2009, p. 10)

Thus, framing is a dynamic process in which frames re-organize their content. Nevertheless, this process is not necessarily limited to the content of the frame itself. Thus, frames are precarious and contingent. On the other hand, following Laclau's work, there is another central characteristic of frame; the system is impossible to completely close as it depends on what remains inside the system and what rests outside (2007). As Paula Biglieri and Gloria Perelló affirm in their article "The Names of the Real in Laclau's Theory: Antagonism, Dislocation, and Heterogeneity", Laclau names dislocation "the failure of the structure to close as such. Every identity (and social object) is dislocated *per se* because it depends on an outside that denies it and, at the same time, is its condition of possibility" (2011, p. 54). Thus, Reality and identities are both dislocated as neither can achieve the status of a closed system.

Combining these two main characteristics, reproducibility is possible because the system is dislocated. On the other hand, precisely because positive identity, understood as a closed identity, is impossible to achieve, subjects can enter multiple and constant identification processes. Their very condition of impossibility is what makes them possible. At this point, fantasy plays a central role; nevertheless, fantasy can be traversed by the very subjects that inhabit Reality. Furthermore, hysterics can take advantage of the moments in which reproducibility and dislocation occur and produce a transgression of such fantasy by developing what multiple authors have denominated as the act or the event. As Glynos affirms,

The 'act' has been invoked by Lacanian scholars as a useful device with which to engage in social, political and ideological critique. Key advantages of taking the act as an analytical and critical category include the shift it often promotes away from the *content* of an intervention to the *form* of an intervention.

(2013, p. 150)

The central element to understand the act and differentiate it from other forms of intervention is its relation to the Real. Again, as Glynos affirms that

The act can be understood, initially at least, in relation to the (Lacanian) real: the *real as impossible*. Qualifying the real as impossible already signals its distance from the *reality* of everyday phenomenal experience. The real, in fact, is in an important sense *opposed* to reality: the real is that which is *impossible* to assimilate into the reality of everyday experience.

(2013, pp. 150–151)

These two central ideas help understand the act as something developed by the hysteric. This shift from content to form has to be read as follows; the act allows understanding the dislocation that the discourse of the hysteric presents. If the Hysteric's Discourse is unintelligible because that who speaks is not supposed nor allowed to speak, it is impossible to prioritize the content. Nevertheless, the act of speaking, the form, is what allows for a moment of dislocation to turn into an act. Second, if the act is related to the Real as impossible, the act is also related to the hysteric, as it is the subject that inhabits such space and who is classified under the Signifier of Pure Threat. Furthermore, Glynos affirms that "[a]ccordingly to Žižek, the act proper is understood to enact just such an impossibility" (2013, p. 151). Such enacting involves grazing or striking the *fantasmatic* object (*a*): Like the successful hysteric discourse, it involves traversing the fantasy. Nevertheless, although I affirm that the act is an intervention proper to the hysteric subject, I am aware that different positions toward the hysteric as the act's agent have been developed. In his book *On belief*, Žižek differentiates between the proper act from the hysterical acting out, the psychotic passage *à l'acte*, and the symbolic act:

> In the hysterical acting out, the subject stages, in a kind of theatrical perfor-mance, the compromise solution of the trauma she is unable to cope with. In the psychotic passage *à l'acte*, the deadlock is so debilitating that the subject cannot even imagine a way out—the only thing he can do is to strike blindly in the real, to release his frustration in the meaningless outburst of destruc-tive energy. The symbolic act is best conceived of as the purely formal, self-referential, gesture of the self-assertion of one's subjective position.
>
> (2001, p. 84)

I differ from Žižek's classification. The proper act and the hysteric acting out rep-resent the two possible outcomes of the act that the hysteric develops. As Glynos affirms by quoting Žižek,

> 'an act retroactively changes the very co-ordinates into which it intervenes' (Žižek 2002a:152) and so retroactively also creates (or fails to create) the conditions of its legitimation. It is for this reason that the same gesture can come to be seen as a genuine act or as a 'ridiculous empty posture', depend-ing on whether and how the socio-symbolic co-ordinates have changed in the wake of the act itself (Žižek 2002a:153).
>
> (2013, p. 152)

In other words, what Žižek sees as the hysteric acting out is just the name given when the outcome of the hysteric act fails to create the condition of its legitima-tion. On the other hand, what Žižek denominates the proper act is precisely the outcome of the hysteric when he or she also creates the conditions of its legitima-tion. Furthermore, the other two acts that Žižek analyzes are not developed by the hysteric subject but by the desiring and the anxious subject. In fact, the psychotic *passage à l'acte* could be seen as the failed traversing of fantasy that woman as *a* develops when she does not engage in the discourse of the analyst. Additionally, I believe that Glynos also offers two other reasons to affirm that the subject of the dislocation is the hysteric.

> The objective dimension suggests that the act shifts the coordinates of the socio-symbolic regime: the act redefines what counts as reality in its descriptive and normative senses. The subjective dimension, on the other hand, suggests that the motivation of the act is ethical: the act is not motivated by pathological considerations.
>
> (2013, p. 152)

The interruption of the Real by the act of the hysteric subject accomplishes both dimensions. Such thought is already present in Walter Benjamin's essay "Critique of Violence" (1996), where we can see the shift from content to form. Benjamin differentiates two dimensions of violence, its conservative dimension; violence is used as a way to preserve something, as a threat, and its creative dimension; violence can be used as a means to achieve a new status or a change. Thus, violence can act as a potent instrument in the reproducibility of frames, and more important, as the primary tool to control the expansion and contraction of such frames. Benjamin differentiates between two main types of violence; sanctioned force (violence sanctioned as power through law) and unsanctioned force (violence outside the law) (1996). From our feminist discursive mediation, sanctioned force and unsanctioned force can undergo a process of Lacanian translation. In this sense, when Benjamin distinguishes between sanctioned force and unsanctioned force, I see a perfect illustration of the distinction between Reality and the Real. The disruption of unsanctioned force that springs from the Real can be seen as an act that the hysteric develops at the moment of dislocation. In this case, in Benjamin's text, violence outside of the law cannot be symbolized entirely since it represents a threat to the power that has already been established through violence. When Benjamin mentions the great criminal, he describes it as a source of legitimization (1996). The great criminal represents an eruption of mythic violence that can disrupt the existing rule and create another law opposite to the one already established. This violence outside the law cannot be read in terms of ends or means. It is a manifestation of discontent or, in Lacanian terms, it is a manifestation of the impossibility to symbolize the Real. Thus, the great criminal can be read as the hysteric, as he or she accomplishes both the subjective and the objective dimensions of the proper act, and furthermore, to read the great criminal's disruption as unintelligible, as a mere outburst of discontent leads us again to Hysteric's Discourse. Simultaneously, as Benjamin affirms in his text, such violence functions as the mechanism through which law can exist. The constant threat of what is outside the law is precisely the principle on which the law rests.

Closing this brief parenthesis, what strikes the most is that authors who describe events that can be homologous of the act or that directly use the Lacanian term act seem to converge on the idea that the form predominates over the content or that the content is unintelligible. From the perspective I propose, the content is unintelligible as long as the existing subject does not engage in the Analyst's Discourse process and can be addressed by the hysteric. Glynos, analyzing Žižek's theorizations, also notices the lack of the analysis of the content,

> What is striking about this account of the act is the absence of any reference to content, whether fantasmatic content or the content of a specific regime […] it is the formal aspects that are emphasized: the *modality* of the act, or the *shift* in the matrix of norms the act produces.
>
> (2013, p. 153)

Nevertheless, Glynos explains and observes the multiple advantages of focusing on the formal dimension of the act. While I agree that this focus has advantages, the lack of reference of the act's content supposes a threat to life itself. While Glynos affirms that

> One advantage of focusing on the formal aspects of the act is that it does not require the a priori specification of the 'true' agent of revolution. What matters is not so much the 'who' of the act, as that there is a shift from one regime to another, a reconfiguration of the socio-symbolic order.
>
> (2013, p. 153)

I believe that such a thing is not an advantage. To omit the analysis of the *who* can derive in defining as acts specific actions developed by desiring or anxious agents. Additionally, while Žižek centers his attention on the effects of the act over capitalism, we believe that capitalism is just an ontic level that rests over an androcentric ontological level. To obviate the analysis of the who can only derive in analyzing hegemonic struggles at the ontic level as acts. Speaking of the "true" agent of revolution does not imply a specific description of the subject, but a description of the ontological level and, therefore, ontological statuses. The true revolutionary agent is who defies the unequal distribution of ontological statuses. In other words, to confine the analysis to the form may lead to seeing the extreme right or every unsanctioned force as revolutionary or as developing a proper act. Translating this to our feminist discursive mediation, what we must analyze in the act is the content of the question it asks. Central authors have overridden the content of the question. Nevertheless, we need to look carefully into the act's content to see if we speak of an act.

To see how the content of the question that the subject poses in the act is a central element of analysis, I have decided to analyze the dislocation of the dichotomous gender structure of androcentric Reality that transgender identities have posed. For Lacan, the hysteric poses a specific question, "Am I a man or a woman?" while the neurotic poses the question of "to be or not to be". Nevertheless, analyzing the ternary relation from the feminist discursive mediation, I have affirmed that the neurotic, anxious subject transforms the question of "to be or not to be" into the question of "What am I to the Other?" From these three questions, I believe that only the one that the hysteric poses creates a shift in Reality. Nevertheless, this question may have been considered unintelligible for a long time. Not long ago, to pose the question of "Am I a man or a woman?" was identified as a non-sensical question; *you are that what your genitalia shows.* In this sense, this act was seen as the acting out of the hysteric more than the proper act. To pose the question of "Am I a man or a woman?" in an utterly sexuated Reality that relies on a hierarchization and classification of humans in two genders poses a radical questioning to Reality. The multiple questions that intersectional feminism and transgender identities have been posing have changed the coordinates in which the question of "Am I a man or a woman?" intervenes.

Transgender identities have been able to transgress fantasy by enacting the impossible, by showing they speak, and they have identities seen as impossible. We are also speaking of different European concepts questioned by different cosmogonies and cosmologies. Another clear example is the idea of sovereignty in Native American culture, where not only are humans subjects of sovereignty but other natural elements.

Summing up, overriding the content of the question, we run the risk of categorizing an intervention as an act when we are facing interventions that do not transgress Reality or fantasy but reinforce them. In other words, if a fascist— the ultimate desiring subject—starts a violent revolt against the expanding of the structure—that is to say, throws an act during dislocation—he or she is not developing an act, but trying to change the parameters of the structure, that is to say, it looks for the closing of the system. However, I believe that the androcentric system has been able to adapt to dislocation and the act. From this perspective, capitalism holds a differential characteristic; it has developed a discursive structure that allows ciphering the act to neutralize and depoliticize it.

References

Benjamin, W. (1996). A Critique of Violence. In M. W. Jeggings (Ed.), *Walter Benjamin, Selected Writings: Vol. 1. 1913–1926* (pp. 236–252). The Belknap Press of Harvard University Press.

Biglieri, P., & Perelló, G. (2011). The Names of the Real in Laclau's Theory: Antagonism, Dislocation, and Heterogeneity. *Filozofski Vestnik, XXXII*(2), 47–64.

Butler, J. (2009). *Frames of War: When is Life Grievable?* Verso.

Fink, B. (1995). *The Lacanian Subject. Between Language and Jouissance.* Princeton University Press.

Fishel, S. R., Fletcher, A., Krishna, S., McKnight, U., du Plessis, G., Shomura, C., Valdés, A., & Voelkner, N. (2021). Politics in the Time of COVID. *Contemporary Political Theory.* https://doi.org/10.1057/s41296-021-00500-1

Glynos, J. (2013). Capitalism and the Act. From Content to Form and Back Again. In Ian Parker & David Pavón-Cuéllar (eds.) *Lacan, Discourse, Event: New Psychoanalytic Approaches to Textual Indeterminacy* (pp. 150–161). Routledge.

Lacan, J. (1998). *On Feminine Sexuality: The Limits of Love and Knowledge*. Norton.

Lacan, J. (2006). Logical Time and the Assertion of Anticipated Certainty. In B. Fink (Ed.), *Ecrits: The first complete edition in English* (pp. 161–175). W.W. Norton & Co.

Laclau, E. (2007). *Emancipations*. Verso.

Valdés, A. (2021). The Facemask Paradigm: Symptoms and Non-neutral Limits during Coronavirus. *Free Associations: Psychoanalysis and Culture, Media, Groups, Politics.*, *81–82*, 18–30. https://doi.org/10.1234/fa.v0i81-82.380

Wittig, M. (1993). One is Not Born a Woman. In H. Abelove, M. A. Barale, & D. M. Halperin (Eds.), *The Lesbian and Gay Studies Reader* (pp. 103–109). Routledge.

Žižek, S. (2001). *On Belief*. Routledge.

Žižek, S. S. (2002a). *Welcome to the Desert of the Real*. London: Verso.

Chapter 5

Toward a Topology of Reality

From the feminist discursive mediation this book offers, the development of a mechanism able to cipher the Real culminates the process of androcentrification, which does not only consist of the Master's discursive operation through which S_1 and $\neg S_1$ are imposed. While the Master's Discourse occurs at the ontological level governing the question of being, other discursive operations occur at the ontic level and govern beings. The discursive operations at the ontic level are best explained by observing the levels upon which specific signifiers are placed through discursive operations. To construct a topology that illustrates the placement of signifiers at the ontic allows observing how the ontic, as the place upon which beings relate to each other, is articulated following the structure of the Borromean knot. The construction of this Borromean knot is a long process characterized by the imposition of three key empty signifiers used to positivize each of the three levels of experience that Lacan developed in his work (Imaginary-Symbolic-Real).

If, at the ontological level, the play of Master's Signifiers resulted in the classification of lives, I aim to illustrate that there is the struggle for hegemony at the ontic level. For a subject to enter in this struggle, they need to be part of the BPC, that is to say, play at the ontological level of being, but more specifically, the subject needs to be able to decide which empty signifiers will positivize the three levels of experience. To analyze the discursive operations at the ontic level, it is necessary to clarify what empty signifiers and the Borromean knot are.

Empty Signifiers and the Borromean Knot

Three empty signifiers occupy vital placements in the cognitive map that this discursive mediation offers. They function as nodal points, as the central knots of the three levels of experience developed by Lacan. Thus, progressively, the $Real_2$—a little two is added to make explicit that this is not the Real, the excluded, the Political, but a fiction that Reality develops—is articulated around an empty signifier that develops a narrative of origin to legitimate Reality. The second main empty signifier articulates the Imaginary, which contributes to constructing an image of the collective. Thus, the discourse of the $Real_2$ is institutionalized. Lastly, there is a progressive establishment of the empty signifier that articulates

DOI: 10.4324/9781003167587-7

the Symbolic in a third level. Thus, this empty signifier is the Master Signifier around which the form of power as coercion and regulation is constituted. It creates the threat of exclusion.

Let me start with a brief analysis of what empty signifiers are and how they intervene at the ontic level. At the ontological level, what is determined is that which can be talked about and those who can speak producing meaning. At the ontic level, there is a different play of signifiers. The signifiers at the ontic level are allowed to enter the signifying chain. Thus, the struggle that occurs at the ontic has to do with which signifiers will occupy the kernel of political discourse and create meaning. In other words, the struggle for hegemony focuses on the struggle to determine which *points de capiton*—or nodal points as Ernesto Laclau denominates them (2007)—will quilt the meaning of the signifying chain in which the discourse of politics consists. While Master Signifiers are the critical element to fix the signifying chain's meaning at the ontological level, the operation and the elements present at the ontic level are different. Central signifiers in politics are not Master Signifiers but empty signifiers, which Ernesto Laclau points out as a central element of politics and political discourse.

In his book *Emancipation(s)*, Ernesto Laclau articulates the Lacanian notion of the empty signifier, which we believe acts as a point de capiton, nodal point in the lexicon of Ernesto Laclau (2007). Empty signifiers and Master Signifiers differ in the type of bonds they create. In the case of empty signifiers, they can construct not only social but affective bonds between subjects. This is the reason why empty signifiers are used consistently in politics to create adhesive relationships (Laclau, 2007, pp. 36–46). Let me first analyze the idea of empty signifiers.

Ernesto Laclau identifies the empty signifier as a signifier without signified that, however, is part of a chain of signifiers (2007, p. 62). That is to say, an empty signifier is a signifier without signified, but which is still used in a language, forming part of the signifying chain. The existence of empty signifiers involves the rupture of the structure of the sign, which implies a "structural impossibility" in the words of Laclau (2007, p. 37). Just because a signifier lacks meaning does not make it incomprehensible because it is already within the signifying structure. As Yannis Stavrakakis notes, "[t]he content of a word is not determined by what it contains but by what exists outside it" (1999, p. 21).

While Ernesto Laclau and Yannis Stavrakakis refer to the importance of nodal points in hegemonic discourses, from this book's approach, empty signifiers are the central elements in the struggle to hegemonize political discourse at the ontic level. This struggle consists of deciding which empty signifiers will create the feeling of universality and heterogeneity that politics needs. Such feeling is created by the imposition of three main empty signifiers that resemble the Borromean knot's structure. This complex articulation would be developed to strengthen the *fantasmatic* support that this discourse needs. In other words, the hegemonic political discourse seeks to generate the three orders resembling the Symbolic, Imaginary, and Real registers to dominate the fields of Reality and the Real through the allocation of empty signifiers. Additionally, each of these empty signifiers comes to be positivized in specific political institutions to reinforce an image of wholeness and the universal within political discourse itself.

In *Seminar XX*, Lacan presents the Borromean knot and defines it as a set of three rings that hang together only by the action of a third: "no two rings of string are knotted to each other, and that it's only thanks to the third that they hang together" (1998, p. 124). Furthermore, it is interesting to look at the Borromean knot (Figure 5.1) as the simplest form of a Borromean chain. As Lacan also illustrates during this seminar, you can create a Borromean chain by adding unlimited strings and break the whole chain by cutting one of the strings.

For me, there are two interesting readings of the Borromean knot that deserve to be introduced, although I will not dwell on them. First, the Borromean knot seems to be connected to the idea of the ternary solution, as Lacan affirms when referring to the Borromean knot, "something begins with three" (Lacan, 2010). This *something begins with three* also reminds one of the idea of love as the ternary solution, in which there are always two plus *a*. Second, the Borromean chain seems to work as the signifying chain. Although Lacan introduces the Borromean knot during *Seminar XX*, his analysis of the knot takes place during *Seminar XXII* (Lacan, 2010). As Evans points out,

> It is in this seminar that Lacan uses the Borromean knot as, among other things, a way of illustrating the interdependence of the three orders of the real, the symbolic and the imaginary, as a way of exploring what it is that these three orders have in common. Each ring represents one of the three orders, and thus certain elements can be located at intersections of these rings.
>
> (1996, p. 20)

However, for our feminist discursive mediation of Lacan's theory, what interests me the most is how Reality manages to construct itself resembling these three

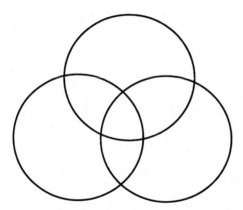

Figure 5.1 Borromean Knot.

levels of experience, creating a Borromean knot. In other words, I am interested in seeing how the ontic, Reality, manages to get structured in the same way that mental experiences; how the structure of the Borromean knot structures Reality; and how empty signifiers follow the structure of the Borromean knot in political discourse. Let me dwell on the Borromean knot idea before developing a feminist discursive mediation to see how Political Reality adapts to it.

In his *Seminar XXII*, Lacan explains that each of the rings in which the Borromean knot consists represents each one of the three orders; however, Lacan affirms that "[n]one of the rings here is different from the others. There is no privileged point and the chain is strictly homogeneous" (1998, p. 130). Thus, although Lacan's teaching's last stage focuses on the Real over the two other registers, this does not imply a hierarchical order among them. This turn to mathemes and topology has to do with the fact that only mathematical language can allow us to get close to the impossible Real. Furthermore, in the three registers' intersections, we find different elements that belong to his psychoanalysis. As Claudio Godoy affirms,

> the zones limited by the crossings are not intersections but, instead, relations and combinations of voids that allow writing, in such crossings, the different types of *jouissance* that Lacan introduced in his teaching: the Other's jouissance (JA) between E and I, meaning between I and S, and phallic jouissance JF between R and S; as well as object a remains placed at the central void delimited by the wedge of the three strings.[1]
>
> (2004, p. 4)

Nevertheless, Lacan goes further and adds a fourth ring to the Borromean knot in his *Seminar XXIII*, which is defined as the *sinthome* or symptom. Zita M. Marks defines this addition as follows:

> Seminar XXIII (1975–76), *Le Sinthome*—the seminar on James Joyce—revises the figure of the Borromean knot; now it can be seen as a four-term figure with the additional loop, the symptom, the 'heart' of the figure tying all the rings together. Lacan identified this fourth loop as that which prevents the other loops from unravelling, which he claimed is what occurs with psychosis. In the case of Joyce, writing was the *sinthome* that held together the Real, the Symbolic and the Imaginary.
>
> (2001, p. 40)

This is a remarkable addition to the feminist discursive mediation we propose. Fantasy can be traversed and transgressed. Thus, the Borromean knot is also vulnerable to breaking. Therefore, if fantasy is the lock of ontological discursive operations at the ontological level, the introduction of the symptom is the lock of discursive operations at the ontic level. Moreover, in both cases, the object around which both fantasy and the Borromean knot are articulated is the *objet petit a.* Thus, the Borromean knot represents the interrelation and interdependence of the three orders. Nevertheless, how does this relate to political discourse? I here depart from an idea that is present in Marcell Marini and that Zita M. Marks quotes:

> A major property of the Borromean knot that identifies the core of Lacan's thought at this time could be the names of the Father under the forms of the Imaginary, the Symbolic and the Real, 'because it is these names that the knot fits' and without it everything falls apart.
>
> (Marini, 1992, p. 75) (2001, p. 41)

The ontological level defines what can be talked about, what forms the signifying chain, and those who can speak, creating a zone of being and that of non-being. On the other hand, the ontic level gives Reality a structure that resembles analytic experience to create a sense of harmony, completeness, and finitude. If the political terms the discursive mediation proposes, politics is structured as a Borromean knot to maintain the Real, the Political, out of the instituted arena of politics. How is it done? As Marini and Zita Marks point out, it is done by the institution of a political discourse in which the Name-of-the-Father is present under the form of the three registers.

Furthermore, this discursive operation creates and imposes specific empty signifiers. As Laclau affirms, the struggle for hegemony consists of being able to fill the empty signifier with meaning (2007, p. 44). Nevertheless, from this book's perspective, hegemony is possible because signifiers have been included and excluded from the signifying chain. Not every signifier can be an empty signifier; additionally, not every subject has a signifier that represents it to another signifier. In this sense, the ontic struggle for hegemony is already conditioned by the sexuation of Reality. Let me analyze the role of empty signifiers more closely.

The Placement of Empty Signifiers within the Borromean Knot

Fantasy can be traversed and transgressed. Thus the ontic level needs to avoid this possibility and the consequent imposition of a new Reality. Political discourse reinforces political fantasy recreating a Borromean knot with empty signifiers that creates a greater sense of harmony and *polemos*, a fictitious antagonism representing a fictitious heterogeneity. The feminist discursive mediation shares the idea that empty signifiers are crucial for politics but affirms that the discursive operation at the ontological already limits the struggle over hegemony at the ontic. Thus, there is a limited play of empty signifiers that a specific Master Signifier governs. Let me analyze how empty signifiers are articulated around the structure of the Borromean knot.

The Empty Signifier of the Register of the Real

The empty signifier that positivizes or represents the register of the Real is in charge of creating the sense of universality, completeness, and wholeness for the ontic, Reality. In European history, some of the most commonly used empty signifiers are *the people* and *nation* also positivized by an institutionalization through the creation of parliaments. Before analyzing this register and to avoid possible misunderstandings, I refer to this discursive register of the Real as Real$_2$. To differentiate between the Real and the Real$_2$ also allows observing the ultimate goal of this empty signifier's imposition, which is the total denial of a Political (Real) that exceeds politics (Reality). To hegemonize this empty signifier allows for a particular group of subjects to represent the totality and creates an original universality. This empty signifier is intimately connected with the Laclaudian Signifier of Pure Being that provides the subject of its existence.

In the case of European liberal democracies, *the people* and *nation* have been key empty signifiers when it has come to the creation of the Real$_2$. Nevertheless, its meaning has fluctuated over time. As this book analyzes in Part II, these terms have traditionally denominated a collective of white, cisgender males. However, this has not stopped current political parties from using the same word when referring to the Political collectively in which women and non-conforming identities also engage. Thus, the empty signifier is still the same, but the filling is contingent. Nevertheless, as this will be discussed later, let me now look at how this empty signifier is also positivized through its institutionalization through parliament.

The people and *nation* are used in liberal democracies as the universal—as the national, which in state-nation politics is the universal—collective entities represented through the parliament. In this sense, *the people/nation* is a particular social group of electors. Thus, this wholeness is understood as the relationship between the individual and the whole/universal provided by *the people* or the *nation*'s definition. The image of wholeness comes from the adaptation of the subject to the whole of *the people* through the parliament. The Real$_2$—imposed by political fantasy to strengthen its discourse—has been institutionalized through the parliament's establishment. Everything that is not representable (the Real) is discarded as part of the universal, as part of the whole. Thus, the parliament is understood as the continent of the original people, as the Real.

The empty signifier *the people/nation* comes to occupy the place of the legitimate Political. It is legitimate because it has managed to turn itself into politics and create a political order that assures harmony and completeness. Nevertheless, this harmony and completeness are fictitious as they are the result of hegemony and exclusion and not of embracing totality. This discourse is false because the Real can never be fully articulated, i.e., the supposed universal or wholeness in which the political fantasy is supported cannot be achieved. Thus, it is an artificial Real constructed by political discourse. Translating this operation to a discursive mediation, the construction of a fictitious ontological dimension at the ontic level occurs. The parliament institutionalizes the empty signifier that seeks to impose an order of the Real managing a total exclusion of the Political.

Nevertheless, the construction of this fictitious political ontology becomes visible in moments of dislocation. Some examples of these moments of dislocation are when particularities not included within the hegemonic particularity engage in the struggle over hegemony, whether by fighting for power or against it. I here refer to different political struggles such as national struggles for national autonomy within nation-states and other political issues that defy the ontic level by provoking a shift at the ontological level, such as the Mediterranean crisis and the refugees' crisis that have shown the inhumanity and lack of memory of the European Union. However, it is important to point here that the parliamentary institution is aware of the impossibility to completely deny the Political as the total inclusion of the Real implies a risk for hegemony itself. Therefore, instead of risking the status quo, another empty signifier is imposed and institutionalized in the Imaginary order.

The Empty Signifier of the Register of the Imaginary

To reduce the risk of dislocation, an empty signifier comes to occupy the central space at the register of the Imaginary. This order is in charge of creating an imaginary collective identity that embraces people who are not part of the $Real_2$ but are at the ontic level. The imaginary order's institutionalization begins because it is realized that parliament cannot and does not want to absorb the Political fully. An image of cohesion is created that seeks to encompass both those who believe in the current government system (desiring subjects) and those who passively submit to it (anxious subjects). This image functions as a defense for the possible dislocation of the Political into politics by producing a perpetual promise of cohesion and possible entry of these excluded subjects into the parliament (the $Real_2$). This is the critical mechanism of political fantasy.

In European countries, the Imaginary order is positivized by the empty signifier *democracy*, which is positivized by the institution of the democratic State. However, State's crises and governments' crises reflect the incapability to sanction our need for identification. In other words, democratic states or government crises are the direct consequence of establishing an image that cannot give what it promises, wholeness. The Other also has a lack. The possible fracture of this level pushes political fantasy to generate a third level; this is in the symbolic order through the institutionalization of the rule of Law, which closes the Borromean knot.

The Empty Signifier of the Register of the Symbolic

While empty signifiers such as *the people*, *nation*, and *democracy* spring from benevolent desires of cohesion, the Symbolic register relies on an empty signifier that functions by creating the threat of exclusion. The Symbolic delimitates the path that the political subject must follow for the culmination of identification processes within the political fantasy avoiding the Real. As an empty signifier, legality is represented by the institution of the Law and presents a shield for the two previous orders. That is to say, perhaps there is a crisis of State or a crisis of government, but the subject clings to the structure created by the symbolic order, understanding that they are doing what is right. The structure created by the symbolic order carries a punishment system for those who do not conform to the imposed premises. The punishment not only consists of a limitation of freedom through the prison, but it also brings the stigmatization of the punished subject, no longer considered equal in the relationship established between the citizens. In other words, it no longer has access to the possible identification promised by the political fantasy. This does not only affect those within the ontic level since every subject, whether it exists or ex-sists, is subjected to the Symbolic, which, in politics, becomes the law.

Summing up, the feminist discursive mediation defends the idea that, at the ontic level, there are three registers represented by different empty signifiers whose content is contingent. Moreover, there are minimum variations of these empty signifiers over time. Thus, the struggle over hegemony does not imply imposing new empty signifiers but filling empty signifiers that seem sacred. The impossibility of adding new empty signifiers implies that the ontological level ultimately conditions what can be found at the ontic level.

Additionally, this triad is visible in two central ideas of European politics. On the one hand, the $Real_2$, the Imaginary, and the Symbolic seem to be the structure of the three political powers in Europe: the Real as the executive, the Imaginary as the legislative, and the Symbolic as the judicial. Additionally, these three registers were also present in Aristotle's rhetoric. Thus, the three modes of persuasion can also be thought of as the three levels. The *ethos* is the Real by establishing the authority of the original; the *logos* as the imaginary that presents the democratic state as the only logical solution; and the *pathos* as the Symbolic that coerces you to obey by telling you that what you do is legal or illegal and therefore, good or bad.

Nevertheless, what differentiates current political structures from previous ones is the capitalist economy's central role in political fantasy as the fourth ring of the Borromean knot that functions as its lock. This fourth ring allows for politics to cipher the Political and finally avoid the risk of dislocation. Let me analyze this idea further.

Note

1 My own translation.

References

Evans, D. (1996). *Introductory Dictionary of Lacanian Psychoanalysis*. Routledge.

Godoy, C. (2004). *El Nudo de Trébol en la enseñanza de J. Lacan*. XI Jornadas de Investigación. (p. 9). Facultad de Psicología - Universidad de Buenos Aires, Buenos Aires.

Lacan, J. (1998). *On feminine sexuality: The limits of love and knowledge*. Norton.

Lacan, J. (2010). *Lacanian Psychoanalysis: Collected Translations and Papers by Cormac Gallagher*. Seminar XXII. RSI (C. Gallagher, Trans.). http://www.lacaninireland.com/web/wp-content/uploads/2010/06/RSI-Complete-With-Diagrams.pdf

Laclau, E. (2007). *Emancipations*. Verso.

Marini, M. (1992) Jacques Lacan: The French Context (trans. A. Tomiche). New Jersey: Rutgers University Press.

Marks, Z. M. (2001). Borromean Knot. In H. Glowinski, Z. M. Marks, & S. Murphy (Eds.), *A Compendium of Lacanian Terms* (pp. 38–41). Free Association Books.

Stavrakakis, Y. (1999). *Lacan and the Political*. Routledge.

Chapter 6

The Void

Ciphering the Real as Reality

The first approximation to the ontic level in the previous chapter allows us to draw the first sketch of a topology of political discourse in Europe (Figure 6.1).

Furthermore, although they are discursive elements, empty signifiers have material consequences; the institutions representing these empty signifiers are situated within the intersections that result between the registers (Figure 6.2).

As I will attempt to illustrate, the core of political discourse relies on the *objet petit a*, which occupies what has been defined by several authors as the void. This

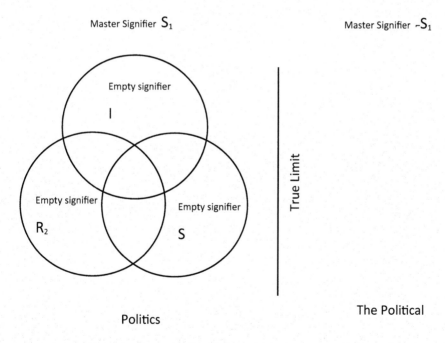

Figure 6.1 A Topology of Discourse.

DOI: 10.4324/9781003167587-8

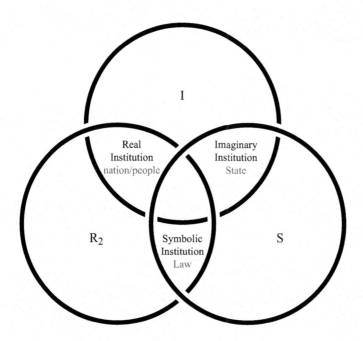

Figure 6.2 Empty Signifiers in the Borromean Knot.

central element is the core of political fantasy, and it is not just related to political power but intimately related to the capitalist economy.

The Void and *Objet petit a*

I agree with Shepherdson when he affirms that the location of the Real is a para-doxical one, the Real "is not simply 'outside' the structure, but is missing from the structure, excluded from within. So, the question is: Just how are we to under-stand this 'belonging' and 'not belonging' to structure, this 'intimate alterity' of the real?" (2008, p. 2). The feminist discursive mediation I defend explains this paradoxical status of inside/outside by affirming that the Real is outside as it is represented by a signifier excluded from the Symbolic. Nevertheless, the Real is also inside, as it functions as a nodal point that attaches the Symbolic order to the Real that it is supposed to exclude (Shepherdson, 2008, p. 21). Thus, what inhab-its the void is precisely the Real. Shepherdson is right when he analyzes Lacan's work and admits that

> In short, one can easily see that the relation between the symbolic and the real cannot be approached if one begins with a dichotomy between inside and

outside. It is rather a matter of a void within the structure. This is of course what the theory of lack in Lacan tries to address.

(2008, p. 3)

The void of the Real makes visible the lack of the ontic level, which is precisely the Real. There is always a rem(*a*)inder that illustrates this lack. Thus, what inhabits the void is precisely the *objet petit a*. Shepherdson affirms that "'object a' emerges in Lacanian theory [...] precisely in order to distinguish between the subject as real and the subject as manifested through the symbolic order" (2008, p. 12). As shown in previous sections, the feminist discursive mediation affirms that *objet petit a*, when translated into political terms, represents a type of political subject that is not fully recognized by the Symbolic but does not inhabit the peripherical space of inhabitancy of the Real. In Shepherdson's work, "the object a—the peculiar object that does not appear in the signifying chain, but that marks a point of pathological attachment, bound to the 'real' of the body, a point of libidinal stasis where desire is lost" (2008, p. 12), on the other hand, in the discursive mediation this book offers, *objet petit a* and the anxious subject share the same characteristic as objet petit a in Shepherdson. When political fantasy articulates a fictitious sexual relationship between male and female, women's role is precisely to attach the desiring subject of the Symbolic to the Real. This idea is also present in Shepherdson when he affirms that the matheme of fantasy "concerns the relation that binds the split subject of the symbolic order ($) to a certain real element that exceeds the symbolic order (*a*)" (2008, pp. 12–13).

Additionally, speaking of *a* as an element that is intimately related to the Real, it is interesting to see how the Real is defined. In the words of Shepherdson, there are two main versions of it. The first version of the Real that Lacan developed had to do with the idea of a pre-symbolic Real "never accessible in itself, but only appears through the mediation of imaginary or symbolic representation (in this case, it tends to correspond to the common meaning of reality)" (Shepherdson, 2008, p. 27). On the other hand, the second version of the Real is defined by Shepherdson as a post-symbolic Real. In this second version, the Real "seems to designate a lack, an element that is missing from within the symbolic order, in which case the real can only be understood as an effect of the symbolic" (Shepherdson, 2008, p. 27). Shepherdson goes into explaining that these two different versions of the Real entail two different modes of being:

In the first case, one can say the real "exists" independently, and then go on to ask whether we can have any knowledge of it independent of our representations. But in the second case, we are led to speak of the 'being of lack'— thereby initiating a whole series of apparently paradoxical claims about the "being" of what 'is not', reminiscent, perhaps, of theological disputes concerning the existence of God.

(2008, p. 27)

In the discursive mediation, the Real is both pre-symbolic and post-symbolic. When the ontic level of politics is imposed, there is already a Real that is not represented in politics because it was not considered part of the ontological. This pre-symbolic Real ex-sists, as the hysteric subject does. On the other hand, it is post-symbolic, as one may be aware of their lack of political subjectivity once androcentrism and patriarchy are established. This leads to a paradoxical status of existing but not fully being that is represented in the anxious subject.

Furthermore, and going back to the role *objet petit a* plays, it is necessary to inscribe it in one of the most relevant ideas of a political translation of Lacan; the act. The act is, as Žižek briefly defines it, "an encounter with the real" (Stavrakakis, 2010, p. 4). Thus, if *objet petit a* plays a central role by attaching the Symbolic to the Real, it must also play a central role in the act. Topologically speaking, the act takes place in the void. Let me now analyze how the individual Lacanian act can be mediated in a feminist and discursive manner to develop our own approach to the political event.

The Lacanian Act, the Political Event

For Stavrakakis, the encounter with the Real that the act represents "only becomes conscious through the failure of the symbolic; and, in addition, it has to be expressed, articulated, registered, within the symbolic" (2010, p. 4). However, as we will see, authors such as Žižek override the relation between the Symbolic and the Real and speak of the real act, of the revolutionary act, as one that does not engage with the Symbolic. From both theoretical articulations, I infer that there needs to be a specific mechanism to prevent the act from losing its radicality in being registered within the Symbolic. As we will see, in order for the act not to lose its radicality, it cannot be ciphered, neither translated, but only inscribed within the Symbolic matrix. As Stavrakakis notes, "[a] proper act, in other words, involves the production of a signifier of the lack in the Other *and* an attempt to *institutionalize* this empty signification" (2010, p. 4). For the discursive mediation, this means that an already existing signifier cannot represent the act, i.e., translated, but it needs to be inscribed with a new signifier. Only by its inscription, and not its ciphering, can the act reconfigure the Symbolic matrix.

One of the most famous theoretical developments of the act is the idea of the radical act in Žižek. As Stavrakakis points out, "Žižek customarily distinguishes between an imaginary form of resistance, a 'false transgression' that ultimately serves to maintain and reproduce the law, and 'the effective symbolic re-articulation via the intervention of the real of an act' (Žižek 1998a: 5)" (2010, p. 2). Stavrakakis continues and affirms, by citing Pluth, that Žižek overrides the relation of the act and the Symbolic. For Stavrakakis, the intimate relation between the Symbolic and the Real within the act is present in Lacan:

> What is the implication of Lacan's locating the act at the intersection of real and symbolic? The constitutive *imperfection* and *impurity* of the act. The perfect

act Žižek idealizes—an act in the real, i.e. Antigone's suicidal gesture—may be an act that, on a first (real) level, succeeds without misfiring, but this is precisely what excludes it from what, according to Lacan, would be a proper psychanalytic act, un *fait de signifiant*—and I would add, a proper *political act*.

(2010, p. 4)

I agree with Stavrakakis, an act, to be political, to radically dislocate and force a re-articulation of the Symbolic matrix, needs to interact with the Symbolic and affect the ontic level, politics.

In his text "From 'Passionate Attachments' to Dis-Identification", Žižek appeals to Judith Butler to differentiate resistance from the act (Žižek, 2002). Žižek vertebrates his text on a critique of Butler's critique to Lacan, a critique widely contested by both Žižek and Laclau (2000). Over this text, Žižek shows his disagreement with Butler's critique of the lack of revolutionary potential in the work of Lacan. For Žižek, Lacanian thought allows for a theory of radicality:

> for Lacan, radical rearticulation of the predominant symbolic order is altogether possible. This is what his notion of point de capiton—the 'quilting point' or the master-signifier—is about. When a new point de capiton emerges, the socio-symbolic field is not only displaced, its very structuring principle changes.
>
> (Žižek, 1998)

The uniqueness of the act relies on its relation to fantasy:

> Act is to be opposed to mere activity. Activity relies on some fantasmatic support, while the authentic act involves disturbing—'traversing'—the fantasy. In this precise sense, act is for Lacan on the side of the object qua real as opposed to signifier—to 'speech act'.
>
> (Žižek, 1998)

Here, the real act, the proper act, seems to deviate itself from the Symbolic for Žižek. The act springs from the Real; it has no relation with speech, with the Symbolic. What seems to underly Žižek's reasoning is that there is no possible way that the act can intervene nor subvert the Symbolic. The only thing left to do is enjoy the space of non-being while knowing that such space is the fair, just, good one.

On the other hand, what is resistance? Alessa Contu, in her text "Decaf Resistance", offers an interesting reading of resistance that Žižek widely inspires (2008). Contu identifies two types of resistance, decaf resistance and the real act of resistance:

> Decaf, because it threatens and hurts nobody. It is resistance without a cost. A Real act of resistance is exactly an act of the impossible. This is because it

> cannot be accounted for and presupposed in and by the Law and its obscene
> undergrowth; as such, it is an impossible act. This impossibility is what
> is foreclosed from our own very discourse on resistance in organization
> theory.
>
> (2008, p. 370)

I believe Contu's distinction is an interesting way of looking at how the anxious
subject may practice the University's Discourse. Nevertheless, I am afraid I have
to disagree with Contu and Žižek, in what I consider their negation of the possibility of the real event. As I shall illustrate in the following section, the act is
potentially disruptive—the possible "decaffeination" of the act springs from how
it is inserted in the Symbolic matrix. Thus, from the discursive mediation, decaf
resistance occurs when the anxious subject, or even the desiring subject, thinks
he or she represents the $\neg S_1$ and sets in motion the University's Discourse. Thus,
the subject is reproducing the signifying chain. More importantly, decaf resistance can also be seen as a mechanism produced by the signifying chain. Decaf
resistance, as Contu affirms, works as the outer kernel upon which ideology rests.
Contu affirms that "Decaf resistance, just as decaf coffee, makes it possible for
us to enjoy without the costs and risks involved. We can have the thing (coffee)
without actually having it" (2008, p. 374). This lack of loss, this lure of disruption,
is not present in the real act, which always involves a cost. As Contu points out,

> A Real act of resistance would be one for which we would have to bear the
> costs. It would be an act that changes the sociosymbolic network in which
> we and our way of life make sense. It would be costly because we depend on
> these sociosymbolic networks. To lose them would be like losing the world.
> In this sense, a Real act of resistance is an impossible act.
>
> (2008, p. 374)

I agree with the cost of the real act; the real act involves costs and losses because
the act's ultimate aim is to inscribe lack and negativity. There cannot be an
inscription of the lack or negativity without dislocation of the Symbolic order.
Therefore, it will always imply a loss for those whose existence is granted by
such Symbolic. Nevertheless, Alessa Contu repeats the real act's impossibility in
a way that makes her sound like Žižek. I thus find in Contu the same problems that
Stavrakakis finds in Žižek. As Stavrakakis affirms,

> Overall, what I find problematic with Žižek's politics of the act is that it
> is over-stressing the unlimited (real) positivity of human action beyond any
> reflexive registering of (symbolic) lack and finitude. Any initial registering of
> negativity – and it is, obviously, initially registered – is eventually disavowed
> in his argument through the perfection with which the act is invested, an
> investment that miraculously transubstantiates negative to positive.
>
> (Stavrakakis, 2010, p. 2)

Thus, Stavrakakis affirms that to conceptualize the radical act in the way in which Žižek does only "discourage active participation, marginalize democratic antagonism and foreclose the possibility of formulating any real, post-capitalist alternatives" (2010, p. 2). Thus, it also seems that Contu's negation of the real act and Žižek's denial of the possibility of the radical act could also be analyzed as extra-ideological kernels.

Although I cannot entirely agree with the real act's impossibility, I find it helpful and engaging to differentiate between decaf resistance and what we shall call the political act. This book aims to show that the act's critical element is not the form but the content as the subject that develops the act. Furthermore, I affirm that these authors miss this question because they do not depart from the differentiation between subjects with different ontological statutes. In other words, they analyze the act from the ontic level while missing the importance of the ontological level in such disruption, thus mistaking acts of resistance or reproduction of the frames with real acts.

On the one hand, Žižek seems to look at the anxious subject; on the other hand, Contu speaks of the desiring subject when speaking of business. I agree that the Real and revolutionary acts are impossible if the agent is the desiring subject or the anxious subject. The only agent able to develop the act is the hysteric subject. In other words, decaf resistance may come from perverse or cynic subjects. However, the act can only spring from hysteria: "Lacan repeatedly insisted that perversion is always a socially constructive attitude, while hysteria is much more subversive and threatening to the predominant hegemony" (Butler et al., 2000, p. 247). The difference between an act that shifts and dislocates the Symbolic order and entails costs, and the decaf resistance of an act, relies on how it breaks into the Symbolic. Additionally, the act can only be potentially disruptive, that is, political, if it springs from the Political, i.e., the hysteric subject.

Ciphering the Real

The void is where the act occurs. Nevertheless, this encounter with the Real may be deactivated. I believe that the deactivation, or decaffeination of the act, relies on how the Symbolic constructs the *objet petit a* within the fantasy that it articulates.

Capitalism entails adding the fourth ring of the Borromean knot. I argue that this fourth ring's role is to transform any act into decaf resistances, thus depoliticizing and deactivating the potential of transformation of the void. Capitalism articulates *objet petit a* as the central element that produces the ciphering of the Real into Reality. This ciphering process's objective is to introduce elements of the Real in Reality by canceling their threat. Let me now illustrate it through topology (Figure 6.3). The void is inhabited by the Lacanian *objet a* and placed at the kernel of the discourse of politics in the total overlapping of the three registers. The lines that link the Political with politics refer to the act and the possible process of ciphering.

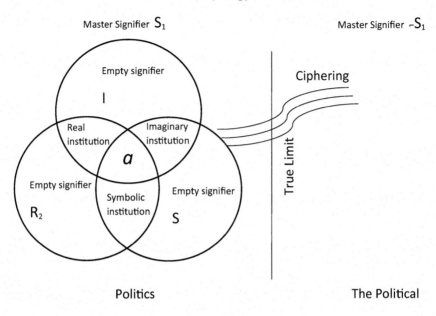

Figure 6.3 A Topology of Discourse and Ciphering.

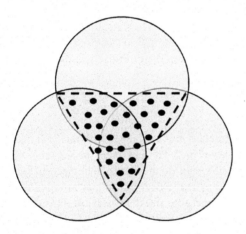

Figure 6.4 Spaces of Inhabitancy.

Furthermore, a symbolic matrix, political syntax, imposes the content of discourse and conditions and limits the subjects that can speak. Thus, it is also necessary to include a topology of inhabitancy that allows observing how subjects are
also placed in this Borromean knot (Figure 6.4).

The core of the Borromean knot corresponds to the space of inhabitancy that assures existence; nevertheless, the desiring subject and the anxious subject enjoy different types of existence. Thus, the desiring subject inhabits the central space of the kernel, represented as a dotted triangle. Within this dotted triangle, the real struggle for hegemony, empty signifiers are filled within this space. In the periphery of this dotted triangle, there is the space of inhabitancy of the anxious subject. A space that illustrates the ambiguity of their existence, within the overlapping of the registers, but not within the triangle of production of meaning. Lastly, the non-overlapping spaces represent the zone of ex-sistence. Although the Master Signifier $\neg S_1$ remains outside of the signifying chain by the need of a true limit, the truth is that subjects that are subjected to the Symbolic, even when their subjectivities are not recognized, are still subjected to the Symbolic.

Closing this parenthesis on topology and coming back to the act, I am interested in showing how capitalism transforms the void, constructs *objet petit a*, and decaffeinates the act. In contemporary politics, this last ring enables the process of ciphering the Real in a way that enables Reality to create new differences within itself to feed the necessity of fake antagonisms that politics needs; but also works as the entrance, as the promise of the excluded to be part of the totality. Before introducing how the capitalist economy ciphers the Real, I first need to explain what the process of ciphering implies in Lacanian thought.

In his book *The Lacanian Subject*, Bruce Fink analyzes how language is created through the allegory of the act of coin tossing used by Lacan in his seminar *The Purloined Letter* (1995, pp. 14–24). Fink observes that Lacan analyzes how a symbolic matrix is created and affirms that it has two main characteristics:

- Impossibility: "related to the *order* in which the category numbers appear as well as to *which* of them can appear if certain positions are predefined" (Fink, 1995, p. 19). We can observe here how political language works. The order is what has been established at the ontological level. The ontological level limits the signifiers that can appear in the signifying chain. On the other hand, certain positions, that of nodal points at the ontic level, are also predefined in the sense that you may struggle to fill the signifier, but it seems impossible to place new empty signifiers.
- Memory: the symbolic matrix "records within itself or 'remembers' its previous components [...] it not only comports an elementary though consequent grammar, but a built-in memory function as well, primitive as it may be" (Fink, 1995, p. 19). Fink goes on and affirms that

constructing a symbolic system that brings with it a syntax—a set of rules or laws—that is not inherent in the 'pre-existing reality.' The resulting possibilities and impossibilities can thus be seen to derive from the way in which the symbolic matrix is constructed, that is, the way it cyphers the event in question.

(1995, p. 19)

The discursive mediation this book introduces affirms that when Reality is created through discursive operations, a symbolic matrix whose main characteristics are impossibility and memory is also created. A symbolic matrix governs political discourse, a political syntax that limits, conditions, and influences how the Real enters or remains outside of Reality. Furthermore, in political terms, the combination of impossibility and memory results in normativity. As Fink affirms, "rather than being remembered by the individual (in an active way, i.e., with some sort of *subjective* participation), things are 'remembered' for him or her by the signifying chain" (1995, p. 20). Thus, normativity is performative because this political syntaxis shapes how the subject thinks of its political existence.

Heteronormativity is a clear example of how political syntax operates. Political syntax did not include women as a political subject until recently. Thus, over centuries, political syntax established women's impossibility to be political subjects; this affirmation acted as impossibility through memory. Women, to be political subjects, needed to dislocate the symbolic matrix. However, how does this dislocation occur? Does it take place by including women in the symbolic matrix, or does it involve the destruction of the previous political syntaxis that denied their existence as political subjects? The entrance of ex-sisting subjects to Reality is possible but is also a process mediated by language in a process that we call ciphering. As Bruce Fink points out, "[i]n Lacan's terminology, existence is a product of language: language brings things into existence (makes them part of human reality), things which had no existence prior to being cyphered, symbolized, or put into words" (1995, p. 25). From my perspective, Postmodernity as the era of the hegemony of the capitalist dream, and the fall of the Eurocommunist one, occurs once capitalism governs the process of ciphering the Real.

As I will attempt to illustrate, the emergence of women as existing results from women's inclusion into a previous political syntax; ciphering. In current capitalist societies, the continuous yet limited introduction of ex-sisting subjects into political syntax occurs through mass consumption and production patterns. Thus, the fifth discursive structure, the Capitalist's Discourse, illustrates the ciphering.

The Capitalist's Discourse

In 1964, during a discourse in Milan, Lacan presented the Capitalist's Discourse (Figure 6.5). Lacan introduces this discourse as "[w]ildly clever, but headed for a blowout" (Lacan, n.d., p. 20).

Again, this book's discursive mediation intervenes Lacan's classical structure and substitutes S2 with ⌐S1 because the core of political discourse relies on the relation between S_1 and ⌐S_1, not on how S_1 intervenes upon S_2. Nevertheless, there is a significant difference between the other four discursive structures and this fifth one. Within the Capitalist's Discourse structure, one cannot differentiate the ontological level and the ontic level because its central goal is to cipher the Real into Reality by blurring and making the existence of two different levels invisible. Let me analyze how this structure functions.

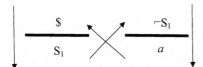

Figure 6.5 Capitalist's Discourse.

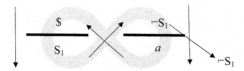

Figure 6.6 Infinite Capitalist's Discourse.

In the agent's position, the desiring subject appeals to its truth, the Master Signifier masculine. From the Master Signifier masculine, we find a direct appellation to its opposite, the other, which results in the production of *a*. Translating this operation to political terms, one can see how ciphering functions. The desiring subject which, as Fabio Vighi affirms, can be defined as "divided by an unknown desire, and at the same time diabolically persuaded that he can access truth, i.e., that he knows exactly what he wants (as the downward vector in Lacan's schema suggests)" (2016, p. 424), appeals to normativity as the truth, there is a Master Signifier that controls political syntax, that Master Signifier must be the truth as the symbolic matrix is considered as being true. The desiring subject appeals with its normativity to the other, to the radical alterity that inhabits the space of existence. It is precisely here where the process of ciphering takes place. You must adequate yourself to the symbolic matrix to obtain your existence. Thus, there is an encounter between the S_1 and $\neg S_1$; in other words, there is an encounter with the Real; there is an act. The process of ciphering occurs when the encounter with the Real results in the creation of *a*. That is to say, the result of the ciphering is the creation of an anxious subject. This newly created subject again appeals to the desiring subject, so the desiring subject finally accepts their existence. Nevertheless, the anxious subject is never fully recognized. This is the reason why, as Fabio Vighi points out, the vectors that constitute the Capitalist's Discourse create the figure of the infinite. However, our discursive and feminist mediation intervenes the structure and divides the idea of product and loss (Figure 6.6).

Not everyone will achieve the status of *a*, *a* is the product, but there is also a loss. Again, the loss is the Real, $\neg S_1$, which falls out of the frame by falling out of the process of ciphering. Therefore, ciphering is successful because it can introduce an aspect of the Real without threatening political syntax continuity. The Real is transformed in its introduction to the Symbolic matrix (there is no prelinguistic Reality, as Lacan says). Nevertheless, not all the Real can be translated into the symbolic Matrix, as $\neg S_1$ is still out of the frame. The subject must wait until the conditions of capitalism need their existence as consumers and or producers. In other words, and again citing Lacan, the subject does not use language, but language uses the subject, which, in our feminist discursive mediation, implies that the subject does not use political syntax, but political syntax uses the subject. The relation between ciphering and capitalism is easily observable in the production of patterns of consumption. Let me first see how different discourses relate to each other for Fabio Vighi:

> This veritable delirium of narcissistic omnipotence of the capitalist subject, who aspires to bypass symbolic castration and related *jouissance* (surplus-enjoyment), establishes a social ontology founded upon a relentless act of recycling: the transformation/distortion of *a* (the senseless residue of the signifying operation and as such object-cause of desire in the Master's discourse) into a universally countable and exchangeable value (University and Capitalist discourses).
>
> (2016, p. 424)

I agree that capitalist ontology creates what Vighi defines as the relentless act of recycling, the transformation/distortion of *a*. Nevertheless, what is missing from Vighi's reading and other authors within the Lacanian Left is this ontology's androcentric dimension. On the other hand, a feminist discursive intervention shows that the narcissistic and omnipotent male capitalist subject is interpellated by the Real, a feminine Real that implies an encounter with the Real. To control this encounter with the Real, the subject of the Master Signifier creates an ambiguous status of existence that *decaffeinates the act that ciphers the Real*. This recycling ontology supposes the continuous transformation of the Real into a transformed or distorted *a*, as Vighi points out. This transformation takes place through the conversion of ontological statuses into consumption patterns.

I thus adhere to the idea of capitalist bulimia that Fabio Vighi develops. Nevertheless, we with a different perspective that leads to assuming that the infinite production of this discourse makes visible not just consumerist bulimia that the subject develops but also the bulimia inherent of capitalism in the creation and disappearance of subjects. Capitalism produces subjects through the process of ciphering by transforming identities into patterns of consumption. Thus, capitalism allows certain subjects to become anxious subjects that aim to be recognized and that appeal to consumption patterns as a way to be recognized by the desiring subjects of a capitalist system. I must be able to consume to exist. Nevertheless, once the hysteric subject becomes anxious and again appeals to the desiring subject, this subject again appeals to the truth of the Master Signifier to again deny the full existence of the subject.

From a Marxist perspective, we face the commodification of ontological statuses into consumption patterns proper of capitalism. This commodification is a common element of critique in the Left. Nevertheless, there is a tendency to mistake commodification of what I refer to as ontological statuses with the idea of difference and identity.

Several authors affirm that speaking of identities is a way to deviate the attention of distributive justice. To think that there are politics that are not related whatsoever to identity is a fallacy. As Catherine Hundelby points out in her article "Androcentrism as a Fallacy of Argumentation", what we see is that to deny the androcentric dimension of Reality, that is to say, to deny that politics, economy, and culture both depart and address the masculine ideal constitutes a fallacy of argumentation (2011).

While the process of ciphering did not imply the commodification of ontological statuses in earlier times; for example, in the bible, Lilith comes to represent an encounter with feminine Real, such encounter puts into risk political syntaxis, Lilith is thus excluded and spat out of Reality and Eve comes into the picture as *a*, as a tamed and ciphered Real. In the case of capitalist ciphering, the subject that belongs to the Real is offered a new identification process that, although it is a failed one due to the absence of recognition of the desiring subject, entails a constant material satisfaction through consumption of goods and services. The symptom is thus *a*, as an anxious ontological status that works as the reminder of the Real but also as the promising horizon of the Real, which deactivates the possible political outburst of the act.

Nevertheless, identities and difference (which sum up to ontological statuses) cannot be overridden or undervalued because capitalism holds the potential to deactivate the radicality of the act that they can enact. The expected critique of identity and difference can come from the idea that identities end up being pure decaffeinated resistance because they all become consumption patterns. Thus, the critique affirms that identity only warrants the capability to consume in an irreverent manner; we are allowed to misbehave. However, I want to conclude this chapter by analyzing the different outcomes that an act may have and shed some light on the mechanisms that allow for the subversion of political syntax. This analysis will be articulated around Žižek's classification of acts.

Encounters with the Real

Žižek suggests that there are one proper act and three other situations that may be conceived as acts but are not. The following classification aims to develop the differences between Žižek's argumentation and the approach on acts that the feminist discursive mediation offers.

- The psychotic *passage à l'acte*: for Žižek, in this situation, the subject feels as in a deadlock; I believe that such deadlock springs from the anxiety of the anxious subject. As a way out of this anxiety, there is an outburst of energy. While Žižek finds this outburst as one of destructive energy, I believe that this outburst is characterized by its energy to reproduce the already given political syntax. What I find in the passage *à l'acte* is the anxious subject's outburst.

From a political perspective, a subject whose political existence is not totally assured neither recognized feels treated as $\neg S_1$ and develops the University's Discourse. As pointed out in earlier sections, this passage *à l'acte* results in reproducing the conditions that political syntax establishes and the continuous emergence of the desiring subject.

- The symbolic act: as analyzed earlier, Žižek defines this act as one that self-asserts a subject's position. From the feminist discursive mediation, this is the act that develops the desiring subject. The desiring subject, who is aware of the conditions of reproducibility of the frame, develops certain acts that aim to reaffirm the exclusivity of its existence. This can be easily seen in national rituals such as military shows on national holidays. Nevertheless, the symbolic act is also present in denying human or civil rights to non-androcentric subjects. Furthermore, the symbolic act is how the Master's Discourse continues to be established within daily life and spaces.

Furthermore, although the form may classify these two moments as proper acts, the truth is that, once one looks at the content of these situations, they are not acts but actions. If the act is an encounter with the Real, one can only speak of acts when the hysteric subject develops it. Let me look at the outcomes of the act.

- The hysterical acting out: I have already defined the hysterical acting out as the failed proper act. This failure takes place when the act is not able to create the conditions of its legitimation. As explained earlier, the hysteric speaks a language that is unintelligible to the Master. This is because the hysteric is (a) someone who is not allowed to speak and (b) someone who speaks of that which lacks a signifier. When the act cannot legitimize itself, there is a disruption that does not imply a change in the Symbolic matrix. Thus, if the condition *sine qua non* of the act is the relation between the Symbolic and the Real, this act fails if it does not manage to inscribe the Real within the Symbolic by introducing a new Master Signifier. I refer to revolutionary outbursts, street demonstrations, or social movements that cannot change the Symbolic. This would be the decaf resistance that Contu developed.
- The proper act: the proper act occurs when the hysteric subject engages in a discursive operation that can address the desiring subject and political syntax. The act is successful because it can create the conditions of its legitimation but, more importantly, because the result of this legitimization is the introduction of a signifier that comes to represent the Real. That is to say, it involves a real change within the symbolic matrix that involves loss and introduces lack.
- The ciphering of the Real: the process of ciphering the Real occurs when a proper act takes place but does not create a new signifier. Instead, the Real is given a pre-existing signifier that allows its entrance but does not guarantee its ontological status as existing, as being. It is a capitalist translation in which the ontological status of ex-sistence becomes a pattern of consumption

that allows the subject to enter into political syntax. The Real is translated into political syntax by assigning it to an already given signifier. There is no creation of signifier, no loss, no cost for the desiring subject.

In order to clarify and systematize the act, the information can be analyzed in Figure 6.7.

Although the analysis of these five different outcomes points out the difficulty of producing a substantial change in political syntax, I want to stress the

	Who	What	Result	Political example
Psychotic *passage à l'acte*	The anxious subject.	The University's Discourse takes place because the anxious subject takes the position of $-S_1$	Political syntax is not subverted neither dislocated.	Transphobic feminist actions.
The symbolic act	The desiring subject .	There is an act that empowers normativity, that reproduces the frame.	The Master's Discourse takes place in a way in which the *status quo* is reinforced.	Denial of LGTBQIA+ rights
The hysterical acting out	The hysteric subject.	The act is not able to create the conditions of its legitimation.	The Hysteric's Discourse takes place, there is an unintelligible act of speaking that does not achieve to enter into the symbolic matrix as a signifier.	Social movements or rebellious acts that do not suppose changes withing politics
The proper act	The hysteric subject.	There is an act able to create the conditions of its legitimation.	The Analyst's Discourse takes place, the hysteric is able to act as *a*, as the actual reminder of *a* and addresses the privileged ontological status.	There is a dislocation and subversion of the symbolic matrix. It involves costs as it is able to inscribe loss and negativity.
The cyphered act		The encounter with the Real is deactivated through capitalist translation.	The proper act is able to create the conditions of its legitimation but undergoes a process of cyphering, of capitalist translation. From ontological status to pattern of consumption.	Feminist movement becomes an Inditex t-shirt.

Figure 6.7 Types of Acts.

possibility of the act. To put all the responsibility of the act, of change, on subjects who usually live in precariousness results in the inactivity of agents who enjoy material conditions and privileged ontological status to formulate a change and enjoy the symptom, enjoy capitalism. Thus, what needs to be developed as a way out of capitalist reality is the act of coalitions.

The idea of the act of coalitions is deeply inspired by the idea of bodily coalitions present in Judith Butler's essay "Bodily Vulnerability, Coalitions, and Street Politics" (2014). In this article, Judith Butler introduces the potential that vulnerable bodies present when creating coalitions that defy the imposed order and normativity. From our feminist discursive mediation, the act of coalitions is a situation in which the anxious subject and the hysteric subject form a coalition to guarantee the event's success. The anxious subject represents the Real, which needs to articulate a relation with the Symbolic for the act's success. On the other hand, as *objet a*, the anxious subject is the reminder that the Real ex-sists and the element that ties the Symbolic to the Real. A reading of feminine fantasy allows observing to see how the act of coalitions needs to take place.

On the one hand, the anxious subject needs to realize that they have already undergone a process of ciphering. In the case of our female cisgender lesbian deputy, she needs to be aware of the privilege of her ontological status and observe the identities that are not present within that political space. She thus becomes aware of her position of *objet a* qua link of the Symbolic with the Real. Nevertheless, once she wants to develop the Analyst's Discourse, she must face that the other that she must address, $, holds her same ontological status. It is here that the act of coalition takes place.

Once she realizes that the other she must address holds her same ontological status, they become aware that what grants her existence is her condition as an educated white cisgender woman, which are dimensions of identity that she shares with other desiring subjects. What is situated in the position of truth in this Analyst's Discourse is precisely $\overline{}\,S_1$. By being aware of the truth and being aware, as Lacan said, that you can never say all the truth as it is impossible (1974), the anxious subject needs to create the conditions that legitimize the hysteric act. In other words, the anxious subject needs to take advantage of the act's dislocation to assure its success. However, how does this take place in political terms?

As seen in previous chapters, I believe that the only way this can be done is by subverting the classical Schmittian relation of friend/enemy and understand that our ontological status is granted through the imposition of antagonisms. Thus, we need to behave in a way in which we establish a coalition with the others in a way in which we understand ourselves as the potential threat to those with the ontological status of ex-sistence (Fishel et al., 2021; Valdés, 2021). In terms of political identities, we need to look at ourselves from an approach that allows us to see the axes of oppression that cross our lives, but more importantly, the axis of privilege that grants our existence. The act of coalitions implies loss and costs; it integrates lack and negativity as a central element of political syntax. The coalition between vulnerable bodies can defy and shift the imposed order through a revolutionary act.

Toward a New Political Relationship

The act of coalitions entails two different radical shifts in how political relationships have been constructed on the grounds of the Schmittian relation of we/they.

The re-articulation of the political relationship that this book articulates departs from the idea of reverse antagonism. Reverse antagonism is a term that I have coined to designate political relationships through a paradigm that does not negate the central space that antagonisms have taken over in liberal democracies. However, as I have argued elsewhere, antagonisms do not need to reproduce the current Symbolic but subvert it (Fishel et al., 2021; Valdés, 2021).

Reverse antagonism, the political bond that springs from and for the act of coalitions, entails reversing the Schmittian traditional reading of antagonism that places the threat outside the Symbolic and not within it. In this sense, *we* can be threatening *them*. In discursive terms, subjects with existence must ask themselves whether their existence is granted by negating another agent's existence. Thus, through self-analysis, we place ourselves in the paradigm of doubt, a paradigm that obliges us to question the very position we inhabit in the topology of discursive Reality and the ontological status it grants us. Thus political self-analysis has to be developed in every situation in which a subject believes they are the oppressed subject to create a reverse antagonistic bond and develop an act of coalitions, an encounter with the Real. It is self-analysis that can lead the subject to develop the Analyst's Discourse instead of the University's.

Seeing how a subject participates in their own submission while acting as masters of others allows re-articulating the political relationship. To put responsibility and empathy as the kernel of political relationships can reverse antagonism as it pushes the subject to evaluate their political position and subjectivity as the potential threat of the external victim (Fishel et al., 2021; Valdés, 2021). Thus, by departing from the feminist discursive mediation that allows analyzing Reality as the product of discursive operations that aim at developing an exclusive and excluding frame upon which politics take place, we can reverse those mechanisms by positing the threat within and not outside the frame from which power relations arise.

In this self-analysis, the anxious subject's question of "What am I to them?" does not change. Nevertheless, it addresses the hysteric subject. By asking, "What am I to the hysteric?" the anxious subject is forced to listen to a so-called unintelligible talk and understand the speaking of the other, obliged to abandon the political matrix. Nevertheless, the re-articulation of the political relation, as the product of the subversion of antagonism, demands us to accept intersectionality and dynamism of political identifications.

In the introduction, I presented how Kimberle Crenshaw (1994; 2006) coined intersectionality not as a position but as a worldview, an active understanding of the world, but several currents within feminism have appropriated the term and interpret it as an ontological position only characterized by the intersection of oppression. This appropriation brings along a crucial risk which is that by adopting intersectionality as a static ontological status—that is to say, avoiding questioning whether intersectionality is situated and therefore my oppression and privilege are dynamic and dependent on the context—we avoid analyzing how women, as an oppressed subject, may also deploy violence and become a threat to other subjects. Thus, as a white cis woman, I am more exposed to sexual violence than a white cis male, but I also need to recognize my superior position while facing a situation in which I may represent a threat to another, for example, a black male refugee in the Mediterranean coast. Thus, we must understand identities as situated in a reading that we appropriate from Haraway. By being aware of our privileges, we can subvert the reading of the other as a potential enemy or threat; we must understand ourselves as potentially threatening the inclusion of identities located in the space of the Real. Thus, the Basic Political Community's frame must be porous to enable the entry of new subjects. This logic can help build reverse antagonistic boundaries and understand how we can become the enemy of the other. Thus, we enter into politics of precaution and care.

The inversion of political antagonisms and the understanding of the Hysteric's Discourse are part of what I have denominated as the act of coalitions. The act of coalitions is the moment in which, facing the constant defeat of the act that should result from the encounter with the Real, the anxious subject and the hysteric subject establish a bond that creates a political coalition. If the political act only succeeds with the inscription of a new signifier within political syntax, the hysteric subject, as belonging to the Real, needs to find an ally within the space of existence. On the other hand, the anxious subject, through self-analysis, needs to become aware of their own contribution in an intricate network of oppression that both oppresses and privileges themselves. For the act of coalitions to occur, the anxious subject must create the conditions upon which the Hysteric's Discourse can be both developed and heard. However, it would be naïve to affirm that this new political relation can occur in current political arenas. I believe that there is a need to create spaces where the act of coalitions can take place.

In his book *Cultura es Nombre de Derrota*,[1] Fernando Broncano develops an intricate and complex reading of the evolution of the left's theoretical body (2018). Furthermore, he articulates the idea of intermediate space, which he defines as spaces of resistance that spring from defeats. He affirms that

> The cultural reaction of defeat [...] implied discovering a new *topos* of resistance, where power constitutes subjectivities, in the short distances of social relations and forms of affection in the second person. It is about the universe of daily life, about the spaces of everyday life where the basic plot of society is inhabited and redone.
>
> (2018, p. 187)

I believe these intermediate spaces spring from the defeat of the feminine act by the masculine Symbolic. Feminist communes in which so-called witches lived could be analyzed as intermediate spaces that allowed a different reading of daily life. They were spaces of resistance in which women gathered to confront or avoid the new hegemonic logic that wanted to establish a new manner of interaction. Furthermore, Broncano also defines intermediate spaces as spaces of intimacy, for Broncano "[i]ntimacy is not isolation, but the production of second-person relationships: 'you to you', 'face to face', where the other counts as someone whose internal states matter for being him or her and for being his or hers" (2018, p. 220).

I believe intermediate spaces subvert the Schimittian logic of the *differentia specifica* principle. Moving or shifting from we/they relationship to second-person relationships allows for the subversion of classical antagonistic political relations. Furthermore, the space of "you to you" allows for communication and care. From a feminist economist paradigm, intermediate spaces are those spaces in which life is placed at the center.

In her book *Subversión Feminista de la Economía*, Amia Pérez Orozco analyzes the current socioeconomic system, which is not only defined as "capitalist but also heteropatriarchal and racially structured, (neo)colonialist and anthropocentric [...] one of the definitory elements of this scandalous Thing is that capitalist markets are in its epicenter" (2017, p. 38). She goes on and affirms that "they are in its epicenter because their mechanism defines how the socioeconomic structure functions; and because the process that is socially guaranteed is that of capital accumulation" (2017, p. 38). From my perspective, this capitalist epicenter is the consequence of a masculine hegemony of Reality that poses markets, as the spaces of inhabitancy of the masculine and capitalist subject, at the center. On the other hand, the periphery responds to non-economical yet reproductive spaces of care, in which feminine subjects are to be found. The alternative to the capitalist economy is the feminist alternative "to put the sustainability of the life at the center" (Pérez Orozco, 2017, p. 39).

Thus, the idea of intermediate spaces and the feminist attempt to put life at the center create a political proposal to confront androcentrification. Intermediate spaces are those spaces of daily life in which lives are put at the center and where the classical Schmittian notion of antagonism is defeated to allow for the act to spring.

Note

1 All quotes belonging from this book are my own translations.

References

Broncano, F. (2018). *Cultura es Nombre de Derrota. Cultura y Poder en los Espacios Intermedios*. Editorial Delirio.

Butler, J. (2014). Bodily Vulnerability, Coalitions, and Street Politics. *Differences in Common. Gender, Vulnerability and Community, 37*, 97–119.

Butler, J., Laclau, E., & Žižek, S. (2000). *Contingency, Hegemony, Universality: Contemporary Dialogues on the Left*. verso.

Contu, A. (2008). Decaf Resistance: On Misbehavior, Cynicism, and Desire in Liberal Workplaces. *Management Communication Quarterly, 21*(3), 364–379. https://doi.org/10.1177/0893318907310941

Crenshaw, K. (1994). Mapping the Margins: Intersectionality, Identity Politics, and Violence Against Women of Color. In M. Albertson Fineman, & R. Mykitiuk (Eds.), *The Public Nature of Private Violence* (pp. 93–118). Routledge.

Crenshaw, K. W. (2006). Intersectionality, Identity Politics and Violence Against Women of Color. *Kvinder, Køn & Forskning, 2–3.* https://doi.org/10.7146/kkf.v0i2-3.28090

Fink, B. (1995). *The Lacanian Subject. Between Language and Jouissance.* Princeton University Press.

Fishel, S. R., Fletcher, A., Krishna, S., McKnight, U., du Plessis, G., Shomura, C., Valdés, A., & Voelkner, N. (2021). Politics in the Time of COVID. *Contemporary Political Theory.* https://doi.org/10.1057/s41296-021-00500-1

Hundleby, C. (2011). *Androcentrism as a Fallacy of Argumentation* (p. 13). University of Windsor.

Lacan, J. (n.d.). *On Psychoanalytic Discourse. Discourse of Jacques Lacan at the University of Milan on May 12, 1972.* Freud2Lacan. Retrieved 3 January 2020, from https://www.freud2lacan.com/docs/DISCOURSE_OF_CAPITALISM-bilingual.pdf

Lacan, J. (1974). *Télévision.* WW Norton & Company.

Pérez Orozco, A. (2017). *Subversión feminista de la economía. Aportes para un debate sobre el conflicto capital-vida* (3rd ed.). Traficnates de Sueños.

Shepherdson, C. (2008). *Lacan and the Limits of Language.* Fordham University Press.

Stavrakakis, Y. (2010). On Acts, Pure and Impure. *International Journal of Zizek Studies, 4*(2), 1–35.

Valdés, A. (2021). The Facemask Paradigm: Symptoms and Non-neutral Limits during Coronavirus. *Free Associations: Psychoanalysis and Culture, Media, Groups, Politics., 81–82,* 18–30. https://doi.org/10.1234/fa.v0i81-82.380

Vighi, F. (2016). Capitalist Bulimia: Lacan on Marx and Crisis. *Crisis & Critique, 3*(3), 415–432.

Žižek, S. (1998). *From 'Passionate Attachments' to Dis-Identification.* https://www.lacan.com/zizekpassionate.htm

Žižek, S. (2002). The Ticklish Subject: The Absent Centre of Political Ontology. *Literature and Theology, 16*(3), 342–345. https://doi.org/10.1093/litthe/16.3.342

Part II

Some Notes for a Genealogy of Sexuation

Introduction

This part aims to apply the discursive tools developed in Part I to analyze Reality and observe how the construction of woman as a political identity in capitalism occurred. Thus, it departs from the already developed idea that the division between what exists and what ex-sists relies on a process of sexuation of Reality. Androcentrification situates masculine elements in the center while relegating feminine elements to the periphery. This androcentrification has a long his-tory and consists of different phases of dynamics that expel the feminine and reject it as valid.

This second part attempts to describe and analyze two different central processes: (a) the process through which women, indigenous, migrant people, and other underrepresented agents are excluded from Reality; and (b) how feminism is being deactivated and depoliticized in current times. These two processes will be analyzed through the application of the feminist discursive mediation developed in Part I. As I will present, the exclusion of feminine subjects from Reality corresponds to their exclusion from political syntax. Such exclusion occurs positioning these subjects under the Signifier of Pure Threat. On the other hand, after analyzing their expulsion, I will analyze how specific agents have been included in political syntax and how such a process entails the deactivation of their potential to subvert. Thus, I will analyze how androcentrification occurs by observing different discursive operations in which this process engages. Thus, we attempt to develop a genealogy that allows us to see the history that backs the division between masculine and feminine.

Androcentrification consists of three different operations. However, they do not create a precise sequence of events but an intricate network in which they also overlap.

- Sexuation of the ontological level: the discursive operation that occurs at this stage is the creation and establishment of the two Master Signifiers that come to divide and organize the ontological level. This discursive operation produces two differentiated ontological statuses and two spaces of inhabitancy that provide subjects with existence or ex-sistence, implementing the Master's Discourse. One can trace back this Master's Discourse as far back

DOI: 10.4324/9781003167587-10

as to Aristotelian thought and that what characterizes the sexuation of the ontological level is the stigmatization of the feminine.

- Masculine hegemony at the ontic level: while the sexuation of ontology is taking place, other discursive operations take place at the ontic level that limit and condition political syntax only to allow the existence of the androcentric subject. In this sense, one can observe that the stigmatization of the feminine at the ontological level results in the expulsion of the feminine from the Symbolic matrix that political syntax is. One can see how specific signifiers representing the androcentric subject are placed as empty signifiers within the Borromean knot in these discursive operations.

- The ciphering of the feminine: this last stage of androcentrification entails creating a mechanism able to cipher the feminine Real into masculine Reality. As seen, this stage implies the deactivation of the potential to disrupt of ex-sisting subjects. In this sense, I believe that this stage entails the climax for androcentrification, as it can assure the continuity of political syntax. In historical terms, the ciphering stage takes place with capitalism, and its culmination coincides in time with the fall of the Eurocommunist dream.

Chapter 7

The Sexuation of the Ontological Level

The feminist discursive mediation this book offers affirms that Reality results from specific discursive operations that work at an ontological and an ontic level. At the ontological level, the discursive operation of the Master's Discourse creates and establishes two opposite Master Signifiers that represent two different modes of existence. On the one hand, S_1 grants the subject with existence; the subject is within political syntax. On the other hand, $\neg S_1$ represents those who do not possess existence but ex-sistence, which implies their absence from political syntax and Reality. Furthermore, this Master's Discourse establishes two opposite Master Signifiers that correspond to the Master Signifier masculine (S_1) and Master Signifier feminine ($\neg S_1$). Thus, the Master's Discourse, which is the origin of Reality, implies its sexuation by creating two different sexual positions toward the Symbolic, represented in the Symbolic matrix.

Although all these discursive operations and ontological classifications have been exhaustively developed and explained in Part I, I now want to show how such operations have been taking place in Europe. In this sense, I aim to illustrate how different philosophical movements and scientific developments have stigmatized the feminine and relegated it to ex-sistence and how such a mechanism can be read in feminist and discursive terms. A central element in our reading of the ontological level's sexuation is the turn from organismic theories to mechanism.

Organismic ontologies are ontologies that do not separate the self from what surrounds it but develop a theory that binds the self to society and the cosmos. As Carolyne Merchant affirms, "organismic theory emphasized interdependence among the parts of the human body, subordination of the individual to communal purposes in family, community, and state, and vital life permeating the cosmos to the lowliest stone" (1989, p. 1). Within the central metaphor of organismic/organic theory, every element has its own specific role. In organic theories, the feminine is identified with nature. In Ancient Greek ontology, like the ones developed by both Aristotle and Plato, the feminine is related to matter as the material that conforms nature and is characterized as a lower form precisely because of its materiality. While ideas, as opposed to matter, were a higher and abstract element related to the masculine. A constant triad of the elements of matter, nature, and the feminine is observable. This triple identification goes as far as to Plato,

DOI: 10.4324/9781003167587-11

"[i]n Platonic and Neoplatonic symbolism, therefore, both nature and matter were feminine, while the ideas were masculine" (Merchant, 1989, p. 10). Nevertheless, although the identification of women with nature is a common element in organic ontologies, it did not imply the same hierarchical system in each of them.

This chapter analyzes discursive operations that implied the stigmatization of the feminine through its connection with negative and threatening ideas. Nevertheless, there was an intense contestation to this discourse that did not hegemonize the ontic but implied and still implies a root for counter-movements. I will argue that the triumph of the androcentric discourse over others relies on the fact that the stigmatization of the feminine entailed the process that transformed the sacred nature into an element created to serve humans for their economic needs and established a new social system. Let me now see how different discursive operations at the ontological level were able to stigmatize the feminine.

Matter and Form

This genealogy of the sexuation of ontology begins with Aristotle's differentiation of matter and form and how this sexuation can be analyzed through our feminist discursive mediation.

Although Aristotle diverged with Plato and understood that matter and form are found within substance, such unification did not imply either a homogenization or a non-hierarchical order among both. In fact, "Aristotelian philosophy, while unifying matter and form in each individual being, associated activity with maleness and passivity with femaleness. Form reigned superior over dead, passive matter" (Merchant, 1989, p. 13). The justification to such sexuation relied on how Aristotle observed and defined reproduction: "[i]n the generation of the offspring, the female constituted the matter or passive principle. This was the material on which the active male principle, the semen, worked in creating the embryo" (Merchant, 1989, p. 13). Jean-Joseph Goux affirms that this metaphysical conception shapes social relations for Aristotle (1973), a theory that Merchant also embraces when she affirms that "Aristotle found the basis for male rule over the household in the analogy that, as the soul ruled the body, so reason and deliberation, characteristic of men, should rule the appetites supposedly dominant in women" (1989, p. 13).

Linda Lange goes one step further in the feminist critique to Aristotelian ontology and affirms that "the important Aristotelian distinctions between 'form' and 'matter', 'mover' and 'moved', 'actuality' and 'potentiality', are all used by Aristotle to distinguish male and female" (1983, p. 2). That is to say, socially, this relation between matter and form, feminine and masculine, legitimizes holistic domination of the masculine over the feminine. Lange also points out that Aristotle's argumentation is full of fallacies and mistakes, which leads us to think that his distinction between matter and form, and the hierarchy that results from such distinction, are not results of the application of a scientific method and observation, but a result of ideological bias. Elizabeth Spelman also concludes that

Aristotle's metaphysics may have been developed to legitimize the status quo of masters over slaves and men over women affirming that society's patriarchal structure shapes Aristotle's metaphysics (1983). This way, Aristotle's political theory, which rests on the relationships of superiority between people—master over slave, men over women—rests in a hierarchical relationship of form—masculine—over matter—feminine. For Spelman, Aristotle's justification of this hierarchy relies on articulating the rule of the rational over the irrational (1983). In other words, the rational elements rule over the irrational just as rational beings must govern and rule irrational ones. Moreover, there is a feminization of kids and slaves.

Spelman analyzes how Aristotle legitimizes the govern of men over women through the rule of the rational over the irrational and finds elements that demonstrate the tautologic dimension of his explanation. She points out Aristotle's definition of women as irrational beings. While two main elements form souls—the rational and the irrational—in women's case, the irrational part overrides the rational one. Nevertheless, naturally, the rational part is to have authority over the irrational, a process that does not take place in women, slaves, and children. Furthermore, as Spelman affirms, the authority of the rational over the irrational does not always take place in men either, as the need for an articulation of ethics and politics shows (1983, p. 19). Therefore,

> the rule or authority he ascribes to the rational part must have to do with entitlement: the rational part has the right to, or ought to, or is intended by nature to rule the irrational part, even if that isn't always what happens.
>
> (Spelman, 1983, pp. 19–20)

Thus, women are irrational—a conclusion shared with Lange's feminist analysis of Aristotle's (1983). Furthermore, if the natural thing is to have the rational ruling the rational, "women are by nature unnatural" (Spelman, 1983, p. 22). It is here where Spelman finds one of the most evident voids in Aristotle's justification of male domination:

> So Aristotle's argument for the natural subordination of women to men is, to put it charitably, wobbly: he holds an inconsistent view about the natural relationship between the rational and irrational parts of the soul, and he begs the question when he claims that the rational element by nature rules in men but does not in women.
>
> (1983, p. 24)

His own rejection of one of his main theoretical elements takes Aristotle to develop a tautological theory for the justification and legitimation of the domination of women by men (Spelman, 1983, p. 26). Thus, Aristotle commits a fallacy driven by his desire to justify an androcentric society by developing an androcentric ontological theory. Nevertheless, and leaving aside Spelman's theory, let me focus now on the analysis that Goux develops over the consequences of this sexuated division.

In his book *Symbolic Economies*, Goux points out the paternal structure domination that results from the sexual differentiation between matter and form, "[i]f (paternal) form is invariant, (maternal) matter is the changing and relative receptacle that possesses no determination or consistency apart from the imprint of this ideal form" (1973, p. 5). This affirmation leads to thinking that men's patriarchal control over nature is necessary for the maternal element. Furthermore, the need for control for an imposed order by a separate or external agent leads me to speak about desire. As Goux affirms, "Aristotle clearly states that matter desires form as the female desires the male. On the female side, there is no order, no principle of internal organization, no generative power" (1973, p. 213). The need for control can be analyzed in terms of this desire and lack of organization. Thus, associating the passivity of matter with desire toward form, and its constant need for control due to its lack of consistency, one can see the perfect mix for masochism. The passivity of the feminine element—matter—would imply the need for an agency—form. It is a subject that interacts as passive in a conscious way to obtain another subject to control it to consummate a desire. In other words, it seems plausible to draw here the connection between masochism and women. There is desire; there is a lack of order; there could also be a desire to overcome that indetermination by control. This domination of form—masculine—over matter—feminine—is defined by Goux as paterialism (1973, p. 243).

Aristotle's theory serves as a mechanism to legitimate the rule of a specific group of people, national men, over others. Here, what concerns me is how Aristotle developed a discursive operation that created two Master Signifiers and modified the ontological level by creating a sexuated division between two different ontological statuses.

From the feminist discursive mediation, one can observe how Aristotle creates two different Master Signifiers representing masculine (S_1) and feminine ($\neg S_1$). Women, slaves, and children are congregated under the same signifier, $\neg S_1$; whether their classification as feminine relies on arguments about their lack of consistency, determination, rationality, or activity, the truth is that they are all congregated under the same signifier. They are $\neg S_1$ because they are not S_1. Nevertheless, I find it interesting to dwell on the relationship between man and woman to see how the absence of sexual relationship and the creation of fantasy takes place in Aristotle.

Although different subjects have been included around $\neg S_1$, it seems that Aristotle's theoretical developments lead him to create a sexuated division spring from his observation of biological reproduction between man and woman. Thus, the relationship between males and females is crucial in Aristotle's politics. In this sense, I find it radically interesting to go back to the idea of masochism. As seen, Goux affirms that it is *the lack of form in matter what makes matter desire form in the same way that female desire the male*. Thus, $\neg S_1$ desires S_1; nevertheless, the sexual relationship between the female and masculine principles is impossible($S_1//\text{-}S_1$). However, affirming that women desire men in the same way in which matter desires form, we also affirm that there is an inherent need in women to be with a man. Thus, the impossibility of the *rapport sexuelle* can be concealed by the idea of heterosexual love, which articulates the desiring subject (man) around *objet petit a* (woman) in the way in which the matheme of fantasy illustrates (\$ ◊ *a*). On the other hand, political fantasy is present in how democracy was built in Ancient Greece; the political fantasy that an ontological division supports is also visible in the political syntax ruling the ontic. Women could not be desiring subjects. Thus, through the feminist discursive mediation, it is observable how to be represented by the Signifier of pure Being allowed you to enter into political syntax by possessing the ontological status of existence. Nevertheless, these discursive mechanisms are not specific to Aristotle. They are present in many other authors and currents of thought. Let me analyze how this sexuated division takes place in different philosophical theories.

Man vs. Nature

If the dichotomic pair of matter and form contributed to the sexuated division of the ontological level, another dichotomic pair that played a central role in such sexuation was that of man and nature. Nevertheless, before dwelling on the Master Signifiers of man and nature, I must first refer to the connection between the feminine and nature.

The connection between nature and matter is previous to Aristotle's theorization on matter and form. In fact, "[i]n Platonic and Neoplatonic symbolism, therefore, both nature and matter were feminine, while the ideas were masculine" (Merchant, 1989, p. 10). Thus, the division between feminine matter and masculine form and between feminine nature and masculine ideas seem to follow the same discursive mechanism. Nevertheless, the fact that nature was feminine did not imply domination of man over nature. However, nature was subordinated to another element, God:

> But nature, as God's agent, in her role as creator and producer of the material world, was superior to human artists both in creativity and in ease of production. She was more powerful than humans, but still subordinated to God.
>
> (Merchant, 1989, p. 10)

Therefore, nature could not produce, nor develop or transform. As Goux writes, when defining Hegel's argument of nature, "[n]ature is fertile but impotent" (1973, p. 213). Such articulation is already visible in Aristotle, as he understands that, although nature does put the material, it needs a masculine, active principle to activate itself. This is easily observable in the definition of reproduction where the semen, and not the womb, possesses the key and central role, but it is also observable in the transformation of wood into a table, in which the active element was always the masculine, the form. As Merchant puts it, "[s]ince no material was ever transferred from the body of the carpenter to the wood, by analogy, the male did not contribute any matter, but rather the force and power of generation" (1989, p. 16). In discursive terms, there is a continuation of the discursive operation already observed in Aristotle's theorization. There are two Master Signifiers, one of them possessing better, more valued characteristics than the other. Nevertheless, the division between feminine and masculine did not imply the same hierarchy in every organic theory.

The Aristotelian identification of the feminine as the passive, the dependent, or the incomplete—as having to be continuously dominated by a masculine element—competes during Renaissance with other views on nature. During the Renaissance, there is a moment in which Aristotelian theories of ontology collide with ontologies that praised nature. As the provider of all life, the figure of Mother Earth, whether seen as benevolent and as the subterfuge or alternative to a sinful life, or as a rebellious and chaotic mother, is the figure of an active agent upon which humanity depended. That is to say, the opposition between masculine and feminine did not have the same consequences in every ontological discourse. The distinction between masculine and feminine did not always imply a hierarchy or a masculine hierarchy. In fact, the distinction could derive into a feminine hierarchy or in the violent opposition between the masculine and the feminine, as the idea of man versus nature illustrates.

Other currents of thought, which directly opposed Aristotle's principles, were also present in Europe. Thus, there were other discourses taking place at the same moment. Gnosticism or Geocosm were currents that took place at the same time that the European philosophical Aristotelian turn. Such currents defined nature as organic and living, but in Gnosticism, there was no hierarchy between masculine and feminine. On the other hand, Geocosm did not only define nature as feminine but also the Earth, which was depicted as a nurturing mother. Nevertheless, it is the Aristotelian formula of form over matter, the one that remains in the collective imaginary. In other words, it is the Aristotelian discourse the one that was able to hegemonize the ontological level and establish a sexuated hierarchy. This hegemony of the Aristotelian discourse has to do with the fact that this discourse allowed for a separation between humans and nature, which was the kernel for economic developments.

In her book *The Death of Nature*, Carolyne Merchant reminds us of the vast plurality of alternative discourses (1989). Thus, as she does, it is necessary to point out that the emergence of a mechanized nature and our relations toward it was not an easy process that did not find resistances. By explaining and demonstrating non-androcentric ontological and epistemological currents, Merchant shows that the androcentric ontology that nowadays governs our European societies is not natural but a social construct naturalized over time. One crucial dimension of some of these alternative currents of thought during the Renaissance is their image of nature. Nature was not just feminine, but the Earth was seen as a "nurturing mother" (Merchant, 1989, p. 29). This incarnation of the Earth as feminine and as a woman led to the endowment of the earth with some specific characteristics (Merchant, 1989). While the organic view conceives earth as living, the sexuation of matter and form conceives earth as feminine. One of the main elements that we must bear in mind when it comes to the androcentrification of Reality is precisely the incarnation of nature with Mother. This incarnation of Earth implies that humans' relations toward nature are endowed with moral constraints, just as human relations are (Merchant, 1989, p. 41). Furthermore, the incarnation is not in the figure of any woman, but the Mother, which provokes a particular interest for a feminist Lacanian reading. Let me analyze how this could be read in discursive terms.

We have seen that symbolic identification and the provision of sexual positions have to do with the fact that the subject needs to enter the Symbolic. Nevertheless, the idea of the Symbolic is not gender-neutral but masculine in Lacan, as Brennan affirmed (1989). In this brief parenthesis, I want to argue that, in organic theories that praised the feminine over the masculine, the Symbolic is governed by the Name of the Mother. In other words, the Symbolic matrix responds to S_1 as feminine. Thus, while the idea of form over matter evolved into man versus nature, that is to say, of the masculine principle as dominating the feminine principle, what organic theories offered was a total subversion of the Symbolic matrix by turning upside down the hierarchy of Master Signifiers.

These different discourses, these different conceptions of nature, shared a challenging historical moment for Europe. While the twelfth and thirteenth centuries had been characterized by an increasing population that derived into the conversion of forestall masses into crops, the European Renaissance starts with the Great Famine (1315–1322), a catastrophe followed by other demographic disasters such as the Black Death (Merchant, 1989, p. 48). A deadly period that Sylvia Federici describes as an "unprecedented demographic collapse profoundly changed Europe's social and political life, practically inaugurating a new era" (2009, p. 44). This demographic collapse produced a restoration of the environment and coincided with the occupation of Abya Yala, and the "[t]echnological improvements associated with the expanding economy based on inorganic, nonrenewable metallic wealth increased the potential for human exploitation" (Merchant, 1989, pp. 61–62). It is in this economic context that the humanization—femininization—of nature produced two opposite outcomes.

On the one hand, one may observe the attitude of those who saw mining as an atrocious act toward the Earth: "[m]oral restraints were thus clearly affiliated with the Renaissance image of the female earth and were strengthened by associations with greed, avarice, and lust" (Merchant, 1989, p. 41). On the other hand, a sector headed by different personalities such as Agricola legitimized mining and did not consider mining or extraction as related to negative notions, but as a natural consequence or result of Mother Earth's characteristics, in fact, "[a]ccording to Agricola, people who argued against the mining of the earth for metals did so on the basis that nature herself did not wish to be discovered what she herself had concealed" (Merchant, 1989, p. 34). In this second definition of nature, nature is an element that exists to cover our needs and help humanity develop in economic terms. Agricola's ideas defended mining and supported extraction and exploitation. The more benevolent and protective attitude toward the Earth could not compete with economic reasoning. The theory that drew nature as an element to enrich humans and improve humans' quality of life started to gain more adepts (Merchant, 1989). This stigmatization of nature—the feminine—as a resource to improve the quality of men's lives takes place at the same time as the witch-hunt—a process that also produced the objectification and instrumentalization of women into a tool to fix demographic maladjustments (Federici, 2009).

In discursive terms, there is a clash between two Master's Discourses taking place simultaneously. While organic theory offered a Symbolic matrix governed by the Master Signifier feminine, the evolution of Aristotelian division between matter and form was evolving into a stronger stigmatization of the feminine—which would, later on, evolve into mechanic philosophy—offered a Symbolic matrix governed by the Master Signifier masculine and that relied on the exclusion of the feminine. On the one hand, the organic discourse, by depicting nature as Mother Earth, reminds one of the incest prohibition. We may not get into her holes and pits—mining, just like we cannot desire those that belong to our mother. On the other hand, Agricola's point of view on mining relied on the idea that, although Mother Earth is hiding or concealing her goods, she wants us to get them. Agricola's vision of Mother Earth relates to feminine masochism. Nature, Mother Earth, may have concealed certain elements, but that does not imply that she does not want us to discover them. The Earth conceals elements that are key to human development. Additionally, these elements can be achieved by sharp, penetrative methods of extraction. This feminine masochism present in Mother Earth is also part of discourses present in rape culture.

It is also quite interesting to add to incest prohibition and feminine masochism, the idea of paterialism that Goux develops. From this perspective, the mechanist turn allows us to see the process through which paterialism establishes paternal social structures; patriarchy. For Goux, the domination of the father over the child functions in three different ways:

> *exogamy* makes women the objects of exchange by male subjects; the *incest prohibition* removes sons from domination by women while confirming women's status as exchangeable goods; and finally, initiation separates the male child from his mother and integrates him, through a symbolic rebirth, into the society of the fathers.
>
> (1973, p. 217)

Extrapolating these three dimensions of the structure of family patriarchy to how Mother Nature was defined in the conflict of mining, one can obtain interesting results on social patriarchy at that time.

- Incest prohibition: the acceptance of mining gives the incest prohibition a new dimension. As children, we must not desire the holes and pits of our mothers, but we may impose a different approach as fathers. Men, as fathers, can get into such holes and pits. In discursive terms, the emergence of the desiring subject through the Master's Discourse imposition occurs. Mining implied a significant advance in the imposition of the masculine as S_1, the subject that comes from being a child controlled by Mother Earth to a man who does not receive the prohibition but imposes it on others. It is necessary to detach men from nature; to detach men from the feminine to become a subject by submitting to a masculine symbolic matrix. It is here where the rejection of *jouissance* occurs.

- Exogamy: being Earth directly connected to woman by its conception as Mother implied the conversion of both nature and women into elements of exchange for desiring subjects. The connection between exogamy (economy) and initiation (acceptance of mining) is also reflected in Merchant's view, as she affirms that

Sanctioning mining sanctioned the rape or commercial exploration of the earth—a clear illustration of how constraints can change to sanctions through the demise of frameworks and their associated values as the needs, wants, and purposes of society change. The organic framework, in which the Mother Earth image was a moral restrain against mining, was literally undermined by the new commercial activity.

(1989, p. 41)

Furthermore, Sylvia Federici refers to how women's body was used as a source of goods for capitalism:

the body has been for women in capitalist society what the factory has been for male waged workers: the primary ground of their exploitation and resistance, as the female body has been appropriated by the state and men and forced to function as a means for the reproduction and accumulation of labour.

(2009, p. 16)

Thus, exogamy and the commodification of nature function in an analogous way.

- Initiation: a social rebirth that allows a child to become a man. As I will argue over this chapter, the desiring subject's initiation is intimately related to the Scientific Revolution. In discursive terms, initiation is the Lacanian Symbolic identification through which the subject appears. The stigmatization of the feminine also takes place in this scientific initiation, in which one can observe how holistic and organic (non-scientific) points of view are seen as archaic, as belonging to past (underdeveloped, childish) conceptions and not to modern (adult and developed) approaches. Furthermore, the result of this masculine and scientific initiation implies what Carolyne Merchant calls the *death of nature*. It is important to note and clarify that nature is killed; it ceases to be a living entity. Therefore, she cannot be incarnated; it ceases to be the Mother.

Following Carolyne Merchant, I believe it is necessary to include the ecological dimension to analyze initiation. She notes the importance of ecologism, affirming that this current "[i]nstead of dichotomizing nature and culture as a structural dualism, it sees natural and cultural subsystems in dynamic interaction" (1989, p. 44). Thus, one could analyze how social conditions affected the environment, specifically "how environmental quality was affected by the transition from peasant control of natural resources for the purposes of subsistence to capitalist control for the purpose of profit" (Merchant, 1989, p. 43). From this approach, one can move on and analyze how such changes affected politics and how the transformation into a mechanistic model "reinforced and accelerated the exploitation of nature and human beings as resources and to a view of conservation as the restoration and management of ecosystems" (Merchant, 1989, p. 43). Carolyne Merchant provides a new tool to analyze a political syntax that excludes natural elements in discursive terms. By adding the ecologist dimension of analysis, one can observe how a long process of economic and political changes.

On the one hand, poor male subjects vastly depended on the land of Mother Nature. For them, Mother Nature was not exchangeable; they had no right to take and exchange her when in the form of the commons. Some landlords saw the dependence of men on Nature as a threat to their domination over the peasants. As Merchant narrates, peasants and artisans were already refusing to use the lord's lands or tools (1989, pp. 48–50). This threat to paternal domination had to be overcome; the existence of a dominating yet nurturing Mother Earth was a double threat. On the one hand, Mother Earth needed to be killed in the wake of human development through mining. On the other hand, there was the need to impose an incest prohibition to remove the mother's domination over the sons and give a more solid ground for exogamy by affirming women's invalidity. Moreover, in discursive terms, one can observe how the desiring subject's emergence did not imply every man's transformation into desiring subjects.

Going back to the relation between exogamy and incest prohibition, they function as two different mechanisms of the same process. Exogamy started with various ecological catastrophes that implied the repurposing of the lands, the draining of the fens, the destruction of forests for croplands and mines, and the lands' enclosures (Merchant, 1989, pp. 42–68). These different processes became normalized and standardized in a developing market-oriented economy through exogamy. A market-oriented economy characterized by the inflation that came with the conquest of Abya Yala. The by-product of exogamy was the dehumanization of nature and the erasure of its domination.

Moreover, the mechanization of labor substantially impacted how nature was conceived, "[b]eginning around 1540 large scale mills and foundries producing paper, gunpowder, cannons, copper. Brass, sugar and saltpetre began to supplement production by domestic workshops" (Merchant, 1989, p. 64). The apparition of workshops and the first underdeveloped factories that appeared during these pre-capitalist times implied the absence of the relation between man and nature; the machine intermediated it. This lack of direct contact and the illusion of domination over natural elements through machinery implied nature's reconceptualization. These last developments in labor, economy, politics, and ontology implied the final shift from organicism to mechanism. The mechanistic turn occurred and implied the stigmatization and the expulsion of the feminine from Reality. It implied the imposition of the Master's Discourse that established the masculine as the only valid Master Signifier and that supposed the creation of a Signifier of Pure Threat—feminine.

To see nature as a legitimate economic resource for mankind required its dehumanization and the abolition of organic theories as they limited the exploitation of nature and feminine agents. The ontological changes that mechanism implied "reinforced and accelerated the exploitation of nature and human beings as resources" (Merchant, 1989, p. 43). Although the environment had time to recover from its prior exploitation by the fifteenth century due to a populational decrease provoked by demographic disasters, a new economy based on extraction took over. Moreover, Abya Yala's occupation boosted the economy based on crafts and trade, which produced the growth of cities and towns and a populational transfer from the rural areas to the urban nucleus.

This new economy fostered the perfect conditions for a change of conscience, implying a total transformation of how mankind thought about itself and what surrounds it. The destruction of the natural grounds upon which the poor lived and that led to male and economic domination through the dependence of poor people on workshops and other early factories alienated men from a now-dead nature. Humanity was also alienated from nature through the populational movement from the rural to the urban areas built around a market-oriented economy.

Thus, in this context, initiation occurs as a change in how humans relate to other humans. The changes in economic and social organization and structures were accompanied by articulating new ontologies, epistemologies, and methodologies. New experiences from new practices and new theoretical articulations took place at the same time. Men were geographically separating themselves from nature and natural environments; they also established complicated relations to a nature that looked even more chaotic after recent scientific discoveries. This separation produced anxiety, which needed to be channeled in theoretical articulations that allowed men to understand Reality. The Aristotelian turn implied the shift from organic theory to mechanism; the mechanistic turn implied the stigmatization of disorder and dynamism (directly related to the feminine). Moreover, it also implied a radical shift that involved the separation between the self and the universe, including the transformation of interpersonal relations. Furthermore, the Cartesian revolution of thought that took place over this period reinforced these changes and implied a new conception of the relation with our bodies, as Sylvia Federici puts it:

> Descartes' doctrines have a double aim: to deny that human behaviours can be influenced by external factors (Such as the stars, or celestial intelligences), and to free the soul from any bodily conditioning thus making it capable of exercising an unlimited sovereignty over the body.
>
> (2009, p. 148)

I argue that the radical alienation these turns implied provoked a status of anxiety in the subject and the apparition of the anxious subject, which I characterized as unable to see the lack of the Other. In the mechanistic turn, a mandate obliges the subject to accept the Symbolic and reject *jouissance*. Man has to separate from Mother Earth, from nature. Nevertheless, this separation process involves anxiety, as the subject cannot see the lack in the Other he cannot separate. Nevertheless, man must overcome this state of anxiety as he is not bound to be the anxious subject. He cannot be the reminder of the Real; instead, he has to be the desiring subject, as the Master Signifier that governs political syntax. This precise status of anxiety derives from a re-articulation of the incest prohibition, which leads to an initiation in which the lack of the other, i.e., the lack of nature; of Mother Nature; of the feminine, needs to be established. I argue that the discursive mechanism that takes place to inscribe the lack of the Other is creating the Cartesian subject (Bordo, 1986), which implied the development of different theories articulated around the notions of order and power to counter the problem of anxiety. As Carolyne Merchant describes, mechanism had a significant impact on the trans-formation of anxiety into control:

> Mechanism, which superseded the organic framework, was based on the logic that knowledge of the world could be certain and consistent, and that the laws of nature were imposed on creation by God. The primacy of organic process gave way to the stability of mathematical laws and identities. Force was external to matter rather that immanent within it. Matter was corpuscular, passive and inert; change was simply the rearrangement of particles as motion was transmitted from one part to another in a causal nexus.
>
> (1989, pp. 102–103)

Susan Bordo agrees and sees the same characteristics in the Cartesian turn of thought (1986). Mechanism allows the total detachment from nature needed for initiation. Initiation thus corresponds to the Cartesian turn needed for the devel-opment of modern sciences. Bordo defines this turn as "a defensive response to that separation anxiety, an aggressive intellectual 'flight from the feminine' rather than (simply) the confident articulation of a positive new epistemological ideal" (1986, p. 441). Bordo also observes the transformation from anxiety to control "[t]he pain of separateness is thus compensated for by the peculiar advantages of separateness: the possibility of mastery and control over those on whom one is dependent" (1986, p. 452). Merchant also analyzes this transformation of anxiety into control, but her analysis goes further and defines control as the sum of order and power:

> In the mechanical world, order was redefined to mean the predictable behavior of each part within a rationally determined system of laws, while power derived from active and immediate intervention in a secularized world. Order and power together constituted control. Rational control over nature, society, and the self was achieved by redefining reality itself through the new machine metaphor.
>
> (1989, p. 193)

Although Carolyne Merchant, Susan Bordo, and myself have used different approaches, we all see how the mechanistic shift, the Cartesian turn, or the Scientific Revolution implied a masculinization. These masculinization processes implied the imposition of a Master's Discourse and a Master Signifier of Pure Being—masculine. Nevertheless, what interests me the most is how this imposition of a masculine Symbolic implied creating two differentiated sexual positions differentiated through their relation to this symbolic matrix, which functions as a political syntax that only allows the entrance of the rational, mathematical, ordered, and controlled. What belongs to political syntax is organized under S_1, the rational man. On the other hand, everything that is not S_1 is $\neg S_1$. Thus, the feminine is not only the category of woman but also of children, slaves, indigenous people, among others. Thus, I affirm that the man who inhabits the symbolic matrix is a specific kind of man—prototypical, normative. To make the anxious man disappear, an exercise of performativity needed to take place through the Master's Discourse. The Cartesian subject, the desiring subject, represents this new masculine sexual position.

Summing up, and as a way to clarify some ideas, scientific initiation consists of two main mechanisms that can be analyzed in terms of discursive theory:

- Mechanical philosophy: a discursive mechanism that implied the death of nature. Mechanism implied that nature was not alive anymore. Mother is dead; the Name of the Father thus rules the Symbolic.
- Cartesian thought: the result of the mother's death creates a status of anxiety in the subject. This anxiety springs from the fact that the subject is unable to see the lack in the Other. Thus, the Cartesian subject's idea emerges from the necessity to inscribe the lack in the Other. The Cartesian subject is thus created out of claims of power, domination, and control over nature.

Mechanism and the Cartesian subject are two of the main elements of the Scientific Revolution that started during the Renaissance. During this time, the stigmatization and expulsion of the Real, the feminine, takes place by establishing a Master's Discourse that implies creating two hierarchized sexual positions. The division in sexual terms of the ontological level has taken place.

References

Bordo, S. (1986). The Cartesian Masculinization of Thought. *Signs, 11*(3), 439–456.

Brennan, T. (1989). Introduction. In T. Brennan (Ed.), *Between Feminism & Psychoanalysis* (pp. 1–23). Routledge.

Federici, S. (2009). *Caliban and the Witch. Women, the Body and Primitive Accumulation (Third)*. Autonomedia.

Goux, J.-J. (1973). *Symbolic Economies. After Marx and Freud*. Cornell University Press.

Lange, L. (1983). Woman is Not a Rational Animal: Aristotle's Biology of Reproduction. In *Discovering Reality: Feminist Perspectives on Epistemology, Metaphysics, Methodology, and Philosophy of Science* (pp. 1–15). D. Reidel; Sold and distributed in the USA and Canada by Kluwer Boston.

Merchant, C. (1989). *The Death of Nature. Women, Ecology and the Scientific Revolution*. HarperOne.

Spelman, E. V. (1983). Aristotle and the Politicization of the Soul. In *Discovering Reality: Feminist Perspectives on Epistemology, Metaphysics, Methodology, and Philosophy of Science* (pp. 17–30). D. Reidel; Sold and distributed in the USA and Canada by Kluwer Boston.

Chapter 8

The Masculine Hegemony of Reality

The ontological level's sexuation implied the stigmatization of the feminine Real and the beginning of its expulsion from Reality. In discursive terms, the Master Signifier masculine is inscribed as the Master Signifier of Pure Being within political syntax. While the Master Signifier masculine works at the ontological level, a different empty signifier represents it within the ontic level. An empty signifier that accepts contingency and multiple fillings without putting at risk the govern of the Master Signifier is imposed. Its primary function is to allow a particular group to represent universality. Nevertheless, this empty signifier of the Real—Real$_2$— does not assure the continuity of political syntax; in other words, the Real is still a threat to Reality. Therefore, two other empty signifiers are established to create a discursive structure that resembles the Borromean knot's topology.

I argue that the Enlightenment created an empty signifier through which only men could be the desiring subject. Moreover, the hegemony of the masculine takes place in both liberal and Marxist theories. Thus neither theory entails strategies from a real dislocation of the symbolic matrix that allows for a feminist re-articulation of the ontological level.

Masculine Hegemony in Liberal Thought

The Enlightenment implied women's expulsion from the legitimate political subject as they were not representable by the subject of reason; women were too emotional. There is an Aristotelian taste in this argumentation. The stigmatization of the feminine implied a process of sexuation visible in the original division between matter and form, an ontological division and hierarchization also present at the ontic level with a social and gendered hierarchy that relied on women's lack of reason. Such lack was supported through the conception of knowledge as a virtue of the masculine subject.

The Enlightenment in Europe was characterized by the Scientific Revolution and various political revolutions and illustrates how the ontological level's sexuation impacts the ontic level by supporting a new political: liberal democracy. Liberal democracy is based on the idea that man is a rational being that can decide

DOI: 10.4324/9781003167587-12

and engage in politics. Nevertheless, this political capacity seems not to be present in every subject.

In the book *The Flight from Woman*, Stern analyzes and compares scientific knowledge and poetic knowledge (1965, pp. 41–57). He takes discursive reason as a method that belongs to scientific knowledge, and intuition, as belonging to poetic knowledge and considers them without considering their sexuated differentiation. He suggests that, while intuition is the consecution of knowledge by union, discursive reason leads us to knowledge by disassembly (1965, p. 42). An example of the former would be the kind of knowledge that a mother gets from her child; for the latter, he explains that it would be the knowledge you obtain from explaining phenomena by other phenomena already explained. The first main difference also corresponds to how the self connects itself to the universe. Intuition has elements of internalization: "a form of knowledge by sympathy, a 'feeling with,'—a union with the knowable" (Stern, 1965, p. 42). Discursive reason corresponds to a mode of knowing by externalization "in which the knowable is experienced as an object, a *Gegen-stand*, something which stands opposed to me" (Stern, 1965, p. 42).

By departing from the hypothesis that the division of these two types of knowledge is not socially constructed but based on reality, Stern affirms that there is no better knowledge; instead, it is a question of "when to use each" (Stern, 1965, p. 49). However, poetic knowledge has acquired a negative connotation after the imposition of scientism, not as a methodology but an ideology. Poetic knowledge related to the past, the woman and the child has been expelled from the field of pure knowledge, and it is to be used purely for specific social issues, as empathy and other emotional elements are needed in specific fields.

Thus, again, there is a dichotomous pair—poetic knowledge versus scientific knowledge—that follows the structure of sexuation. Rational and scientific knowledge belongs to man and allows him to engage in politics. On the other hand, poetic and emotional knowledge belongs to woman. Their lack of scientific knowledge and their relations toward the Earth and children inhibit women from engaging in politics. However, a well-known enlightened feminist critique claimed women's rights (O'Brien, 2004, p. 622).

The liberal feminist critique demanded the equivalence of man's rights to women. In discursive terms, the anxious subject attempts to reach the desiring subject's position. Nevertheless, as seen in the process of cyphering the Real, the taming and controlled entrance of hysteric subjects is governed by the rhythm of political syntax and the market's needs. I argue that women who led this struggle for gender equality did not embrace every woman, either every feminine subject. In fact, while certain women were fighting for their political subjectivity as desiring subjects, hysteric subjects, in this case, non-white people, were being stigmatized in the Real, thus, reinforcing the idea of the Real as the Pure Threat visible in the use that enlightened male writers did of peripheric cultures.

Enlightenment writers continued to use the idea of the despotic East as a means not only of demonstrating but also of making the case for greater freedom in the West, associating the question of female liberation with arguments about national and racial difference.

(O'Brien, 2004, p. 625)

The antagonistic relation between Reality and the Real is constructed around a different axis. Wealthy and educated women are not the problem; the Real antagonism consists of the relationship between social classes and against *under-developed* cultures. Thus, there is a conversion of certain women, women who hold a specific socioeconomic position, into anxious subjects.

Thus, the ontological division in which two Master Signifiers are established as pure antagonism impacts the ontic level. Nevertheless, to analyze liberal discursive operations for a masculine hegemony of the ontic, it is necessary to analyze contract theory. As I will argue, contractualism implies the construction of the Real$_2$ allowing for the Borromean knot and masculine hegemony of the ontic.

Contract Theory

Contractualism establishes a before-and-after picture of a society and conditions its government. More specifically, and following the line of argumentation that Carol Pateman develops in her book *The Sexual Contract*, what interests me the most is how the empty signifiers of the origin of politics—Real$_2$—imply women's total exclusion desiring subjects (1988). The importance of contractualism in how European politics are shaped is crucial. As Carole Pateman affirms,

> The story, or conjectural history, tells how a new civil society and a new form of political right is created through an original contract. An explanation for the binding authority of the state and civil law, and for the legitimacy of modern civil government is to be found by treating our society as if it had originated in a contract.
>
> (1988, p. 1)

I agree with Pateman. The idea that societies sprung from a social contract creates a narrative that affirms that an original group of people is entitled to politics. The main characteristic of this original group of people, i.e., the people that sign the contract, is precisely that they are men. In fact, Pateman goes as far as to affirm that

> The standard commentaries on the classic stories of the original contract do not usually mention that women are *excluded* from the original pact. Men make the original contract. The device of the state of nature is used to explain why, given the characteristics of the inhabitants of the natural condition, entry into the original contract is a rational act. The crucial point that is omitted is that the inhabitants are sexually differentiated and, for all the classic

writers (except Hobbes), a difference in rationality follows from natural sexual difference.

(1988, p. 5)

When I spoke of how the desiring subject appears in the discursive operation of the Master's Discourse, I said *that man is man because a man established the Master Signifier masculine and defined what a man is, man gives birth to Father in order for a son to emerge.* In the Enlightenment, man gives birth to the fraternity for brothers to emerge. Thus, emancipation from paternal and maternal figures spring from the Enlightenment, and a new empty signifier of the Real appears. This is the transition from patriarchy to fraternal patriarchy that Pateman describes:

> Political right originates in sex-right or conjugal right. Paternal right is only one, and not the original, dimension of patriarchal power. A man's power as a father comes after he has exercised the patriarchal right of a man (a husband) over a woman (wife). The contract theorists had no wish to challenge the original patriarchal right in their onslaught on paternal right. Instead, they incorporated conjugal right into their theories and, in so doing, transformed the law of male sex-right into its modern contractual form. Patriarchy ceased to be paternal long ago. Modern civil society is not structured by kinship and the power of fathers; in the modern world, women are subordinated to men *as men*, or to men as a fraternity. The original contract takes place after the political defeat of the father and creates modern *fraternal patriarchy*.
>
> (1988, p. 3)

Following the feminist discursive mediation, the Father's rule rests on the sexuated division between S_1 and $\neg S_1$, not on a rule of S_1 among S_2. Thus, I switch from S_2 to $\neg S_1$. To maintain S_2 as the central element upon which S_1 acts would imply an original rule of a man (Father) over the others, which would annulate the hypothesis that the Symbolic matrix is supported upon sexuation. Furthermore, when Pateman affirms that contract theorists did not wish to defy the original patriarchal right, one can deduce that they did not want to generate a shift at the ontological level that could imply the imposition of a Name-of-the-Mother as Symbolic. Instead, they aimed to reinforce the patriarchal right by extending this right to other men.

On the other hand, a specific mechanism is necessary to shield the govern of S_1, this mechanism is fantasy. Fantasy in fraternal patriarchy is created through conjugal right. Following Pateman's train of thought, I affirm that modern civil society rests upon the idea of androcentric heterosexual love, present in the *matheme* of fantasy. Women, thus, as anxious subjects, are subordinated by men. As she points out, women are subjected to men, as men, not as Father, women are subordinated to men as fraternity and, as I will argue, the fraternity that springs from the social contract is structured through the empty signifier of the Real. Fraternity is the Real$_2$.

In the Old Regime, the agent was S$_1$ as Father, the King, the desiring subject. The existence of the King was founded on the idea of an S$_1$. In other words, there was a subject (the King) represented by a Master Signifier (Father) that precisely emanated from this subject. Thus, the agent Father develops the discursive structure because it emanated from a truth that allowed its existence. In other words, the Father relies on the King's existence to hold its power simultaneously that allows the King to emerge as subject. Contractualism does not challenge the original patriarchal right; it does not pose $\neg$S$_1$ as the discourse agent. Instead, it extends the patriarchal right to more subjects. This extension springs from the changes occurring at the ontological level through scientific initiation. That is to say, the emergence of a more plural subject responds to the very necessity of reproducibility of the frames. Thus, contract theorists create a new desiring subject, *men as men, not men as Father*. In this sense, Master Signifier masculine comes to be represented as fraternity. This new adaptation of the Master Signifier masculine is founded on the truth of the men who hypothetically signed a contract. Thus, the idea of fraternity is what allows men as the original, as Real$_2$. Nevertheless, Pateman gives conjugal right a central role in this new fraternal patriarchy. Thus, how is women's political subjectivity constructed in the New Regime? I believe that Pateman points toward a fascinating idea of women's political subjectivity under this fraternal patriarchy:

> Women have no part in the original contract, but they are not left behind in the state of nature-that would defeat the purpose of the sexual contract! Women are incorporated into a sphere that both is and is not in civil society. The private sphere is part of civil society but is separated from the 'civil' sphere. The antinomy private/public is another expression of unnatural/civil and women/men. The private, womanly sphere (natural) and the public, masculine sphere (civil) are opposed but gain their meaning from each other, and the meaning of the civil freedom of public life is thrown into relief when counterposed to the natural subjection that characterizes the private realm.
>
> (1988, p. 11)

Through a feminist discursive mediation, one can see how women are incorporated in the state of nature but not in the original contract because they need to remember what has been lost through the contract. Pateman affirms that leaving women out of the picture of the state of nature would defeat the purpose of the sexual contract. From my perspective, erasing women from the state of nature would make the sexual contract impossible as it follows the structure of the *matheme* of fantasy ($\$\lozenge a$). For fantasy to work, the desiring subject needs an *a* around which to articulate his desire. In this case, women have to be constructed as *a*. I believe that Pateman illustrates how women become *objet a* through the inhabitancy of a space between existence and ex-sistence. Thus, by being relegated to the private sphere, women can inhabit the space of existence, but they cannot occupy the civil sphere, as such space belongs to Real$_2$; fraternity. The relation that Pateman establishes between women, the private sphere, and the natural; and men, the public sphere, and civility, allows seeing how women are being expelled from the Real only to function as *a* for the purpose to establish the conjugal right.

However, intersectionality is missing from Pateman's analysis, leading to the erasure of kids, slaves, nature, and other agents. If women are bound to act as *a* within the space of existence, the rest of the subjects not represented inhabit the space of ex-sistence needed for political antagonism. In fact, as seen, when English men spoke of the terrible East, alterity was already being used as the Signifier of Pure Threat. Thus, I believe that Pateman avoids articulating non-female identities as feminine identities. Carole Pateman affirms that the social contract is also a sexual contract as she analyzes that:

> The original pact is a sexual as well as a social contract: it is sexual in the sense of patriarchal – that is; the contract establishes men's political right over women – and also sexual in the sense of establishing orderly access by men to women's bodies. The original contract creates what I shall call, following Adrienne Rich 'the law. of male sex-right'. Contract is far from being opposed to patriarchy; contract is the means through which modern patriarchy is constituted.
>
> (1988, p. 3)

Furthermore, the social contract is a sexual contract in a double manner. First, the contract is sexual as it generates a new rule of men over women. As seen, establishing a male original is part of the process of sexuation. Second, the contract is sexual because it allows access of men to women's bodies. This is where Pateman's theorization of marriage and the idea of fantasy as hetero-sexual androcentric love converge. Marriage creates a middle ground between Reality and the Real created for women. This ground grants women the status of *objet a*. It is through marriage that woman is expelled, confined to the private sphere. Through marriage, the ontological division continues by creating a fantasy that allows men to overcome the anxiety resulting from the mother's separation. In other words, the idea of androcentric heterosexual love, the fantasy that supports an androcentric Reality, is thus constructed upon the idea of the sexual contract and marriage.

Consequently, after the Real$_2$ has been introduced through the idea of a social contract and a sexual contract that established a masculine empty signifier of the Real, two other empty signifiers come to occupy the positions of the Symbolic and the Imaginary as a way to construct the structure that emulates the Borromean knot.

In liberal democracies sustained by contract theory, I find institutionalization of this Real$_2$ through Parliament, resulting in political syntax that allows for a total exclusion of the Real. However, the parliamentary institution knows that the complete absorption of Real is impossible and undesirable. Thus, a second empty signifier that comes to resemble the Imaginary is created to function as a deterrent to possible disruptions. The empty signifier that contributes to the collective image (Imaginary Order) creates a collective identity that embraces the anxious subject. Thus, those who are not part of the $Real_2$ are also appealed as necessary. The empty signifier that comes to introduce the Imaginary Order in liberal democracy is precisely democracy. Women are not desiring subjects; nevertheless, they are included within political syntax as the secondary subjects of democracy through the conjugal contract.

Nevertheless, the empty signifier of the Imaginary is unable to cope with the vast plurality of identities that are not present within the Real. In fact, crises of the State and crises of government reflect its incapability to sanction our need for identification. In other words, democratic crises are the direct consequence of establishing an image that cannot give what it promises, wholeness. Whether they came from working-class subjects or liberal women, revolutionary outbursts challenged the idea of liberal democracies. The possible fracture at the Imaginary level pushes the generation of a third level, the Symbolic Order, by institutionalizing the rule in law, closing the Borromean knot. At the level of the Symbolic, one finds the empty signifier legal. As an empty signifier, legality is represented by the Law's institution and presents a shield for the two previous orders. That is to say, perhaps there is a crisis of State or a crisis of government, but the subject clings to the structure created by the Symbolic Order, understanding that *they are doing what is right*. The structure created by the Symbolic Order carries with it a system of punishment for those who do not conform to the imposed premises. The punishment not only consists of a limitation of freedom through the prison, but it brings with it the stigmatization of the punished subject, no longer considered equal in the relationship established between citizens. In other words, he no longer has access to the possible identification promised by the political fantasy.

Masculine Hegemony in Marxist Thought

In liberal theory, one finds a state of nature and a contractual society. In Marxist thought, there is also a state of nature (primitive communism) and a society that emerges from a contractual relation, waged labor. This contractual society leaves specific subjects again out of the picture.

The Wage Contract

Marx affirmed that fully developed capitalism can be found in the eighteenth century because capital accumulation arises in that moment of history (1992). To explain the mechanism that enables that accumulation of capital, Marx analyzes how forces and relations of production have changed and developed since the abolition of serfdom. His research is based upon England's study case, where Marx estates that serfdom had disappeared, at least in practice, by the end of the fourteenth century. In purely economic terms, Marx explains this historical process as follows:

> the accumulation of capital presupposes surplus-value; surplus-value presupposes capitalist production; capitalist production presupposes the availability of considerable masses of capital and labor-power in the hands of commodity producers. The whole movement, therefore, seems to turn around in a never-ending circle, which we can only get out of by assuming a primitive accumulation (the 'previous accumulation' of Adam Smith[1]).
>
> (1992, p. 873)

If we were to draw a scheme of Marx's chronology of capitalism, it would be as follows (Figure 8.1):

As this scheme shows, there cannot be capital accumulation in a society that does not generate a surplus. A person can obtain a surplus by expropriating the product from the direct producer in an environment in which the producer's wage remains lower than the money that can be obtained by the commercial activity in which the product engages. Consequently, to produce a surplus, society needs to be articulated around capitalist production, principally characterized by the producer's separation from the means of production, which enables the wage relation. Furthermore, if contract theorists focused on a social contract as the kernel of civic society, from a Marxist point of view, the contract that works as the kernel of capitalist society is precisely the labor contract, the wage contract. However, within this new wage society, how do we control lower wages to guarantee that a surplus will be generated? Capitalist production depends on the availability of vast amounts of both capital, understood as different means of production and raw materials—which we will name from now on in this section as non-human conditions for capitalism, and labor force—which from now on will be defined as human conditions for capitalism.

The process that makes both human and non-human conditions for capitalism available is what we call primitive accumulation. Marx sees that this process

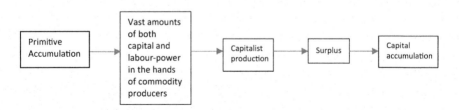

Figure 8.1 Marx's Chronology of Capitalism.

"is nothing else than the historical process of divorcing the producer from the means of production" (1992, pp. 874–875). However, I believe that it is also a process that implies the division of work into labor and non-labor, a division sustained upon the sexuated division at the ontological level. Thus, that which is considered labor belongs to the masculine, and that what is considered non-labor belongs to the feminine, resulting in a sexuated, not just sexual, division of labor. Nevertheless, to prove this hypothesis, I first need to observe how Marx defines in his theory the primitive accumulation of human and non-human conditions.[2]

For Marx, the capitalist relation's main feature is the "complete separation between the workers and the ownership of the conditions for the realization of their labor" (1992, p. 874), which implies the worker's subordination to the owners of non-human conditions for capital. Moreover, through establishing such a relation of subordination, non-human conditions for capitalism become capital themselves (Marx, 1992, p. 874).

The mechanisms through which primitive accumulation occurred implied the use of violence (Marx, 1992, p. 875). Furthermore, although the result was the apparition of free proletarians, they were still rightless because both citizenship and rights were still linked to property. This lack of rights and citizenship profoundly impacted this first proletarian identity, which implied an ambiguous status, that of the anxious subject. However, Marx conceives the male proletariat as the hysteric subject, as the subject of the Real. This misconception of the proletariat drives Marxist theory to obviate the political status of women and other feminine subjects.

Marx ignores the primitive accumulation of proletarians.[3] The conversion of money, commodities, and means of production into capital creates two confronted classes, a capitalist class and a working class. Thus, Marx finds the true limit $(S_1//\neg S_1)$ between the bourgeois class and the working class. In discursive terms, Marx assigns $\neg S_1$ to the working class, while the capitalist class is defined as S_1, resulting in the antagonistic relation between S_1 and $\neg S_1$. Nevertheless, by analyzing the process of primitive accumulation of human conditions for capitalism, the male proletariat is not $\neg S_1$, but an anxious subject that later on results into the desiring subject.

The new relation between capitalist and worker is based on the wage the capitalist gives to the free and rightless proletariat in exchange for his work and product. One of the mechanisms that enabled capitalists to establish low wages was the excess of unemployed workers. However, contrary to what the capitalists might have imagined, not every unemployed worker was willing to become a proletarian. Thus, harsh legislation against unemployed people was imposed with two main objectives. The first one was to stigmatize those who did not want to work, defying mechanisms that guaranteed lower wages. On the other hand, the second result of this legislation was that, as a punishment, it allowed slavery of these unemployed criminals, making it possible to obtain labor force at a cost of zero (Marx, 1992, p. 896).

I infer from Marx's analysis that the accumulation of non-human conditions was not enough to transform pauperized peasants into the available workforce. The conversion to the proletariat is not natural. During the fifteenth and sixteenth centuries, lower wages did not guarantee sufficient economic support to maintain a family that maintained itself during serfdom, which led many peasants to revolt against wage labor. The stigmatization of those who refused to adapt to the new logic and new ethic of capitalism needed to be reinforced by creating an evil image linked to non-productive agents. This criminalization had, as a result, the naturalization of capitalist discipline. Once fully established, capitalism allowed more expansive formal freedom for proletarians as they had reached a total dependence on capitalism and had interiorized capitalist discipline (Marx, 1992, p. 899).

Thus, although it may seem that the antagonistic relation takes place between capitalists and producers, such clean polarization is not visible. A vast number of abled workers did not fit within the specific capitalist relation. In fact, this relation in the genesis of capitalism was not a real reflection of society. As Marx points out, "[t]he class of wage-laborers, which arose in the latter half of the fourteenth century, formed then and in the following century only a very small part of the population" (1992, p. 900). This intricate social network led to coalitions and alliances between capitalist and proto-capitalist (artisans and independent peasants) subjects that needed the imposition of the dichotomy of the capitalist relation to increasing their profits. Although Marx is aware of this fact, he thinks that this exclusion of unemployed proletarians disappeared by the eighteenth century, and those capitalist relations of production took over society. This way, Marx can affirm that by the eighteenth century, with industrial capitalism, the process of primitive accumulation is over.

However, from the fourteenth century to the seventeenth century, I believe that what takes place is the establishment of fraternal patriarchy, in which capitalists and waged proletarians engage. The relation among the working class—in its orthodox version—and capitalists is what Chantal Mouffe denominates as agonistic relation. On the other hand, the real antagonistic relation occurs through the sexual and international labor divisions. The process through which proletarians interiorize capitalist discipline responds to the process through which the proletariat, which at a first moment could have been seen as $\neg S_1$ becomes S_1. Marx's main mistake was to take the same male collective as the constant hysteric subject. In fact, the conversion of the economic masculine $\neg S_1$ into an economic masculine S_1 through the wage contract implied creating an economic feminine $\neg S_1$. By taking into account the creation of an economic feminine $\neg S_1$, one can see how the possibility to introduce capitalism relies on the very construction of non-capitalist subjects.

By acquiring a feminist and decolonial approach to primitive accumulation, one can demonstrate that primitive accumulation is not a temporal stage whose aim is to accumulate capital in a specific given time, but a constant mechanism of capitalism that aims to maintain non-capitalist production and relations to maintain capitalism. In other words, and analyzing this process from the feminist discursive mediation, while proletarians and capitalists are subjects of a wage contract that allows them to be classified under S_1, capitalism relies on non-capitalist relations. The subjects that engage in these latter relations of production are precisely those who rest under $\neg S_1$. As a way to start our critique of Marx's lack of analysis of human conditions, we shall analyze Luxemburg's critique of the accumulation of capital.

The International Division of Labor

Rosa Luxemburg's critique relies on the idea that capitalism does not purely rely on the capitalist mode of production nor capitalist relations of production. Both the origin and the later development of capitalism take place in a non-capitalist *milieu*. This affirmation already questions Marx for as, although he was aware of capitalism's feudal origin and the influence that fifteenth-century imperialism had in capitalism's genesis, he continued his analysis on capitalism's development by assuming abstraction and isolation of capitalist societies from non-capitalist societies. Rosa Luxemburg affirms that "[c]apitalism requires non-capitalist forms of production for its existence and further development" (2015, p. 367). Furthermore, these non-capitalist forms of production may be used in different ways to fulfill capitalism's needs for capital accumulation:

> It requires non-capitalist social strata as a market in which to realize its surplus value, as a source for its means of production and as a reservoir of labor-power for its wage system. Forms of production based on a *natural economy* are of no use to capital for any of these purposes.
>
> (Luxemburg, 2015, p. 367)

The feminist discursive mediation allows observing how capitalism creates an $\neg S_1$ that serves its purposes. Thus, although hysterical subjects do not form part of political syntax through the engagement in a wage contract, they are subjected to political syntax. Thus, one finds the status of subjects subjected to a symbolic matrix but are not subjectified through it. In the case of the expropriation of material goods from the colonies and the trade of slaves or childrearing and child birthing, those actions are not part of the conception of labor. Thus, reproductive work or natural goods are excluded from the wage contract; they do not imply labor. In other words, they are not economic activities.

Furthermore, to study how non-capitalist relations and production function as the base for capital accumulation, Luxemburg divides this process into three different stages based on three different struggles that capitalism must overcome to obtain the necessary means for capital accumulation: capital vs. natural economy, introducing the commodity economy, and division of agriculture and handicraft (2015). For Luxemburg, capitalism needs a constant expansion that is based on an ongoing accumulation. Moreover, while Marx considers that accumulation has to be read in terms of how constant capital produces surplus accumulation,

Luxemburg considers that it is not what produces surplus but who produces it, variable capital, that needs to be analyzed. Thus Rosa Luxemburg affirms that capitalism does not solely rely on the capitalist relation established between capitalist and worker, but it relies on non-capitalist relations that, to her, can be found in imperialist relations. If capitalism needs a constant non-capitalist *milieu*, capital accumulation is a process through which non-capitalist formations are absorbed to cover capitalism's needs. Thus, Marx's closed schema on capital accumulation is wrong because it would imply a dead point for capital accumulation.

Luxemburg's main point about primitive accumulation is that there is always a capitalist need for having non-capitalist formations. In other words, just like the Master's Discourse is not a punctual but a continuous form of discourse that reinforces the govern of S_1, primitive accumulation is a process in charge of creating a constant $\neg S_1$ through which to feed capitalism. Although Luxemburg introduces a very complex and right critique of Marx, her critique also implies a dead point to primitive accumulation. In other words, if the antagonism that relies on the opposition of non-capitalist formations and capitalist formations merely responds to imperialist processes, once capitalism works at a global level, capitalism would end as there are no more non-capitalist formations that allow for capitalism to survive. In other words, if accumulation by antagonism is a condition *sine qua non*, we need to look at different contexts in which such opposition takes place.

Furthermore, what I attempt to illustrate is that primitive accumulation and capital accumulation are two differentiated processes. On the one hand, capital accumulation has as its objective the accumulation of means of production. In contrast, primitive accumulation's main objective is the accumulation of producers, that is to say, creating an economic-political subjectivity that consists of a continuous classification of certain subjects under the Master Signifier $\neg S_1$.

Thus, the true limit that Laclau articulates is, in capitalist terms, a relation that dehumanizes—femininizes, and therefore exploits, human beings to conform non-capitalist formations upon which primitive accumulation can be achieved. The idea of primitive accumulation as an accumulation of producers is best explained in Yann Mouliere-Boutang's book *De la esclavitud al trabajo asalariado. Economía histórica del trabajo asalariado embridiado.*[4] While Traditional lectures have considered labor as waged labor, Mouliere-Boutang extends labor to every type of dependent labor; this means that non-capitalist formations are also included in his analysis of labor. This definition of dependent labor is also more accurate for current times since it provides a wider angle from analyzing every kind of waged labor, unpaid labor, and waged slavery. Moulier-Boutang affirms that "capital's primitive accumulation is the accumulation of the proletariat" (2006, p. 11). On the other hand, he affirms that "labor process and the process of composition/decomposition/re-composition of the working class and antagonism are intimately tangled" (2006, p. 12).

Thus, Luxemburg's critique and Mouliere-Boutang's analysis allows affirming that, in primitive accumulation, there is a process through which certain subjects are excluded from the Symbolic matrix that governs the economy. In other words,

⌐S₁ needs to be created to function as the reservoir of the proletariat that allows for wage control, work at cost zero, consumers of capitalist goods and services, and also function as a source of means needed for capitalism. Nevertheless, neither of these authors can see that the process through which primitive accumulation of human conditions for capitalism is characterized by its sexuating dynamics. Furthermore, to analyze primitive accumulation from a feminist approach, Silvia Federici considers three critical dimensions of analysis.

> (i) the development of a new sexual division of labor subjugating women's labor and women's reproductive function to the reproduction of the work-force; (ii) the construction of a new patriarchal order, based upon the exclusion of women from waged work and their subordination to men; (iii) the mechanization of the proletariat body and its transformation, in the case of women, into a machine for the production of new workers.
>
> (2009, p. 12)

Although Silvia Federici focuses her book *Caliban and the Witch* on how primitive accumulation took place over the sixteenth and the seventeenth centuries through the witch hunt (2009), her analysis allows seeing how feminine sexual position is constructed as excluded from the wage contract. Thus, the wage contract is what grants existence, while the expulsion from the productive system implies the state of ex-sistence visible in women and in slaves, children, or anyone who did not engage in the wage contract. A feminist critique on primitive accumulation as the accumulation of a non-capitalist proletariat is present in Maria Mies's *Patriarchy Accumulation on a World Scale* (2001). If capitalism, as Rosa Luxemburg defended, depends on non-capital formations and relations, Maria Mies offers an interesting analysis on how the sexual division of labor works as a constant resource for capitalist relations.

Sexual Division of Labor

This sexual division takes place through two different dynamics; a sexual division of labor that expulses women from political syntax by not considering reproduce work and care work forms of labor and through conjugal right, which introduces women in political syntax as an economic appendix of the male worker through what Maria Mies calls the classic capitalist couple (2001).

Through the feminist discursive mediation, the witch hunt served to classify reproductive and other feminine forms of work under the ⌐S₁. Silvia Federici points out that

> the political lesson that we can learn from Caliban and the Witch is that capitalism, as a social-economic system, is necessarily committed to racism and sexism. For capitalism must justify and mystify the contradictions built into its social relations—the promise of freedom vs. the reality of widespread

coercion, and the promise of prosperity vs. the reality of widespread penury—by denigrating the 'nature' of those it exploits: women, colonial subjects, the descendants of African slaves, the immigrants displaced by globalization.

(2009, p. 17)

As one can see in Federici's quote, creating an $\ulcorner S_1$ that englobes the exploited as a group of people who do not deserve to inhabit political syntax is necessary for capitalism's normal functioning. This $\ulcorner S_1$ is inhabited by women and subjects with the feminine position in an androcentric Reality. However, as feminine subjects, women hold a differential status in an androcentric Reality upon which heterosexual love is mandatory. This specificity is observable in Maria Mies's book *Patriarchy Accumulation* where the author addresses the question of the intimate yet obscured relation between patriarchy and capitalism (2001). Rosa Luxemburg pointed out the capitalist necessity to rely on non-capitalist formations and how imperialism and an international division of labor function. In comparison, Maria Mies provides an approach that considers the international and the sexual divisions of labor. Mies's analysis of the sexual division of labor within marriage relates to the idea of conjugal rights developed by Carole Pateman. In fact, Maria Mies points out the sexual division of labor that results from marriage and that classifies wife and husband into housewife and breadwinner:

> by defining women as housewives, a process which I then called 'housewifization', not only did women's unpaid work in the household become invisible, unrecorded in GDP (Waring 1988), and 'naturalized' - that is, treated as a 'free good' - but also her waged work was considered to be only supplementary to that of her husband, the so-called breadwinner, and thus devalued. The construction of woman as mother, wife and housewife was the trick by which 50 per cent of human labor was defined as a free resource. It was female labor.

(2001, p. ix)

Thus, feminine work is not considered labor because the contract that characterizes women's economic activity is not the wage contract but the sexual contract in marriage. Nevertheless, many subjects cannot engage in the wage contract or the marriage contract, such as slaves. The marriage contract produces a new political status for married women; this status is the one that we have defined as the anxious subject's status.

In this book, *The Origin of the Family*, Engels mentions Morgan's division of history (2010). Furthermore, while Morgan put the accent on human's progress over food production as the indicator for his historical division, Engels affirms that "[t]he development of the family takes a parallel course, but here the periods have not such striking marks of differentiation" (2010, p. 51). Thus, Engels compares different family conceptions across cultures; nevertheless, as his coevals, Engels understands that there are different stages of the family structure. These stages determine the level of evolution of society. In this sense, Engels differentiates four different stages. I am here interested in the fourth stage; the monogamous family describes how the marriage contract creates a division of labor as Mies describes and creates the fundamental institution for non-paid reproductive work. Engels defines the monogamous family as

> based on the supremacy of the man, the express purpose being to produce children of undisputed paternity; such paternity is demanded because these children are later to come into their father's property as his natural heirs. It is distinguished from pairing marriage by the much greater strength of the marriage tie, which can no longer be dissolved at either partner's wish. As a rule, it is now only the man who can dissolve it and put away his wife. The right of conjugal infidelity also remains secured to him, at any rate by custom.
>
> (2010, p. 86)

The monogamous family is visible since Ancient Greece and, as we can see, is already articulating a situation of inequality among men and women. Furthermore, Engels dwells into the origin of monogamous marriage and affirms that

> when monogamous marriage first makes its appearance in history, it is not as the reconciliation of man and woman, still less as the highest form of such a reconciliation. Quite the contrary monogamous marriage comes on the scene as the subjugation of the one sex by the other; it announces a struggle between the sexes unknown throughout the whole previous prehistoric period.
>
> (2010, p. 89)

In discursive terms, sexuation and the construction of monogamous marriage as an institution of love and reconciliation were occurring. Thus, the idea of androcentric heterosexual love in monogamous marriage is a way to make up for the absence of the sexual relationship. Furthermore, it seems that Engels was also aware of the sexual division of labor that this familial institution brought with it.

> In an old unpublished manuscript written by Marx and myself in 1846, I find the words: 'The first division of labor is that between man and woman for the propagation of children.' And today I can add: The first class opposition that appears in history coincides with the development of the antagonism between man and woman in monogamous marriage, and the first class oppression coincides with that of the female sex by the male.
>
> (2010, p. 89)

Thus, if Marx recognized the sexual division of labor within reproduction, and Engels is aware of the role of both marriage and monogamous family, why do I speak of Marxism as a current that departs from a sexuated division of the ontological, allowing for a masculine hegemony of the ontic? The answer is explained by analyzing Marxism's discourse from the theoretical body developed in Part I.

To analyze the discursive operations that Marxism develops, I need to consider that the countries where I focus the analysis (Central countries, i.e., Western European Countries and North America) are societies in which the liberal Master's Discourse is present. Thus, one finds societies in which the ontic level, politics, is governed by the Borromean knot presented in the previous section. In other words, I am not referring to Marxist discursive operations within countries in which communisms achieved power. Instead, I am interested in seeing how Marxism articulates discursive operations that can be read as counterhegemonic in liberal countries. The main objective is to analyze whether the left has been able to develop a discursive operation in the Analyst's Discourse parameters, i.e., a discourse able to embrace the Real and shift liberal political syntax. If liberal discourse followed the structure of the Master's Discourse, what I find in Marxism is the University's Discourse.

In the University's Discourse, an agent who believes that they are $\neg S_1$ addresses a as the others that hold similar political subjectivities. In Marxism, the male proletariat is $\neg S_1$. The male proletariat is supposed to hold all the oppression from the capitalist system of production. Nevertheless, the male proletariat ends up in the space of existence through its engagement in the relation of waged labor. Thus, in the case of Marxism, as well as it happens in liberalism, males who did not hold political power enter into the space of existence by establishing a contract that somehow situates them in a position of heterogeneity, but not of pure antagonism. In other words, the conversion of peasants and serfs through the wage contract may be conceived as a cyphering of subjects of the Real. Additionally, to conceive the male proletariat as the subject of revolution while being aware of different oppressions such as gender or race through a sexual and international division of labor takes Marxist theory to hold the denial of intersectionality.

Thus, when Marxism addresses women as secondary victims of capitalist, or sexism as a by-product of capitalist relations, or obviates the impact of continuous primitive accumulation in imperialism and the sexual division of labor, one finds an operation through which the anxious subject believes he is the hysteric subject. As seen in the analysis of the University's Discourse, the product of the addressing operation of this supposed $\neg S_1$ toward a is $\$$. In other words, by prioritizing and universalizing the male proletarian struggle, Marxist theory reinforces the sexuation of the ontological level. Thus, by taking the hysteric subject's place, the anxious subject, who holds a status of privilege over hysteric subjects, prioritizes the agonic political struggle of the ontic level between desiring and anxious subjects over the agonistic political struggle that takes place between $\neg S_1$ and S_1.

Thus, and as a way to conclude the analysis of these two currents of thought, I find that liberalism imposed a Borromean knot at the level of the ontic that guarantees the hegemony of the masculine through the creation of liberal democracies. On the other hand, Marxist discursive operations are not articulated outside of the political syntax that excludes hysteric subjects. Instead, it takes a subject with existence as the agent of the Real. In this sense, Marxism cannot provoke a shift within political syntax able to provoke a contra against the ontological level's sexuation. Furthermore, if the social contract allows men to create a new political syntax, the waged contract allows working-class men to enter this political syntax. Nevertheless, how have certain women (cis abled white) entered this political syntax? I believe that, after these three registers have been masculinized through liberal discourse, a fourth ring is created in later capitalist developments that allows a process of cyphering for other hysterical subjects into anxious subjects. Let me analyze this final idea.

Notes

1 'The accumulation of stock must, in the nature of things, be previous to the division of labour' (Adam Smith, Wealth of Nations, Bk II, Introduction).
2 Although we understand that there is a direct and close relation between the two types of conditions for capital and that they cannot therefore be clearly or possibly divided, we do explain them separately in order to make a clearer exposition.
3 The conceptualization of primitive accumulation as the accumulation of proletarian belongs to Moulier-Boutang and will be analyzed throughout this chapter.
4 The book was originally written in French. Nevertheless, the Spanish edition has been widely corrected by the author himself, that's the reason why we have chosen to work with this edition. Also, the book hasn't been translated into English. The translations that appear in this text have been made by me.

References

Engels, F. (2010). *The Origin of the Family, Private Property and the State (epub)*. Penguin Classics.

Federici, S. (2009). *Caliban and the Witch. Women, the Body and Primitive Accumulation (Third)*. Autonomedia.

Luxemburg, R. (2015). *The Complete Works of Rosa Luxemburg: Vol. II* (P. Hudis, P. Le Blanc, D. Fernbach, J. G. Fracchia, G. Shriver, & N. Gray, Eds.; epub). Verso.

Marx, K. (1992). *Capital_ Critique of Political Economy Volume 1*. Penguin Classics.

Mies, M. (2001). *Patriarchy and Accumulation on a World Scale: Women in the International División of Labour*. Zed.

Mouliere-Boutang, Y. (2006). *De la esclavitud al trabajo asalariado. Economía histórica del trabajo asalariado embridado*. Akal.

O'Brien, K. (2004). The Feminist Critique of Enlightenment. In M. Fitzpatrick, P. Jones, K. Knellwolf, & I. McCalman (Eds.), *The Enlightenment World* (pp. 621–635). Routledge. http://site.ebrary.com/id/10093881

Pateman, C. (1988). *The Sexual Contract*. Stanford University Press.

Stern, K. (1965). *The Flight from Woman*. Farrar, Straus and Giroux.

Waring, M. (1988). *If women counted: A new feminist economics*. San Francisco: Harper and Row.

Chapter 9

Ciphering the Feminine

This chapter aims to illustrate that *objet a* is located in the void and how the Real is integrated into Reality through ciphering. Women's possession of masculine sexual position relates to how political fantasy creates an ideal image of woman as wife, housewife, and consumer. This transformation occurs in the void and establishes the image to which women have to subject themselves to achieve existence. Nevertheless, the conversion of the void into a ciphering space is not fully completed until the void becomes the space in which political subjectivities become consumption patterns. Thus, the process of ciphering is double. One can find an exercise of performativity through which the ideal of woman as *objet a* is imposed through violent means, i.e., the witch-hunt, and an exercise of commodification through which the ideal of woman is converted into a pattern of consumption.

A primordial question of processes of ciphering is rhythm. As seen in the previous section, the conversion of the patriarchy into fraternal patriarchy implies introducing certain subjects into political syntax through the social contract. Later on, economic changes implied a new opportunity to introduce subjects in political syntax through the wage contract. Both processes imply a process of ciphering in which certain subjects are inscribed into political syntax. Moreover, I classify these inclusions as decaf resistances since they did not imply the introduction of an empty signifier able to shift political syntax to the point of threatening the ontological sexuation.

Additionally, male subjects' entrance into fraternal patriarchy as desiring subjects is also granted by another ciphering process in which certain women become anxious subjects through the marriage contract's ciphering mechanism. In other words, once the desiring subject has undergone a process of transformation, the *objet a* needs to undergo another process of redefinition. It is the process through which women are constituted as the *objet a* needed for fraternal patriarchy on which I want to focus.

Ciphering Women: The Marriage Contract

The sexual contract and the marriage contract are established at the same time the social and the wage contract are established. This marriage or sexual

DOI: 10.4324/9781003167587-13

contract creates what Maria Mies identifies as the *classic capitalist couple* (2001). Nevertheless, Maria Mies focuses on the analysis of colonization and house-wifization as processes derived from the new subordination of nature that the Scientific Revolution implied (2001, p. 77). However, I believe that colonization and housewifization have very different dynamics and consequences.

On the one hand, I believe that white, cisgender, heterosexual women undergo housewifization as a ciphering process that grants them a masculine sexual position that guarantees them existence. On the other hand, people from the colonies, migrants, non-white people, the LGTBIQA+ community did not undergo the same process and did not achieve a masculine sexual position. I believe that the process of housewifization has a direct consequence on the division of the subjects from the Real, which results in the confrontation of different feminine subjects in the struggle for recognition—*Dīvide et īmpera*. Thus, I will focus on how housewifization, as a double process of performativity and commodification, is a clear example of a ciphering process.

In her analyses on the subordination of women, nature, and colonies, Maria Mies illustrates how women go from being under the control of the paternal figure to that of the fraternal figure (2001). Thus, Maria Mies also sees a clear relation between the Scientific Revolution and marriage. From my perspective, within the current international division of labor, international affairs in which the North still dominates, invades, and interferes in foreign countries, and the climate emergency have a clear different status from those related to gender in our societies. I believe then that nature and countries that were colonized are still part of the Real, while women have managed to engage in political syntax.

If primitive accumulation and the formation of the male proletarian through the extension of the wage contract was a painful process in which males suffered consequences of what Marx denominated bloody legislation, women also underwent a process of subordination through violence; this process is the witch-hunt. For Maria Mies, the witch-hunt

> raged through Europe from the twelfth to the seventeenth century was one of the mechanisms to control and subordinate women, the peasant and artisan, women who in their economic and sexual independence constituted a threat for the emerging bourgeois order.
>
> (2001, p. 81)

As one can see, the witch-hunt did not address every woman, but it targeted women who did not engage in the marriage/sexual contract, women who did not engage in the classical capitalist couple. Maria Mies defines the classic capitalist couple as "the 'free' wage earner or 'free' owner of means of production and his dependent housewife" (2001, p. 119).

The classic capitalist couple is the economic translation of the fantasy, heterosexual androcentric love from the feminist discursive approach. The desiring subject, in this case, the free male wage earner, articulates his desire around *objet a*, the anxious subject that depends directly on him. Thus, the ciphering of women that occurred with the marriage contract in the first stage only succeeds in those families in which the breadwinner's wage was invested in the family and was enough to maintain the family. Therefore, the classic capitalist couple is only observable in the capitalist class, while poor women were left out of the ciphering due to their socioeconomic conditions. It is toward widows, single mothers, working women, and sex workers that the witch-hunt was addressed. Thus, women who could not construct their subjectivities within the classic capitalist couple's parameters suffered the process of expulsion from political syntax. Thus, one already sees how the ciphering of women, the construction of women as wives, takes place through performativity through the housewife's image's imposition. The expulsion from political syntax was not a mere process of lack of political and civic rights. Instead, the witch-hunt was a violent process that stroke bodies and served scientific purposes.

> The persecution and burning of the midwives as witches was directly connected with the emergence of modern society: the professionalization of medicine, the rise of *medicine* as a 'natural science', the rise of *science* and of *modern economy*. The torture chambers of the witch-hunters were the laboratories where the texture, the anatomy, the resistance of the human body - mainly the female body was studied.
>
> (Mies, 2001, p. 83)

Maria Mies introduces how the witch-hunt targeted midwives as they were considered a threat to the classical capitalist couple. Furthermore, the witch-hunt was initiated as a mechanism to assure the sexuation of the ontological and the subordination of nature, as a process that we would denominate the taming of the Real. This taming process aims to persuade, through violent means, the hysteric subject to leave the Real. It is a process that, through coercion, tries to cipher the feminine. One of the mechanisms of this coercion is the division of the subjects with ex-sistence. This division is done by establishing categories that separate the feminine subject between those who are good and therefore allowed to enter into political syntax; those who are able and willing to adequate to the image presented by *objet a*, and those who are related to evil as they do not achieve the position of *objet a*. Thus, the ciphering process continues the stigmatization of the Real that was taking place at the ontological level. Nevertheless, the ontic level offers women a tamed position. The witch-hunt's main objective is to cancel out a possible emergence of the Real introducing women as *objet a* in political syntax. Thus, Maria Mies defines the witch-hunt as follows:

> It seems plausible that the whole fury of the witch-hunt was not just a result of the decaying old order in its confrontation with new capitalist forces, or even a manifestation of timeless male sadism, but a reaction of the new male-dominated classes against the *rebellion* of women. The poor women' freed',

that is, expropriated from their means of subsistence and skills, fought back against their expropriators.

(2001, p. 81)

Nevertheless, the witch-hunt found resistance within women just as the process of proletarianization, as Maria Mies affirms:

> Recent feminist literature on the witches and their persecution has brought to light that women were not passively giving up their economic and sexual independence, but that they resisted in many forms the onslaught of church, state and capital. One form of resistance were the many heterodox sects in which women either played a prominent role, or which in their ideology propagated freedom and equality for women and a condemnation of sexual repression, property and monogamy. Thus the 'Brethren of the Free Spirit', a sect which existed over several hundred years, established communal living, abolished marriage, and rejected the authority of the church. Many women, some of them extraordinary scholars, belonged to this sect. Several of them were burnt as heretics (Cohn, 1970).

(2001, p. 81)

Thus, the witch-hunt also functions as a weapon against possible revolutionary acts derived from the encounter with the Real that the introduction of women supposes. The sexual and the marriage contracts hold a central role in this stage of the process of ciphering. Their centrality is explicable following the feminist discursive mediation. The sexual/marriage contract implies the imposition of heterosexual normativity, which is a crucial element for patriarchy, visible in the construction of fantasy. Heterosexual androcentric love—the fantasy that makes up for the absence of sexual relationship $(S_1 // \neg S_1)$—relies on the idea of inequality and female submission. The feminine needs to be tamed into a delicate and dependent subject. The witch-hunt plays a central role in classifying women between those who are economically and sexually dependent on a man and those who are evil. In other words, women need to be ciphered because of their condition as subjects from the Real. Politics, the law, and economics provided the witch-hunt with multiple tools to create a division among women. Sylvia Federici analyzes state control over women's bodies through policies that encourage families and penalized celibacy (2009). Furthermore, the codification of reproductive crimes is a precise way to see how political syntax imposed a division between those who could inhabit the space of existence and ex-sistence. In Federici's analysis, one can also observe how complex, intricate, and proper of political syntax was the witch-hunt:

> Women could not have been totally devalued as workers and deprived of autonomy with respect to men without being subjected to an intense process of social degradation; and indeed, throughout the 16th and 17th centuries, women lost ground in every area of social life.

(2009, p. 100)

This social degradation consisted of legal infantilization, division of public spaces, and a sexual division of labor that affected social constructions of gender. They invested each gender with vices and virtues, creating the canons of the masculine and feminine. Besides the witches' case, two other cases call our attention from a psychoanalytical perspective: the cases of the sex worker and the lesbian. On the one hand, the sex worker traverses fantasy by becoming the desiring subject because she becomes the subject of desire and not the *objet a* around which desire is articulated. She is thus sexually and economically independent from men. On the other hand, the lesbian traverses the fantasy by refusing to be man's *objet a*; a *matter* that does not desire *form*. In Monique Wittig's text "One Is Not Born a Woman", the idea of the lesbian as the threat and defiance to heterosexuality is extensively analyzed (1993). Wittig affirms that the lesbian "destroys the artificial (social) fact constituting women as a 'natural group'" (1993, p. 103). Furthermore, she affirms that lesbians' refusal to be woman, understood as their rejection of the social construction of woman, "is the refusal of the economic, ideological, and political power of a man" (1993, p. 105).

From the manners in which social degradation of women took place, I find it essential to emphasize the idea of legal infantilization since I believe that the law, as the Lacanian Symbolic, is the crucial mechanism of coercion through which hysterics subject are called to submission. Legal infantilization is the process through which women cease to be existing subjects. This process of legal infantilization took place once women ceased to have a male companion, whether husband or father:

> One of the main rights that women lost was the right to conduct economic activities alone, as *femme soles*. In France, they lost the right to make contracts or to represent themselves in court, being declared legal "imbeciles." In Italy, they began to appear less frequently in the courts to denounce abuses perpetrated against them. In Germany, when a middle-class woman became a widow, it became customary to appoint a tutor to manage her affairs. German women were also forbidden to live alone or with other women and, in the case of the poor, even with their own families, since it was expected that they would not be properly controlled. In sum, together with economic and social devaluation, women experienced a process of legal infantilization.
> (Federici, 2009, p. 100)

Women had to choose between being a witch or a wife; between becoming the *objet a* of androcentric fantasy or remaining hysteric subjects.

Summing up, the witch-hunt, which occurred from the twelfth to the seventeenth century in Europe, can be analyzed as one of the mechanisms through which women's ciphering took place by its taming. The taming process that the witch-hunt implied was violent, and it accompanied the imposition of heteronormativity that the sexual and the marriage contracts needed. Through the imposition of an ideal *objet a* adapted to the structure of patriarchal fantasy, the witch-hunt also worked as an exercise of both performativity and stigmatization. The encounter with the Real that women represented defied patriarchal political syntax and had to be suffocated through the imposition of a fantasy that entailed the taming of the feminine. Thus, in a way, the act that the encounter feminine Real implies was deactivated, as Sylvia Federici notes when explaining the consequences of the witch-hunt:

> Out of this defeat a new model of femininity emerged: the ideal woman and wife—passive, obedient, thrifty, of few words, always busy at work, and chaste. This change began at the end of the 17th century, after women had been subjected for more than centuries to state terrorism. Once women were defeated, the image of femininity constructed in the "transition" was discarded as an unnecessary tool, and a new, tamed one took its place. While at the time of the witch-hunt women had been portrayed as savage beings, mentally weak, unsatiably lusty, rebellious, insubordinate, incapable of self-control, by the 18th century the canon has been reversed. Women were now depicted as passive, asexual beings, more obedient, more moral than men, capable of exerting a positive moral influence on them.
>
> (2009, p. 103)

As the space in which the Real finds its paradoxical location of being not merely outside neither entirely inside, the void loses its potential for disruption. The act that can take place in the void is deactivated. However, this deactivation is not produced just by the witch-hunt. Performativity and stigmatization could not assure the obedience of women and their transformation into *objet a*. There is a further process through commodification that converts women into wives to assure the deactivation of the act.

Ciphering through Production and Consumption

Once the myth of the wife is imposed, another process of ciphering takes place, the process of housewifization. The process of housewifization described by Maria Mies is the process through which women become housewives. In this process, the housewife becomes the ideal, *objet a* is now related to economics. Thus, the void as the core of political fantasy comes to be founded on capitalist economy. Let me see how the process of housewifization is closely related to economic elements. As Maria Mies affirms,

> defining women as housewives, a process which I then called '*housewifiza-tion*', not only did women's unpaid work in the household become invisible, unrecorded in GDP (Waring 1988), and 'naturalized'—that is, treated as a 'free-good'—but also her waged work was considered to be only supplementary to that of her husband, the so-called breadwinner, and thus devalued. The construction of woman as mother, wife and housewife was the trick by which

50 per cent of human labour was defined as a free resource. It was female labor.

(2001, p. ix)

Marx affirmed that primitive accumulation finished by the eighteenth century and the witch-hunt finished over the seventeenth century. Thus, once the witch-hunt is over and women have undergone a process of total social degradation that has forced them to transform into wives as *object a*, political syntax then allows them to enter into economics as subjects with existence. Nevertheless, as anxious subjects, their existence is conditioned to the needs of capitalism. Thus, if women can enter into political syntax as wives, they can enter into economics as housewives. To analyze the housewife's role in the patriarchal economy, production, reproduction, consumption, and how women are articulated around them need to be analyzed.

Reproduction and Production

The division between productive and reproductive work derives from the sexual division of labor analyzed in previous chapters. Thus, productive work takes place within the household and is mainly executed by women. I refer to childrearing, housework, care labor such as taking care of elders and sick, affective work, and aesthetic work (Valdés, 2019). As seen in our analysis of Marxism, production, and not reproduction, is the kernel of economic analysis, which results in the male proletariat's construction as the subject of history and revolution. It is interesting to note that, while economic analyses from the neoclassical approach address the study of means of production and raw materials, they have left behind the study of the creation of labor force, that is, reproduction and care of workers until they can work. This lack of analysis responds to the fact that reproduction is not seen as an economic variable since it is developed by women in the household. Thus, it is not a job but a female's natural role in society.

The separation between the private and public sphere and the sexual division of labor, through which women are responsible for taking care of future workers in an altruist manner, allows observing how women are already positioned out of the economic system because of their condition as wives. Thus, the ciphering of women through the reproductive dimension of economy converts women into *objet a* as housewives, free laborers whose social and economic function is understood as their natural destiny. Moreover, Maria Miles affirms that "[t]he concept of labor is usually reserved for men's productive work under capitalist conditions, which means work for the production of surplus value" (2001, p. 45). Therefore, the female agency will not be able to be constructed in terms of a productive member of society, not even in the cases where working-class women will work as maids since such work does not produce surplus and only responds to women's natural role in society.

The sexual division of labor in capitalist production was the key element to separate the private and the public spheres, and therefore, to divide the spaces in which women and men would respectively construct their identities under capitalism. Thus, the construction of gendered identities under capitalism follows the same pattern of the male desiring subject and the female *objet a* of patriarchal fantasy. Brenner and Laslett affirm that the private and public sphere's gendered separation was highly institutionalized during the nineteenth century because the separation between the private and public sphere "has been central to the organization of gender in modern industrial society" (1989, p. 386). Women's power inside and outside the home was a central question when analyzing changes within social reproduction and family. The reproductive element in feminine genitalia was not the only root of the women-nature binomial relationship. The separation of the public and private sphere reinforced this binomial relationship by assuming that women were naturally more prepared for childcare (Laslett & Brenner, 1989, p. 387). Women were more connected to nature; they were also domestic. Moreover, as Maria Valverde shows in her paper "When the Mother of the Race Is Free", white middle-class women's groups advocated for women's power in society due to a natural moral superiority that came from motherhood and the importance of reproduction for social and racist purposes (1992).

It is important to notice two elements when talking about the feminine dimension of the private sphere. On the one hand, the association of the private sphere with femininity does not imply that women were the central character within the home. Male pleasures and needs were the central elements; women would work inside the home to fulfill them. On the other hand, middle-class women and working-class women did not face the same situations nor attained the same results due to the separation between the public and the private sphere. Since working-class men had salaries insufficient to sustain an entire family, working-class women usually had to take jobs outside the home. This happened first in other homes as maids, and in the late nineteenth century, white-collar jobs for women in retail stores appeared. Thus, while women from high socioeconomic backgrounds could perform the role of *objet a* without deviations, some women had to play *objet a* within political syntax at the same time they held a different position in the economic realm. Nevertheless, although low-class women and migrants, poor kids, and sex workers held positions within the productive realm, their work was devalued.

In summary, women faced several difficult obstacles to construct female agency related to their productive activity in early capitalism. The nature-women binomial and the separation between spheres influenced the appearance of a sexual division of labor that did not just classify jobs by gender but created a hierarchy which led women's work to (a) not be paid and (b) not provide women with the status of producer or breadwinner. Working-class women who were not excluded from the productive system were misrepresented, and not defined as workers or breadwinners, unlike their male counterparts. Furthermore, the need to work within the productive realm left working-class women in an ambiguous status in which they could not adapt themselves to the ideal of the wife or house-wife imposed during the witch-hunt. Summing up, women's ciphering in the capitalist productive system was that of *objet a*, women could not achieve the status of desiring subject. Women were to remain invisible whether their work was confined to the household's limits or developed within the spaces for male production. Nevertheless, women's role in capitalist society had another dimension, their dimension as consumers.

Consumption

Capitalism depends on production and consumption. While capitalism gave men the role of producers, women were given the roles of reproducers and consumers. Thus, women's role as *objet a*, as the necessary political subject of second-order, is visible in three ways: their position in patriarchal fantasy as the reminder of the Real, which derives in their secondary position within the political system; their secondary position in the productive system by the devaluation of reproductive work; and their secondary position in consumption through their entrance in consumerism as wives and housewives.

As Frank Trentmant affirms, "[i]f there is one agreement between theorists of Modernity and those of Postmodernity, it is about the centrality of consumption to modern capitalism and contemporary culture" (2004, p. 373). Consumption, production, and urban planning have always been deeply interrelated. Ever-growing production needed better and more expansive paved surfaces for the transport of goods. Retailers needed to make their products visible to pedestrians; they needed their shops to work as small-scale world exhibitions that promoted consumption. Overall, capitalism required the city to undergo a massive reorganization to reinforce consumption and facilitate transportation. These new needs were covered by Paris' public urban planning policies and the new architecture that would from then on characterize Paris.

The arcades, which Benjamin studied and analyzed in depth in his *Arcades Project*, started appearing during the 1830s, but it was not until the 1850s that Paris would undergo a complete transformation by Haussmann (1999). The arcades are large glass-roofed corridors where several shops were placed, which Benjamin defines as the early spaces of consumerism. For Benjamin, there are two critical conditions for the appearance of the arcades, the rise of the textile trade that required large stores to keep larger product stocks and the emergence of iron construction. It was the beginning of a new production model that would later give birth to mass consumption. These new production patterns and consumption entangled with a new type of society, a society based on spectacle. The logic of this new market and this new society is visible in World Exhibitions. World Exhibitions focused on and increased the exchange-value of commodities, leaving aside the use-value of such products, as Benjamin defined them, "World Exhibitions are places of pilgrimage to the commodity Fetish" (1999, p. 17). Commodities that were not valuable due to their use, but rather due to their exchange-value, could be seen by an audience of consumers in a new type of spectacle that endorsed consumerism. This spectacle could be observed on a small scale in the arcades by the appearance of storefronts that would always display large quantities of new products targeted, in most cases, to women. Visual elements, such as advertisements and storefronts, transformed how people moved around the city. Men had always been allowed to move freely around the city regardless of their socioeconomic status, as the tramp, the ragpicker, and the *flâneur* illustrate. On the other hand, the appearance of consumption spaces was a significant change for women, who traditionally belonged to the private sphere. Open spaces, such as the corridors, or large avenues filled with stores, created a new arena where women would become public and visible agents.

From the analysis of the urban changes related to early capitalism, one can deduce that the city's new structure serves as the perfect ally to establish a new behavior focused on consumption and converts commodities into the city's central element. Furthermore, the re-articulation of the public space implied a new inclusion of women in the public sphere. This alliance between the city and commodities, the emergence of storefronts—with glass windows that displayed the store's interior and reflected the viewer's image—played a crucial role in women's activity through the new urban structure. As previously stated, women's activity was confined to the interior of the house. Middle-class women were harassed when leaving the house, while the labor performed by working-class women outside the interior of the familial house was devalued. The fact that women were supposed to remain in the family space conditioned the kinds of activities they could also engage publicly.

Brenner and Laslett analyze the department store as crucial in developing the feminine identity during early capitalism (1989). On the one hand, middle-class women became critical consumers of such stores. Women mainly consumed, apart from goods to cover basic needs, household, and retail goods. Although their duties were confined to the household, many products and goods were entering the house, taking women's activities to retail stores to buy the necessary goods. The number of middle-class housewives and mothers who appeared in department stores and shopping centers in the capital led to the necessity to have female workers within department stores, such as new white-collar jobs as shop assistants or waitresses in female-only restaurants and restrooms (Laslett & Brenner, 1989). Women entered the public scene, but this scene was built for men by men. The need to have female workers in the places where middle-class women were becoming visible was vital. Furthermore, middle-class women could freely move around early shopping centers without the fear of being defined as prostitutes or as women of a low socioeconomic class (Laslett & Brenner, 1989). That is to say, women could engage in certain earlier forbidden activities without the risk of being expulsed from the political syntax for not conforming to the role assigned as *objet a*.

I argue that this allowed introduction into public spaces responds to a new articulation of the ideal of *objet a*. Women, as *objet a* in a capitalist system, were allowed to engage in public capitalist consumption due to the proper necessity of capitalism for consumers. The thesis that supports that women's role as consumers of luxury goods was a crucial element for the development of capitalism is well known. Nevertheless, I read this process with the feminist discursive mediation.

The emergence of capitalist mass consumption allowed women to enter the public sphere not through their production role but in consumption, which was only affordable by women with high socioeconomic statuses. On the other hand, working-class women were taking more visible jobs in department stores. The sexual division of labor was now blurred as it could not be confined to the sexual division of spaces. I believe that, within the public sphere, specific spaces addressed women's production and consumption; this is visible in how low-class women were given specific spaces in department stores. As Laslett and Brenner note,

> Although, in the first instance, department store appeals were made more to middle-class women with discretionary income than to working-class women, the principle of free entrance without an obligation to buy and the development of special sections for women with less money (the bargain basement) expanded the culture of consumerism to the working-class as well. Department stores became like museums of the modern, fashionable life, open without charge to all women (Leach 1984).
>
> (1989, pp. 394–395)

Whether in the form of window-shopping, the austere consumption of working-class families, or the excessive consumption by middle and high-class families, the truth is that family consumption rested on the hands of mothers and wives. Consequently, as women became the primary consumers of this early capitalist society, they also became advertisements' targets. This new and early industry of advertisement portrayed a new kind of feminine and new way of behaving like a woman. The idea of the perfect housewife changed; women would not only be seen now as caretakers, housewives, and mothers; from then on, women would also be seen as individual agents with material desires and needs to be covered by consumerism, "[t]he 'new woman' was an ideal attainable by a very small minority at the turn of the century" (Laslett & Brenner, 1989, p. 395). Women faced an ideal model characterized by consumption, which most women could not reach, but an ideal that seemed reachable due to bargain sales in different department stores. Creating a feminine agency based on consumption can be deduced from early capitalism's necessity to create new publics and new niches for consumption. The birth of the capitalist system needed new consumers to sell the goods from a new production process.

In her book *Patriarchy Accumulation*, Maria Mies also analyzes the process of housewifization concerning the changes in consumption patterns in women analyzing the consumption of luxury goods as the other side of colonialist exploitation and expropriation (2001, p. 101). Furthermore, Maria Mies introduces Sombart's ideas on women's role in capitalist consumerism; for Sombart, capitalism was born out of the consumption and trade of luxury goods (2001, p. 101). This consumption and trade are, for Sombart, the result of the engagement of women in the economy. Furthermore, as Maria Mies points out, "Sombart identifies certain trends in the luxury production, which he, as we have seen, attributes to the passions of a certain class of women" (2001, p. 102). These trends are a *tendency toward domesticity*, which illustrates that people exhibit their luxury within the confines of the house. Thus, Sombart identifies the consumption of luxury products in the household as a female vice; a *tendency toward objectification*, people demonstrated their wealth through goods and commodities; and last, a *tendency toward contraction* of time, which implied that the consumption of luxury could take place during any time of the year (Mies, 2001, pp. 102–103). Maria Mies affirms that

> the tendency towards domestication and privatization certainly had a great impact on the construction of the new image of the 'good woman' in the centres of capitalism in the nineteenth and twentieth centuries, namely, woman as *mother* and *housewife,* and the family as her arena, the privatized arena of consumption and 'love', excluded and sheltered from the arena of production and accumulation, where men reign. In the following, I shall trace how the ideal of the domesticated privatized woman, concerned with 'love' and consumption and dependent on a male 'breadwinner', was generalized, first in the bourgeois class proper, then among the so-called petty-bourgeosie, and finally in the working class or the proletariat.
>
> (2001, p. 103)

Thus, the conversion of the housewife consists of the transformation of the housewife—as a political identity of second-order, as an *objet a* dependent of a desiring subject—into a pattern of consumption that is spread from higher socioeconomic classes to lower ones implies the political ciphering of feminine subjects and the ciphering of women into capitalist subjects. From this book's approach, the consumption and trade of luxury goods as a way to insert women as the necessary demand for capitalist goods occurs when the reproducibility of frames produces a moment of dislocation in which the frame opens up for the inclusion, at this point of women into the capitalist system. Thus, women are not just *objets a* that depend on the male political subject. They are also given a false promise of conversion into desiring agents through consumption.

Once housewifization is over, that is to say, once the idea of the good woman, as a housewife, wife, and consumer is transformed into a pattern of consumption, the ciphering of women into a subject with a masculine sexual position is complete. That is to say, by the end of the twentieth century, women may not be able to engage in the productive system as men—they still have the responsibility of reproductive work, there is still a wage gap and a ceiling glass—nevertheless, they have been given a different fantasy. This different fantasy corresponds to the application of the masculine fantasy ($\Diamond a$) in capitalist terms.

If masculine fantasy is a mechanism upon which political syntax is supported, women engage in a different masculine subject concerning economics. Patriarchy holds its power through the fantasy of heterosexual love where the desiring subject is master, but patriarchy is aware that this fantasy may not be sufficiently strong, and a new fantasy is created. Within this fantasy, woman as a consumer believes she is a desiring subject and articulates her desire around *objet a*, which are commodities. In other words, the introduction of the fourth ring of the Borromean knot implies the imposition of a capitalist fantasy in which any subject can believe he or she is a desiring subject because he or she can articulate desire around an *objet a*. This last process of ciphering implies the complete introduction of women in political syntax. Through their subjection to capitalist patriarchal political syntax as consumers, women achieve the status of existence. Women as wives and consumers obtain the status of anxious subjects in political syntax and cease to hold a feminine sexual position to a masculine one. Nevertheless, their continuity as anxious subjects is assured by developing a capitalist fantasy through which women believe she has evolved into the desiring subject.

The *Sinthome*

From our feminist Lacanian analysis, the introduction of this purely economic dimension to patriarchy corresponds to the fourth ring's introduction into the Lacanian Borromean knot. Consequently, fraternal patriarchy is not a mere political system, but it also involves an economic system, capitalism. In other words, the contingency of woman as *objet a* is conditioned by the needs of the market; the normative woman is shaped through the capitalist market. In historical terms, the process through which the introduction of this fourth ring starts at the end of the nineteenth century and culminates once the Eurocommunist dream is defeated.

As the fourth ring, the symptom is added to the Borromean knot as the lock of the other three. It hosts the process of capitalist ciphering through which feminine subjects are tamed into subjects with masculine sexual positions through the conversion of their identities into patterns of consumption. Thus the feminist discursive analysis of patriarchy allows affirming that capitalism is a system that springs from patriarchy and makes possible its continuation. Thus, the introduction of capitalism as the symptom involves the apparition of different elements.

- Capitalist fantasy: the main element that springs from capitalism is the apparition of capitalist fantasy. Within this fantasy, the anxious subject can articulate a fake identity that resembles that of the desiring subject. While her subjectivity in political syntax is still one of subjugation, capitalism, through consumerism, can create a new process of identification, which we denominate object identification. In this fantasy, $, the capitalist subject, articulates their desire around *a*, *a* being the commodity. Thus, object identification entails the identification of the subject with a commodity. When the subject engages in capitalist fantasy, they become blind to political fantasy. In other words, this subject cannot see they are the *objet a* that sustains political syntax. It is essential to highlight that, as well as political fantasy affects every subject, whether the subject inhabits the space for existence or ex-sistence, capitalist fantasy also affects the hysteric subject. If capitalist production depended on non-capitalist formations and relations, capitalist consumerism also depends on non-capitalist formations and relations.

• Capitalist discourse: the introduction of a new ring, a new register, also introduces a new discursive structure. In this case, the Capitalist's Discourse, which is in charge of ciphering acts. This ciphering takes place by the introduction of a third element between the anxious subject and the Real. This third element is the commodity that comes to represent the Real.

• Objectual identification: objectual identification occurs in the act's ciphering and comes after imaginary and symbolic identification. If imaginary identification fails and symbolic identification is a harmful act that supposes a painful rejection and is a process not even available to everyone, a third identification with positive outcomes needs to be articulated. Objectual identification has a positive outcome in the sense that it provides *material wellbeing* to the subject. It offers a new status of the subject through the acquisition of goods whose objective is to offer the subject a needed identity based on the goods that it consumes.

Furthermore, this fourth ring's imposition entails a radical deactivation of the act's disruptive potential in a very intricate way. Being aware of the fact that the anxious subject may realize that they do not hold the status of the desiring subject, the patriarchal capitalist system produces a final mechanism able to cipher possible encounters with the Real, which takes place through a new discursive operation; the capitalist discourse analyzed in previous chapters. Let me see how this discursive operation takes place with women.

As an anxious subject, woman has a closer relation to the Real than the desiring subject. In moments of political or economic discontent, this relation with the Real may entail a threat to political syntax. The anxious subject may realize that they are not the desiring subject and wish to subvert political syntax by developing the act. Such an encounter needs to be ciphered.

By engaging in capitalist fantasy, woman thinks of herself as a desiring subject. Thus, the desiring subject, in this case, woman as the capitalist subject ($), appeals to normativity as the truth (S_1). That is to say, woman thinks that she can generate a change within political syntax. Once the subject has appealed to normativity, it addresses the other ($\neg S_1$). In this case, $\neg S_1$ represents feminism as a philosophy and a political position that belongs to the Real. The encounter between normativity and feminism has the double outcome of loss and product that we have seen in earlier chapters. On the one hand, the addressing operation's product is a, as *objet a* within capitalist fantasy, a commodity. On the other hand, what is lost is ⌐S₁, which cannot be commodified if it does not adapt to political syntax. In more pragmatic words, what is occurring here is that feminism (the Real) becomes a commodity. One clear example is the empowered woman who buys a t-shirt that says *Girls Rule!* in a store owned by Inditex. In the encounter of this woman with feminism, in the encounter with the Real, what is produced is *a*, the t-shirt, and what is lost is feminism. The encounter with the Real has been ciphered by the intermediation of a commodity and the transformation of a political position into a consumption pattern. This example makes visible the conversion of an act into an act of decaf resistance.

As a way to conclude, the symptom, the fourth ring of patriarchy, is precisely capitalism. Capitalism offers a new mechanism to stabilize and to secure the continuity of patriarchy through the imposition of a new fantasy in which everyone fits; a new discursive operation in charge of ciphering the act into decaf resistance; a new process of identification that can provide the frame with a mechanism that blocks the threat in moments in which the frame needs to open up.

References

Benjamin, W. (1999). *The Arcades Project*. The Belknap Press of Harvard University Press.

Cohn, N. *The Pursuit of the Millenium* (Paladin, London, 1970).

Federici, S. (2009). *Caliban and the Witch. Women, the Body and Primitive Accumulation (Third)*. Autonomedia.

Laslett, B., & Brenner, J. (1989). Gender and Social Reproduction: Historical Perspectives. *Annual Review of Sociology, 1*, 381–404.

Leach, W. R. (1984). Transformations in a culture of consumption: women and department stores, 1890-1925. *The Journal of American History, 71*(2), 319–342.

Mies, M. (2001). *Patriarchy and Accumulation on a World Scale: Women in the International División of Labour*. Zed.

Trentmann, F. (2004). Beyond Consumerism: New Historical Perspectives on Consumption. *Journal of Contemporary History, 39*(3), 373–401.

Valdés, A. (2019). Can erotic capital subvert masculine economy? Aesthetic work and the post-feminist approach to economics. *Recerca: Revista de Pensament i Analisi, 24*(2), 87–108.

Valverde, M. (1992). When the Mother of the Race is Free: Race, Reproduction, and Sexuality in First-Wave Feminism. In *Gender Conflicts. New Essays in Women's History* (pp. 3–26). University of Toronto Press.

Waring, M. (1988). *If women counted: A new feminist economics*. San Francisco: Harper & Row.

Wittig, M. (1993). One Is not Born a Woman. In H. Abelove, M. A. Barale, & D. M. Halperin (Eds.), *The Lesbian and Gay Studies Reader* (pp. 103–109). Routledge.

Conclusions

Notes for a Feminist Political and Economic Praxis

This book has developed an attempt to articulate a feminist discursive mediation of Lacan's work through the theory developed by the Lacanian Left, especially Butler's work, to create a new framework for political theory and praxis. Thus, I have tried to demonstrate how a feminist discursive reading of the Lacanian concept of sexual position allows for a more complex reading of how political identities are constructed in our European and androcentric society. With the introduction of this variable for political analysis and with a new approach to political identities through nosology and discursive ontological statuses, one can analyze, in a different and renewed manner, how capitalism, heterosexuality, and androcentrism shape political identities and discourses to strengthen the intricate system of oppression that produces inequalities. This last section thus presents the theoretical innovations that this dissertation proposes and sketches some ideas for a feminist praxis from the feminist Lacanian Left.

The Introduction of Sexual Position for Politics

The inclusion of sexual position as a variable of political analysis within a feminist discursive mediation of Lacan's work allows observing how the grounds upon which politics occur result from different discursive operations that entail establishing a Symbolic that divides subjects into feminine and masculine subjects. Thus, one can define patriarchy as an intricate and complex system of submission and oppression that affects every subject oppressing certain subjects and privileging others. Furthermore, the introduction of sexual position as a variable of analysis also allows seeing how oppressed subjects take part in their submission through the development of the University's Discourse when mistaking sexual position they possess. I believe that the mistake or weakness of the institutional feminism has been its misconception of the oppressed. Nevertheless, its bias or misconception can be overcome by introducing sexual position, which allows European women to draw a bigger picture to analyze their role in the intricate network of the systems of oppression that patriarchy implies. It is through such analysis that responsibility becomes *corresponsability*. In other words, only by assuming their role and their privilege in patriarchal systems can women shift the ontological level upon which

DOI: 10.4324/9781003167587-14

patriarchy rests. As seen, avoiding self-analysis and self-criticism can only lead women to develop a University's Discourse that reproduces that of the Master.

What Is to Be Done?

In his article "On Acts, Pure and Impure", Stavrakakis sheds some light on what he believes is the path that the Lacanian Left should engage:

> what the Lacanian Left needs is to move in the direction of articulating an alternative conception of the act, one which may link Lacan's insights (operating at both the real and symbolic levels) with a radical democratic project, able to promote the idea of a continuous *re-enacting of the act* as well as to imagine and construct a (conceptual, affective and material) space where such *re-enacting* becomes possible here and now.
>
> (2010, p. 8)

This book's articulation of the act through the act of coalitions within intermediate spaces is a good departing point for articulating an alternative conception of the act that will finally produce a shift at the ontological level. However, I am aware of the possible critique of a lack of practical examples of how the act of coalitions and or intermediate spaces may function or be developed. Žižek developed a harsh critique toward Stavrakakis's book *The Lacanian Left* by pointing out its lack of examples (2008). Stavrakakis addresses this topic in his article "On Acts, Pure and Impure", in which Stavrakakis faces Žižek's critique as follows:

> To start with, it is true that although a variety of examples is offered in *The Lacanian Left*, I do refrain from fully elaborating the empirical implications of the ethico-political orientation put forward. And this is not only due to limitations of space. It is partly intentional. It is done in an explicit attempt to frustrate any demand for closure, to deconstruct the idea of any simplistic 'application' of theoretical principles, to keep alive the imagination of the reader and to stimulate new articulations between the formal level and the challenges each and every one of us is facing in her/his own particular context. No matter how many examples are presented, theoretical and analytical discourse can neither predict and command nor accomplish the act – any act, that is, beyond its own (limited) elaboration. Nothing would be more alien to psychoanalytic discourse, which locates itself beyond any naïve.
>
> (2010, p. 14)

Furthermore, Stavrakakis keeps replying to such critique by pointing out the objective of his book:

> This is why The Lacanian Left was never envisaged as a political manifesto. This is made clear already from the first pages of the book: 'This is

an exercise in political theory and critical analysis and not a political manifesto' (Stavrakakis 2007: 13). It limits itself to offering a commentary on the character of the act, reflexively articulating some of its formal conditions of possibility/impossibility: an act is always impure, imperfect, located at the intersection between real and symbolic, but, instead of repressing or camouflaging it, it thematises this imperfection, registering it within its own fabric.

(2010, p. 15)

I agree with Stavrakakis that leaving specific unresolved questions may work as an incentive for other authors to keep alive the theory. Moreover, I have already pointed out how the theoretical framework articulated in this book may be applied to different oppressed subjects. Nevertheless—although this book is not a political manifesto either—from a feminist commitment, I believe that to propose a new paradigm to look at feminist political theory without sketching some notes for a feminist political and economic praxis entails an exercise of irresponsibility. The person who creates knowledge should take the responsibility to sketch how such knowledge can be implemented. Thus I find it necessary to finish this book by sketching a political and an economic feminist alternative to masculine Reality. However, it is also necessary to point out another critique theoretical books face.

On the one hand, some academic books are criticized for their lack of proposals for applying their theory. On the other hand, another common critique is that these books are rejected for their utopian horizon when articulating a proposal on applying their theoretical frameworks. This is visible in how major works on feminist economics that propose economics beyond the neoclassical paradigm have been the target of capitalist critiques that affirm that the feminist alternative economic system is utopian and unreachable.

However, being aware of the possible critique on the "utopian" dimension of the application of the act this book proposes, I still believe that the articulation of a possible praxis is necessary to void developing the University's Discourse.

Toward an Application of the Act of Coalitions

As seen in Chapter 6, the act of coalitions heavily relies on corresponsability, affection, and the creation of bonds based on care through reverse antagonism (Fishel et al., 2021; Valdés, 2021). The act of coalitions thus needs to reject alienation as the mechanism that separates individuals.

Although alienation is a mandatory element in Lacanian identifications, I believe that current political systems, through individualism, impose different types of alienating processes, producing a continuous status of political anxiety that drives the subject to a state in which they feel threatened. Alienation can be thus analyzed as a common element in the multiple processes of masculinization typical of the construction of Reality. I believe there are three different fields in which alienation works:

- Corporal alienation: corporal alienation comes from denying the bodies' interdependence and their dependence on infrastructure and elements external to them (Butler, 2014). The denial of interdependence is palpable when the political relationship is understood in Schmittian terms of friend/enemy. This corporal alienation implies the community's dismemberment and produces fragmentation of the commons by establishing the law of competition for survival. On the other hand, body alienation allows the human body to be separated from the natural environment, thus preparing the ground for an ecological crisis.
- Political alienation: political alienation can be analyzed in two different phenomena. First, as the separation between subjects—the political—and political structures and institutions—politics. In other words, political alienation is visible in the division between the ontic and ontological levels introduced in this book. One example is the mandatory obligation to have a specific administrative status to vote, which expulses political subjects from political institutions. Furthermore, this alienation is enhanced by levels of organization and power based on structures such as nation-states. The lower democratic proportionality of political systems of macro populations implies a detachment and disinterest in politics, thus alienating the sovereign subject from the development of their power. On the other hand, political alienation can be understood as a by-product of bodily alienation. This second form of political alienation is observable in the Schimittian relation of friend-enemy analyzed throughout the book. This political alienation based on antagonistic relations implies creating political bonds that do not embrace or include everyone as political subjects; instead, they are based on the antagonistic Schmittian relation.
- Economic alienation: economic alienation occurs through the delocalization of production and bodily alienation between producers and consumers. The delocalization of production and bodily alienation, which rejects the interdependency of bodies and the environment, supposes the invisibilization of the consequences of mass production on the environment. Furthermore, economic and bodily alienation also work together by dismembering and erasing the relation between consumers and producers through the invisibility of working conditions in third countries.

Alienating processes play a crucial role in shaping what I have been denominating as the Basic Political Community. Summing up the different mechanisms exposed in this book, one could affirm that the subject faces an intricate process of alienation based on the exclusion of the other from the political space through the distribution of unequal ontological statuses. The introduction of sexual position allows seeing how this process of distribution of different ontological statuses can be both analyzed and overcome by creating a shift at the ontological level able to include new signifiers within the Symbolic by developing the act of coalitions. However, for the act of coalitions to occur, anxious and hysteric subjects need to share a political and economic agenda able to create intermediate spaces for reverse antagonisms to arise. Let me now introduce two different projects that allow the apparition of intermediate spaces.

Community Currency as a Feminist Economic Praxis

The first project I would like to introduce relates to how intermediate spaces can emerge in economics. I believe that the feminist articulation of community currencies can eliminate the three levels of alienation that the process for masculinization entails creating an intermediate space. Thus I seek to examine how social currencies can entail a subversion of feminist economics while shifting the ontological level of masculine Reality. Thus, one must first ask what kind of objectives should a feminist community currency have.

In their article "Feminist Economics: Theoretical and Political Dimensions", Agenjo-Calderón and Gálvez-Muñoz point out different objectives present in different branches of feminist economy: (a) a more integral comprehension of the processes that support life and social provision and the processes of inclusion and exclusion and an understanding of gender as a fundamental category; (b) the need to value unpaid domestic work and caregiving; (c) the use of human wellbeing as a measure of economic success; (d) the implementation of intersectional analysis, considering the different social layers that define people's lives and identities; and (e) the belief in the importance of social action and the need to incorporate ethical judgments in economic analysis (2019, pp. 141–142).

I believe that it is impossible to embrace these objectives and articulate an accurate solution for them without shifting the ontological level of Reality and considering the role of sexual positions in the economic system. Furthermore, I believe that these five key points are intimately related to the eradication of alienation. However, I understand that the idea of community currencies must go beyond the proposals of the feminist economy and must touch on political and ontological praxis.

Although community currencies are already active tools within our societies (Hughes, 2015), the truth is that they do not necessarily lead to a feminist subversion of the economy. Furthermore, the current analyses on community currencies focus more on their potential for de-growth and 'green' dimension (Seyfang & Longhurst, 2013) than on their potential for a feminist subversion of the economy. I understand that community currencies must be conceptualized in a specific way to reverse alienation and, more important, to shift the Symbolic by producing intermediate spaces. Thus, departing from the point of view that the economy's masculinization is based on alienation, we have to generate a community currency that manages to reverse such processes.

As I have analyzed before, bodily alienation occurs through the denial of interdependence between the bodies and the denial between the body and the environment upon which the body is dependent. The denial of bodily interdependence lives in the myth of the *homo economicus*, which is defined by Rhonda M.

Williams as "the offspring of a separative worldview that understands the nonself and self as totally independent" (Williams, 1993). This denial of interdependence implies a negation of care and reproductive work as it leads to obviate the need for reproductive work and self-rearing during childhood (Federici, 2014; Mies, 2001; Pérez Orozco, 2017). We understand that the myth of *homo economicus* helps interpersonal alienation as soon as it denies unpaid female work.

As a revaluation of bodily interdependence, creating a feminist community currency must necessarily include the revaluation of reproductive work and care work during the entire life cycle (Agenjo-Calderón & Gálvez-Muñoz, 2019). Within a feminist economic system, care and reproductive work need to be defined as economic activities (Pérez Orozco, 2017). For the bodily alienation between the body and the natural environment, community currencies must benefit and stimulate local production and consumption. The ecological crisis we face is based on the relocation of production, which makes the effects of mass production over the environment invisible. Being partakers of production and witnessing its effects would make us aware of the need to return to different consumption and production patterns that assure a livable life for every subject. Additionally, by relocating production and valuing reproductive work, we create a community network with which to be able to break the dichotomy between altruism and selfishness by renegotiating the commons. Lastly, I believe that a community currency based on local consumption and production can make economic relations visible as social relations.

Thus, this new economic network aims to break the dichotomy between altruism and selfishness (Ferber & Nelson, 1993), making economic relations visible as social relations and making explicit interdependence. This network then allows for creating intermediate spaces based on ethical consumption and production that encourages coalitions.

Nevertheless, is a re-articulation of the economy through community currencies enough to generate a system in which every life can be put at the center? As I have mentioned, political and economic alienation are intertwined and based on bodily alienation. Thus, to achieve a system that makes it possible to place every life at the center involves a redefinition of the Basic Political Community. Therefore, it is also necessary to sketch some notes for feminist political praxis.

Municipalism as a Feminist Political Praxis

Municipalism is not a novelty (Bookchin & Colau, 2019). Debbie Bookchin affirms that "[m]unicipalism asks key questions. What does it mean to be a human being? What does it mean to live in freedom? How do we organize society in ways that foster mutual aid, caring and co-operation?" (2019, p. 15) I agree with Bookchin and add that, from the feminist discursive mediation this book articulates, these fundamental questions can be reduced to questions concerning precariousness, existence, ex-sistence, and inclusion in the Basic Political Community. Thus, this brief section aims at illustrating how Municipalism does not only pose key questions but allows for the creation of intermediate spaces in which reverse antagonism can occur.

I understand that feminist political praxis has to reverse masculinization processes of the ontic and ontological levels. It must be able to generate a shift at the ontological level. In the introduction to this section, I have affirmed that the denial of bodily interdependence relies upon the alienation proper to the friend/enemy Schmittian relationship (Schmitt, 2007). This relationship imposes artificial boundaries between bodies and subjects. They are created based on the potential threat of introducing new subjects into the Basic Political Community that may result in a loss of privileges in distributing power and resources or may involve a threat to the supposed harmony governing the Basic Political Community.

As a revaluation of bodily interdependence, feminist Municipalism has to offer a new articulation of the political relationship. Chantal Mouffe refers to a paradigm shift in the political relationship by transforming relations between enemies into a relationship between competitors, which she defines as agonistic relationships (Mouffe, 2005). However, as I have argued in Part I, I understand that the relationship between competitors and non-enemies already occurs within the Basic Political Community. The real antagonism occurs in the division between the Basic Political Community and the subjects excluded from it because the members of the Basic Political Community are already competitors for hegemony, while those outside it are seen as enemies and threats to it. Thus, a political shift at the ontological level has to go beyond the agonistic relationship. This political shift, I believe, is produced by reverse antagonisms.

At the beginning of this section, I affirmed that political alienation could be analyzed in two different elements: (a) alienation produced by the separation between political agents and political structures, and (b) alienation proper to the Schmittian political relation. On the one hand, while the idea of reverse antagonisms has already been articulated in this book and elsewhere (Fishel et al., 2021; Valdés, 2021), I find it now interesting to advocate for Municipalism as a political system within which reverse antagonisms can take place.

Remunicipalization—as the relocation of micropolitics and daily politics at the center of the political agenda (Bookchin & Colau, 2019)—can reverse antagonism by making explicit and visibilizing bodily and political interdependence through direct democratic participation. However, direct democratic participation does not necessarily allow people with irregular administrative statutes. In other words, remunicipalization, to generate an ontological shift, needs to allow the introduction of subjects with ex-sistence to the Basic Political Community. In this sense, I believe that Municipalism needs to work toward creating intermediate spaces, thus generating spaces in which antagonism is reversed for the act to arise. The spaces of resistance in daily life and second-person politics need to be articulated around the local and the commons.

Municipalism helps to bring closer political decisions with the needs of the population itself. In political systems that present great separations between political institutions and sovereign subjects, vital needs are relegated to a second-order due to the centralization of macroeconomic needs. In the article "Municipalism in Small Towns and Rural Areas", there is an interesting analysis on how Municipalism can play a central role in the feminization of politics:

> On the other hand, small towns and rural areas can enjoy a greater sense of community and more of a culture of the commons than their urban counterparts. Mutual support between residents is both more necessary and more feasible in smaller, more isolated communities, and the need to manage common goods such as water and soil make the unit of the community more important than that of the individual or even local public administrations. Since women are central to community life, albeit often in deeply gendered roles, this can give them increased capacity to influence shared goals and ways of working.
>
> (Boulton et al., 2019, p. 74)

However, I believe that a further move needs to be made for an ontological shift that will assure women's participation and grant direct political participation and inclusion to the Basic Political Community. In other words, I see here how women may engage in what Mouffe classified as agonistic relationships. However, there must be a further articulation for reverse antagonism. I believe that the way we can reverse antagonism through a clear political strategy is to practice assemblearism in every dimension of our lives.

In the article "How to Create a Participatory Municipalist Candidacy", there is a list of recommendations on participating in a municipalist assembly created by Marea Feminista, a municipalist feminist group (Shea Baird et al., 2019, p. 38). Within these recommendations, we find several tips on avoiding treating the other as a threat or as someone to whom you must act as a master or professor. I believe these indications are valid as direction on how not to construct antagonisms but reverse antagonisms in which we must think of ourselves as potential threats to others and create intermediate spaces for the act of coalitions.

Remunicipalization along community currencies helps erase political and bodily alienation between subjects and between bodies and their surroundings by adding an ecological component in which both the local and well-being of each subject are put at the center of political and economic decision-making.

References

Agenjo-Calderón, A., & Gálvez-Muñoz, L. (2019). Feminist Economics: Theoretical and Political Dimensions. *American Journal of Economics and Sociology, 78*(1), 137–166.

Bookchin, D. (2019). The Future We Deserve. In D. Bookchin & A. Colau (Eds.), *Fearless Cities: A Guide to the Global Municipalist Movement* (pp. 12–16). New Internationalist.

Bookchin, D., & Colau, A. (2019). *Fearless Cities: A Guide to the Global Municipalist Movement*. New Internationalist.

Boulton, J., Amich Vidal, M., & Bergés, L. (2019). Municipalism in Small Towns and Rural Areas. In D. Bookchin & A. Colau (Eds.), *Fearless Cities: A Guide to the Global Municipalist Movement* (pp. 68–75). New Internationalist.

Butler, J. (2014). Bodily Vulnerability, Coalitions, and Street Politics. *Differences in Common. Gender, Vulnerability and Community, 37*, 97–119.

Federici, S. B. (2014). *Caliban and the witch* (2., rev. ed). Autonomedia.

Ferber, M. A., & Nelson, J. A. (Eds.) (1993). *Beyond Economic Man: Feminist Theory and Economics*. The University of Chicago Press.

Fishel, S. R., Fletcher, A., Krishna, S., McKnight, U., du Plessis, G., Shomura, C., Valdés, A., & Voelkner, N. (2021). Politics in the Time of COVID. *Contemporary Political Theory*. https://doi.org/10.1057/s41296-021-00500-1

Hughes, N. (2015). The Community Currency Scene in Spain. *International Journal of Community Currency Research, 19*, 1–11. http://dx.doi.org/10.15133/j.ijccr.2015.017

Mies, M. (2001). *Patriarchy and Accumulation on a World Scale: Women in the International División of Labour*. Zed.

Mouffe, C. (2005). *On the Political*. Routledge.

Pérez Orozco, A. (2017). *Subversión feminista de la economía. Aportes para un debate sobre el conflicto capital-vida* (3rd ed.). Traficnates de Sueños.

Schmitt, C. (2007). *The Concept of the Political* (Expanded ed.). University of Chicago Press.

Seyfang, G., & Longhurst, N. (2013). Growing Green Money? Mapping Community Currencies for Sustainable Development. *Ecological Economics, 86*, 65–77. https://doi.org/10.1016/j.ecolecon.2012.11.003

Shea Baird, K., Delso, C., & Zechner, M. (2019). How to Create a Participatory Municipalist Candidacy. In D. Bookchin & A. Colau (Eds.), *Fearless Cities: A Guide to the Global Municipalist Movement* (pp. 32–40). New Internationalist.

Stavrakakis, Y. (2007). *Lacanian Left*. Edinburgh University Press.

Stavrakakis, Y. (2010). On Acts, Pure and Impure. *International Journal of Zizek Studies, 4*(2), 1–35.

Valdés, A. (2021). The Facemask Paradigm: Symptoms and Non-neutral Limits during Coronavirus. *Free Associations: Psychoanalysis and Culture, Media, Groups, Politics, 81–82*, 18–30. https://doi.org/10.1234/fa.v0i81-82.380

Williams, R. M. (1993). Race, Deconstruction, and Feminist Economic Theory. In M. A. Ferber & J. A. Nelson (Eds.), *Beyond Economic Man: Feminist Theory and Economics* (pp. 144–153). The University of Chicago Press.

Žižek, S. (2008). *In Defense of Lost Causes*. Verso.010237470Information Classification: General00Information Classification: General

Index

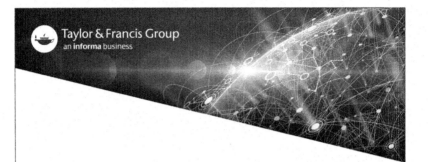